INTRODUCTION TO COMPANY LAW

Prof (Dr) Jaikishan Sahu
Dr. Siddharth Rewadikar

SAMANT PUBLISHING

ISBN : 9788169244251
Edition : First, May 2026
Title : Introduction to Company Law
Author : Prof (Dr) Jaikishan Sahu, Dr. Siddharth Rewadikar

Published by

SAMANT PUBLISHING

An Imprint of **Taneesha and Prachi NextGen Publication**

Plot No. 48, Khasra No. 646, Road No. 2,
Suman Nagar, Haridwar - 249402, Uttarakhand (India)
Website : www.samantpublishing.com
E-mail : support@tpnextpub.com
Phone : 01334 388 862

Printed by :
Techshresta Solutions Private Limited
Hebbal Kempapura, Bangalore, Karnataka - 560024, India

Dedication

This book is humbly dedicated to

the students of commerce and law,
who have chosen the noble path of understanding
the intricate world of business and corporate governance,

and to the teachers, mentors, and well-wishers
who have inspired me throughout my academic journey.

Preface

The law relating to companies in India has undergone a major transformation with the enactment of the Companies Act, 2013. This Act replaced the Companies Act, 1956 – a legislation that had governed the corporate sector in India for over half a century. The 2013 Act reflects the changing economic landscape of India, the globalisation of business, the rise of information technology, and the growing importance of corporate governance and transparency. It has introduced several new concepts such as One Person Company, Corporate Social Responsibility, class action suits, key managerial personnel, and mandatory rotation of auditors, among others.

This book, 'Business Law (Specially Company Law),' has been written with the specific objective of providing a comprehensive, student-friendly, and up-to-date treatment of the subject. It is primarily designed for the students of B.Com, BBA, MBA, LLB, CA, CS, and CMA courses, but it will also be useful to practicing professionals, company secretaries, chartered accountants, cost accountants, and anyone interested in understanding the legal framework of companies in India.

Special attention has been given to the Indian context. Examples have been drawn from well-known Indian companies such as Tata, Reliance, Infosys, HDFC, and others. Landmark Indian cases such as Satyam, Sahara, and HDFC-HDFC Bank merger have been discussed to illustrate the practical application of the law. The book also explains the interaction between the Companies Act and other related laws such as SEBI regulations, FEMA, and the Insolvency and Bankruptcy Code.

I am fully aware that company law is a vast and ever-evolving subject. Despite my best efforts, there may be errors or omissions in this book. I would be grateful to readers – students, teachers, and professionals – who bring such matters to my notice so that they can be corrected in the next edition. I also welcome suggestions for improvement.

I hope this book will serve as a useful companion to students in their study of company law and that it will contribute, in some small measure, to a better understanding of the legal framework that governs the corporate sector in India.

Dr Jaikishan Sahu
Indore, Madhya Pradesh
2026

Acknowledgements

The writing of a book is never a solitary Endeavour. It is the result of the support, encouragement, and inspiration of many people who have contributed to the author's journey in various ways. I take this opportunity to acknowledge, with deep gratitude, all those who have helped me in the preparation of this book.

I am indebted to the many authors and scholars whose works have shaped my understanding of company law. The classical texts of N.D. Kapoor, M.C. Shukla, Avtar Singh, A. Ramaiya, and Taxmann Publications have served as invaluable references. I also acknowledge the guidance received from the bare text of the Companies Act, 2013, the various rules made thereunder, and the decisions of the Supreme Court of India, various High Courts, the NCLT, and the NCLAT, which have illuminated the practical application of the law.

I would like to thank my students, whose questions and curiosity have often led me to explore topics in greater depth and from different perspectives. Their feedback and enthusiasm have been a constant source of motivation. A special word of thanks is due to the technology and resources that have made this book possible. The online resources of the Ministry of Corporate Affairs (MCA), the Securities and Exchange Board of India (SEBI), and the Insolvency and Bankruptcy Board of India (IBBI) have been extremely useful in ensuring that the book reflects the most current legal position. I am profoundly grateful to my family for their love, patience, and support throughout the writing of this book. Their understanding during the long hours of research and writing has made this work possible. Without their encouragement, this book would have remained a distant dream. Finally, I humbly bow before the Divine, whose grace has guided me throughout this academic journey. Any merit in this work is due to the grace of teachers and well-wishers; any shortcomings are entirely my own.

CONTENTS

PART – I : GENERAL PRINCIPLES OF BUSINESS LAW

Chapter 1

Introduction to Business Law

1.1 Meaning and Definition of Business Law

In every society, whether simple or complex, there are certain rules and regulations which govern the conduct of the people. Without such rules, no society can function properly. When we talk about business, there are thousands of transactions happening every day – buying and selling of goods, entering into contracts, forming companies, hiring employees, paying taxes and so on. All these activities need to be regulated by law. The branch of law which deals with such commercial and business activities is called Business Law.

Business Law, in simple words, is that branch of law which is directly concerned with trade, commerce, and mercantile transactions. It lays down the rules relating to the rights and obligations of persons engaged in business and commercial activities. It is also known as Commercial Law or Mercantile Law in many textbooks.

Definitions

According to **M.C. Shukla**, "Business Law means that branch of law which comprises laws concerning trade, industry, and commerce."

According to **N.D. Kapoor**, "Mercantile Law or Commercial Law may be defined as that branch of law which comprises all those laws that are applicable to or related to the rights and obligations of mercantile persons arising out of mercantile transactions in respect of mercantile property."

According to **Justice Oliver Wendell Holmes**, "The prophecies of what the courts will do in fact, and nothing more pretentious, are what I mean by the law." This definition tells us that the true meaning of law can be understood only by studying what the courts actually decide.

From the above definitions, we can understand that Business Law is not a single statute or act. It is a collection of various laws and enactments which together regulate business and commercial activities in a country.

Note: The term 'Business Law' is wider than 'Mercantile Law' because Business Law includes not only laws relating to mercantile transactions but also covers company law, taxation law, industrial law, intellectual property law and other laws which affect business.

1.2 Nature and Scope of Business Law

To understand Business Law properly, it is necessary to know about its nature and the area which it covers. Business Law is not a static subject. It keeps on changing with the changing needs of the society and the business world. As new forms of business emerge, new laws are also framed to regulate them. For example, the Information Technology Act, 2000 was enacted to deal with matters of electronic commerce which did not exist earlier.

Nature of Business Law

(a) It is a part of Civil Law: Business Law primarily falls under the category of civil law. It deals with the rights of private individuals and regulates their relationships. If a person breaks a contract, the other party can file a civil suit for damages. It does not generally deal with crimes, though some business offences like fraud under the Companies Act, 2013 may attract criminal liability as well.

(b) It is largely based on English Law: The foundation of Indian business law was laid during the British period. Most of our commercial laws like the Indian Contract Act, 1872, the Sale of Goods Act, 1930, and the Negotiable Instruments Act, 1881 were based on the principles of English common law and equity. However, Indian courts and legislature have made significant modifications over the years to suit Indian conditions.

(c) It is dynamic in nature: Business law is not fixed or rigid. It changes according to the needs of the time. The Companies Act, 1956 was replaced by the Companies Act, 2013 to bring Indian corporate law at par with international standards. Similarly, the Insolvency and Bankruptcy Code, 2016 was a landmark legislation which completely changed the way business failures are handled in India.

(d) It is both substantive and procedural: Substantive law defines the rights and duties, while procedural law prescribes the method of enforcing those rights. Business law contains both elements. For example, the Indian Contract Act tells us what a valid contract is (substantive), and it also tells us what remedies are available in case of breach (procedural).

Scope of Business Law

The scope of Business Law is very wide. It is not confined to any single legislation. In the Indian context, the following major areas are covered under Business Law:

Area of Business Law	Relevant Legislation in India
Law of Contract	Indian Contract Act, 1872
Law relating to Sale of Goods	Sale of Goods Act, 1930
Law relating to Negotiable Instruments	Negotiable Instruments Act, 1881
Law relating to Partnership	Indian Partnership Act, 1932
Company Law	Companies Act, 2013
Law relating to Limited Liability Partnership	LLP Act, 2008
Consumer Protection Law	Consumer Protection Act, 2019

Law relating to Insolvency	Insolvency and Bankruptcy Code, 2016
Law relating to Information Technology	Information Technology Act, 2000
Law relating to Intellectual Property	Patents Act, 1970; Trademarks Act, 1999; Copyright Act, 1957
Law relating to Foreign Exchange	FEMA, 1999
Competition Law	Competition Act, 2002

It must be noted that the above list is not exhaustive. With the growth of new forms of business like e-commerce, fintech, and start-ups, the scope of business law is continuously expanding.

1.3 Sources of Business Law in India

The business law of India has developed over a long period of time. It draws its principles from various sources. Understanding these sources is important because they tell us where the law comes from and how it has evolved over the centuries.

(A) English Mercantile Law

The English Mercantile Law is the most important source of Indian business law. During the British rule in India, the English merchants brought with them the principles of English commercial law. Most of the early Indian commercial statutes were drafted on the pattern of the corresponding English legislation. The English Mercantile Law itself has three main sources:

(i) Common Law (or Judge-made Law): This is the law which has been developed by the English judges over a period of several centuries through their decisions in various cases. When there was no written statute on a particular point, the judges decided the disputes on the basis of customs, usages, and their own sense of justice. These decisions, over the years, became established principles of law. The doctrine of 'stare decisis' (i.e., to stand by the previous decisions) made these judicial decisions binding on the lower courts. In India also, the decisions of the Supreme Court are binding on all courts under Article 141 of the Constitution.

(ii) Equity: The rules of equity were developed by the Court of Chancery in England to supplement the common law. Common law was sometimes rigid and did not always do justice. The equity courts gave relief where the common law courts could not. Principles like specific performance of contracts, injunctions, and the doctrine of estoppel came from equity. In India, many equitable principles have been incorporated into our statutes. For instance, Section 10 of the Specific Relief Act, 1963 deals with specific performance which is an equitable remedy.

(iii) Law Merchant (Lex Mercatoria): This was the body of commercial customs and usages which were followed by the merchants in Europe during the medieval period. These customs related to bills of exchange, partnership, insurance, sale of goods, and shipping. Gradually, these customs were recognised by the English courts and became part of the common law. In India, many of these principles have found a place in our various commercial statutes.

(B) Indian Statute Law (Legislation)

This is the most important source of Indian business law at present. The Parliament and State Legislatures in India have enacted various laws to regulate business activities. Some of the important statutes are:

(a) Indian Contract Act, 1872 – This is the most fundamental law governing all types of contracts in India.

(b) Sale of Goods Act, 1930 – It was originally a part of the Contract Act and was separated in 1930.

(c) Negotiable Instruments Act, 1881 – It deals with promissory notes, bills of exchange and cheques.

(d) Indian Partnership Act, 1932 – It governs the formation and working of partnership firms.

(e) Companies Act, 2013 – It is the principal law governing the formation, management, and winding up of companies in India. This Act replaced the earlier Companies Act, 1956.

(f) Limited Liability Partnership Act, 2008 – It provides for a new form of business organisation.

(g) Consumer Protection Act, 2019 – It provides protection to consumers against unfair trade practices.

(h) Insolvency and Bankruptcy Code, 2016 – It deals with the resolution of insolvency in a time-bound manner.

(C) Judicial Decisions (Case Law / Precedents)

The decisions of the courts, particularly the Supreme Court and the High Courts, constitute an important source of business law. Under the doctrine of judicial precedent, the decisions of the higher courts are binding on the lower courts. The Supreme Court of India has, through its various judgments, interpreted and clarified many provisions of business law. In many cases, the courts have also filled the gaps in the statutory law.

Case: Mohiri Bibi v. Dharmodas Ghose (1903)

The Privy Council held that an agreement with a minor is void ab initio (void from the beginning). This is one of the most famous cases in Indian contract law. The court said that since a minor is not competent to contract under Section 11 of the Indian Contract Act, any agreement entered into by a minor is absolutely void and not merely voidable.

(D) Customs and Trade Usages

Customs and usages of trade are an important source of business law. Many rules of business law have their origin in the customs followed by merchants and traders over a long period. Section 1 of the Indian Contract Act saves the usage and custom of trade. Similarly, Section 9 of the Sale of Goods Act provides that in the absence of an express contract, the terms may be implied from the course of dealing between the parties or from trade usage.

Note: For a custom to be recognised as a source of law, it must be (a) certain and definite, (b) reasonable, (c) in conformity with the law, and (d) followed continuously for a long period.

(E) Personal Law

In some cases, the personal law of the parties also becomes relevant in business transactions. For example, the capacity of a person to enter into a contract may depend on his personal law. Under Hindu law, a joint Hindu family can carry on a business through its karta (head of the family). The Hindu Succession Act, 2005 (as amended) has given equal rights to daughters in the coparcenary property, which has implications for family business.

1.4 Classification of Law

For a better understanding of business law, it is helpful to know the broad classification of law. Law can be classified in many ways. The following are the main classifications:

(I) On the Basis of Content

(a) Substantive Law: Substantive law defines the rights and obligations of the parties. It tells us what the law is. For example, the Indian Contract Act defines what a valid contract is, what are the essential elements, and what happens if a contract is broken. Similarly, the Companies Act, 2013 defines the duties of directors, the rights of shareholders, and the procedure for formation of a company.

(b) Procedural Law (or Adjective Law): Procedural law deals with the process or method of enforcing the rights given by substantive law. It tells us how the law is to be enforced. The Code of Civil Procedure, 1908 and the Code of Criminal Procedure, 1973 are examples of procedural laws. Without procedural law, the substantive law would remain only on paper.

(II) On the Basis of Nature

(a) Public Law: Public law regulates the relationship between the State and the individuals. It includes Constitutional Law, Criminal Law, Administrative Law, and Tax Law. For example, the Income Tax Act, 1961 is a part of public law because it deals with the relationship between the taxpayer and the Government.

(b) Private Law (or Civil Law): Private law governs the relationship between individuals. It includes the law of contracts, the law of property, family law, and the law of torts. Most of the business law falls under private law because it regulates the relationship between business persons, between companies and their members, between employer and employees, and so on.

(III) On the Basis of Application

(a) General Law: General law is the law which applies to all persons in the country without any distinction. For example, the Indian Contract Act and the Sale of Goods Act apply to all persons who enter into contracts or sell goods, irrespective of their religion, caste, or personal status.

(b) Special Law: Special law is the law which applies to a particular class of persons or a particular type of activity. For example, the Companies Act, 2013 applies only to companies, the Partnership Act applies only to partnership firms, and the Banking Regulation Act, 1949 applies only to banking companies. Where there is a conflict between general law and special law, the special law prevails over the general law. This is based on the legal maxim 'generalia specialibus non derogant' (general things do not derogate from special things).

Table 1.1: Classification of Law at a Glance

Basis	Type	Example
Content	Substantive Law	Indian Contract Act, 1872
Content	Procedural Law	Code of Civil Procedure, 1908

Nature	Public Law	Income Tax Act, 1961
Nature	Private Law	Indian Contract Act, 1872
Application	General Law	Sale of Goods Act, 1930
Application	Special Law	Companies Act, 2013

1.5 Importance of Business Law

In the modern world, no business can be carried on without the knowledge of business law. Whether it is a small shopkeeper or a large multinational corporation, everyone has to follow certain laws. The importance of business law can be understood from the following points:

(1) Provides a legal framework for business: Business law provides the basic framework within which all business activities must be conducted. It defines the rules of the game. For example, the Companies Act, 2013 prescribes the procedure for incorporating a company, the rights of shareholders, the duties of directors, and the requirements for maintaining books of accounts. Without such a framework, there would be no orderly conduct of business.

(2) Protects the rights of the parties: Business law protects the rights of all parties involved in a business transaction. The law of contracts ensures that promises are kept. The Sale of Goods Act protects the buyer as well as the seller. The Consumer Protection Act, 2019 gives special protection to consumers against defective goods and deficient services.

(3) Provides remedies for grievances: When a person's rights are violated, business law provides various remedies. A person can sue for damages, seek specific performance of a contract, or get an injunction from the court. The National Company Law Tribunal (NCLT) under the Companies Act, 2013 provides a specialised forum for resolution of corporate disputes.

(4) Regulates unfair practices: Business law prevents unfair trade practices and promotes fair competition. The Competition Act, 2002 prevents anti-competitive agreements and abuse of dominant position. The SEBI Act regulates the securities market to protect the interests of investors.

(5) Encourages foreign investment: A strong and transparent legal system attracts foreign investors. If the business laws of a country are clear, fair, and properly enforced, foreign companies will have confidence to invest. The liberalisation of Indian economy after 1991 was accompanied by several changes in business law to make India more investor-friendly.

(6) Helps in dispute resolution: Business disputes are inevitable. Business law provides mechanisms for resolving such disputes. Apart from regular courts, the Arbitration and Conciliation Act, 1996 provides for alternative dispute resolution through arbitration and mediation, which is faster and less expensive than court litigation.

(7) Promotes ethical business conduct: Many provisions of business law are aimed at promoting honesty and ethical conduct in business. For example, Section 447 of the Companies Act, 2013 imposes severe punishment for fraud. The Prevention of Money Laundering Act, 2002 prevents the use of proceeds of crime in business. These provisions discourage dishonest practices and promote a culture of compliance.

(8) Essential for professional studies: Knowledge of business law is essential for students of commerce, management, law, and professional courses like CA, CS, and CMA. Business law is a compulsory subject in most university syllabi because it equips students with the legal knowledge required in their professional life.

Case: Salomon v. Salomon & Co. Ltd. (1897)

This is a landmark English case which established the principle of separate legal entity of a company. The House of Lords held that once a company is incorporated, it becomes a separate legal person, distinct from its members. This principle has been adopted in Indian company law and is the foundation of the corporate form of business organisation.

Chapter 2

Indian Contract Act, 1872 – An Overview

2.1 Meaning and Essentials of a Valid Contract

Every day, we make a number of promises and agreements. A father promises to buy a toy for his child. A friend agrees to lend his book. A shopkeeper agrees to sell goods at a fixed price. But the question arises – are all these promises enforceable by law? The answer is no. Only those agreements which satisfy certain conditions laid down by the Indian Contract Act, 1872 become contracts and can be enforced in a court of law.

The Indian Contract Act came into force on 1st September, 1872. It extends to the whole of India except the State of Jammu and Kashmir (now applicable to J&K after 2019 reorganisation). It is not a complete code dealing with all branches of the law of contracts. It deals with the general principles applicable to all contracts. The special contracts like sale of goods, partnership, negotiable instruments, etc. are governed by separate Acts.

Definition of Contract

Section 2(h) of the Indian Contract Act defines a contract as: "An agreement enforceable by law is a contract."

This definition tells us two things. First, there must be an agreement. Second, that agreement must be enforceable by law. If an agreement is not enforceable by law, it is not a contract.

Section 2(e) defines an agreement as: "Every promise and every set of promises forming the consideration for each other is an agreement."

Section 2(b) defines a promise as: "When the person to whom the proposal is made signifies his assent thereto, the proposal is said to be accepted. A proposal, when accepted, becomes a promise."

From the above definitions, the following formula can be derived:

Proposal (Offer) + Acceptance = Promise (Agreement)

Agreement + Enforceability by Law = Contract

It follows that all contracts are agreements, but all agreements are not contracts. An agreement becomes a contract only when it is enforceable by law. An agreement which is not enforceable by law is said to be void [Section 2(g)].

Essential Elements of a Valid Contract

According to Section 10 of the Indian Contract Act, "All agreements are contracts if they are made by the free consent of parties competent to contract, for a lawful consideration and with a lawful object, and are not hereby expressly declared to be void."

On the basis of Section 10 and other provisions of the Act, the following are the essential elements of a valid contract:

(1) Offer and Acceptance: There must be a lawful offer by one party and a lawful acceptance of that offer by another party. The offer and acceptance must result in an agreement. The terms of the offer must be definite and the acceptance must be absolute and unconditional.

(2) Intention to Create Legal Relations: The parties to an agreement must have the intention to create legal relations. If there is no such intention, no contract comes into existence. For example, if a person invites his friend for dinner and the friend fails to come, the host cannot sue for damages because there was no intention to create legal relations. Agreements of social and domestic nature generally do not create legal relations. However, commercial and business agreements are presumed to be made with the intention to create legal relations unless otherwise proved.

Case: Balfour v. Balfour (1919)

A husband promised to pay a monthly allowance to his wife while she was staying in England for medical treatment. The husband failed to pay. The wife sued him. The Court of Appeal held that this was a domestic agreement and the parties did not intend to create legal relations. Therefore, it was not a contract and the wife could not recover the amount.

(3) Lawful Consideration: Consideration means 'something in return.' An agreement without consideration is void (with certain exceptions under Section 25). The consideration must be lawful, i.e., it must not be illegal, immoral, or opposed to public policy.

(4) Capacity of Parties (Competence to Contract): The parties to a contract must be competent to contract. According to Section 11, every person is competent to contract who (a) is of the age of majority (i.e., 18 years), (b) is of sound mind, and (c) is not disqualified from contracting by any law to which he is subject.

(5) Free Consent: The consent of the parties must be free. According to Section 14, consent is said to be free when it is not caused by coercion, undue influence, fraud, misrepresentation, or mistake. If the consent is not free, the contract is voidable at the option of the aggrieved party (except in case of mistake where the contract may be void).

(6) Lawful Object: The object or purpose of the agreement must be lawful. Section 23 says that the object of an agreement is not lawful if it is forbidden by law, is of such nature that if permitted it would defeat the provisions of any law, is fraudulent, involves or implies injury to the person or property of another, or is immoral or opposed to public policy.

(7) Agreement Not Expressly Declared Void: The Act has specifically declared certain agreements as void. These include agreement in restraint of marriage (Section 26), agreement in restraint of trade (Section 27), agreement in restraint of legal proceedings (Section 28), agreement the meaning of which is uncertain (Section 29), agreements by way of wager (Section 30), and so on. If an agreement falls under any of these categories, it cannot be a valid contract.

(8) Certainty: The terms of the agreement must be certain and not vague or ambiguous. Section 29 provides that "Agreements, the meaning of which is not certain, or capable of being made certain, are void." For example, A agrees to sell to B 'a hundred tons of oil.' There is nothing whatever to show what kind of oil was intended. The agreement is void for uncertainty.

(9) Possibility of Performance: The agreement must be capable of being performed. Section 56 provides that an agreement to do an impossible act is void. For example, A agrees with B to discover treasure by magic. This is a void agreement because the performance is impossible.

(10) Legal Formalities: Generally, a contract may be oral or in writing. However, certain contracts are required by law to be in writing and/or registered. For example, a contract for the sale of immovable property must be in writing and registered under the Registration Act, 1908. Similarly, a promissory note must be in writing under the Negotiable Instruments Act, 1881.

Note: If any one of the above essential elements is missing, the agreement will not be a valid contract. It may be void, voidable, illegal, or unenforceable, as the case may be.

2.2 Classification of Contracts

Contracts can be classified on various bases. A proper understanding of this classification is very important for the study of the law of contracts. The following are the main types of classification:

(A) On the Basis of Enforceability

(i) Valid Contract: A valid contract is an agreement which satisfies all the essential elements prescribed by the law. It creates legal obligations between the parties and is enforceable in a court of law. For example, A agrees to sell his car to B for Rs. 5,00,000. B accepts the offer. This is a valid contract if all essentials are satisfied.

(ii) Void Contract [Section 2(j)]: A contract which ceases to be enforceable by law becomes void when it ceases to be enforceable. A void contract is not void from the beginning; it was a valid contract when it was made but has subsequently become void due to change in law or impossibility of performance. For example, A contracts to marry B.

Before the time fixed for the marriage, B goes mad. The contract becomes void.

(iii) Voidable Contract [Section 2(i)]: An agreement which is enforceable by law at the option of one or more of the parties thereto, but not at the option of the other or others, is a voidable contract. A voidable contract continues to be valid until it is avoided (set aside) by the party entitled to do so. Contracts obtained by coercion, undue influence, fraud, or misrepresentation are voidable contracts.

(iv) Void Agreement [Section 2(g)]: An agreement not enforceable by law is said to be void. A void agreement is void ab initio, i.e., it has no legal effect from the very beginning. For example, an agreement with a minor, an agreement without consideration (subject to exceptions), an agreement in restraint of marriage – all these are void agreements. There is a difference between a void agreement and a void contract. A void agreement is void from the beginning while a void contract was valid initially but has subsequently become void.

(v) Illegal Agreement: An agreement which is forbidden by law or which is of such a nature that, if permitted, it would defeat the provision of any law, is an illegal agreement. Every illegal agreement is void but every void agreement is not necessarily illegal. The difference is that an illegal agreement is punishable by law whereas a void agreement is not punishable. Also, collateral transactions to an illegal agreement are also void, but collateral transactions to a void agreement are not necessarily void.

(vi) Unenforceable Contract: An unenforceable contract is one which is actually valid but cannot be enforced because of some technical defect such as absence of writing, absence of registration, absence of stamping, time barred by the Limitation Act, etc. If the defect is removed, the contract can be enforced.

(B) On the Basis of Formation (Mode of Creation)

(i) Express Contract: When the terms of the contract are stated in words (spoken or written), the contract is said to be an express contract. For example, A says to B, "I offer to sell my house for Rs. 30 lakhs." B says, "I accept your offer." This is an express contract.

(ii) Implied Contract: When the terms of the contract are inferred from the conduct of the parties or from the circumstances of the case, the contract is said to be an implied contract. For example, when a person enters a bus, there is an implied contract that he will pay the fare. When a coolie picks up the luggage of a traveller at a railway station without being asked to do so, there is an implied contract that the traveller will pay reasonable charges.

(iii) Quasi-Contract: A quasi-contract is not a contract in the strict sense of the term. It is an obligation which the law creates in the absence of any agreement. The law implies a promise and imposes an obligation on one party to prevent unjust enrichment. Sections 68 to 72 of the Indian Contract Act deal with quasi-contracts. For example, if A supplies necessities of life to B, who is a lunatic, A is entitled to be reimbursed from B's property (Section 68).

(C) On the Basis of Performance

(i) Executed Contract: When both the parties to a contract have performed their respective obligations, the contract is said to be executed. For example, A goes to a shop and buys a book by paying Rs. 500. Here both parties have performed – the shopkeeper has delivered the book and A has paid the price. This is an executed contract.

(ii) Executory Contract: When one or both the parties to a contract have not yet performed their obligations, the contract is said to be executory. For example, A promises to deliver goods to B after one week and B promises to pay the price on delivery. Until the goods are delivered and the price is paid, the contract is executory. If one party has performed and the other party's obligation is pending, the contract is said to be partly executed and partly executory.

Table 2.1: Classification of Contracts at a Glance

Basis	Type	Key Feature
Enforceability	Valid	All essentials present; fully enforceable
Enforceability	Void	Was valid, now unenforceable
Enforceability	Voidable	Enforceable at option of aggrieved party
Enforceability	Void Agreement	Void from the very beginning
Enforceability	Illegal	Void + punishable; collateral also void
Formation	Express	Terms stated in words
Formation	Implied	Terms inferred from conduct
Formation	Quasi-Contract	Obligation imposed by law
Performance	Executed	Both parties have performed
Performance	Executory	Obligations still pending

2.3 Offer and Acceptance

The foundation of every contract is an offer (or proposal) by one party and its acceptance by the other party. Without offer and acceptance, there can be no agreement, and without agreement, there can be no contract. Therefore, a clear understanding of the law relating to offer and acceptance is fundamental to the study of contract law.

Offer (Proposal) – Section 2(a)

Section 2(a) defines a proposal as follows: "When one person signifies to another his willingness to do or to abstain from doing anything, with a view to obtaining the assent of that other to such act or abstinence, he is said to make a proposal."

The person who makes the proposal is called the 'proposer' or 'offeror' or 'promisor.' The person to whom the proposal is made is called the 'proposee' or 'offeree' or 'promisee.'

Essentials of a Valid Offer

(a) It must be made with the intention to create legal relations. A casual invitation to dinner is not an offer in the legal sense.

(b) The terms of the offer must be definite, clear and certain. A vague or ambiguous offer cannot be accepted. For example, A says to B, "I will sell you my car at a reasonable price." This is not a valid offer because the term 'reasonable price' is not certain.

(c) It must be communicated to the offeree. An offer is effective only when it is communicated to the offeree. An offer which has not come to the knowledge of the offeree cannot be accepted.

(d) It may be express or implied. An offer made by words (spoken or written) is an express offer. An offer inferred from the conduct of a person is an implied offer.

(e) It may be specific or general. An offer made to a specific person is a specific offer and can be accepted only by that person. An offer made to the world at large is a general offer and can be accepted by anyone who has knowledge of the offer.

Case: Carlill v. Carbolic Smoke Ball Co. (1893)

The Carbolic Smoke Ball Company published an advertisement offering to pay £100 to anyone who caught influenza after using their smoke ball as directed. Mrs. Carlill used the smoke ball and still caught influenza. She claimed £100. The company refused to pay, arguing it was merely an advertisement. The Court held that the advertisement was a general offer to the whole world. Mrs. Carlill had accepted the offer by performing the conditions mentioned therein. She was entitled to the reward. This is one of the most famous cases in contract law.

Offer Distinguished from Invitation to Offer

An invitation to offer (or invitation to treat) is not the same thing as an offer. It is merely an invitation to others to make offers. The person making the invitation does not intend to be bound by it. He is only inviting others to come forward and make offers which he may accept or reject. Examples of invitation to offer include display of goods in a shop window with price tags, advertisements in newspapers, catalogues and price lists, menu cards in restaurants, prospectus issued by a company, and tender notices.

Case: Pharmaceutical Society of Great Britain v. Boots Cash Chemists (1953)

The question was whether display of goods on shelves of a self-service shop constituted an offer. The Court held that the display of goods with price tags was only an invitation to offer. The customer makes the offer when he takes the goods to the cashier. The contract is completed when the cashier accepts the offer and receives the payment.

Acceptance – Section 2(b)

Section 2(b) defines acceptance as follows: "When the person to whom the proposal is made signifies his assent thereto, the proposal is said to be accepted. A proposal, when accepted, becomes a promise."

Rules Regarding Valid Acceptance

(1) Acceptance must be absolute and unconditional (Section 7): The acceptance must be of the whole offer, without any modification. If the offeree adds conditions or changes the terms of the offer, it is not an acceptance but a counter-offer, which destroys the original offer. For example, A offers to sell his house for Rs. 20 lakhs. B says he will buy it for Rs. 18 lakhs. This is a counter-offer and not an acceptance. The original offer of A stands rejected.

(2) Acceptance must be communicated (Section 4): The acceptance must be communicated to the offeror. Mere mental acceptance or silent acceptance is not sufficient. However, in the case of a general offer, performance of the conditions of the offer itself amounts to acceptance.

(3) Acceptance must be according to the prescribed manner: If the offeror prescribes a particular mode of acceptance, the acceptance must be given in that manner. If no mode is prescribed, the acceptance must be given in some usual and reasonable manner.

(4) Acceptance must be given within a reasonable time: If a time limit is specified, the acceptance must be given within that time. If no time limit is specified, the acceptance must be given within a reasonable time. What is a reasonable time depends on the facts and circumstances of each case.

(5) Acceptance must be given before the offer lapses or is revoked: An offer can be revoked before it is accepted. Once an offer lapses or is withdrawn, it cannot be accepted.

(6) Acceptance must be by the offeree or his authorised agent: Only the person to whom the offer is made (or his duly authorised agent) can accept it. A third person cannot accept an offer on behalf of the offeree without authority.

Section Reference: Communication of Offer, Acceptance and Revocation: Sections 3, 4 and 5 of the Indian Contract Act deal with the communication, acceptance, and revocation of proposals. Under Section 4, the communication of acceptance is complete – as against the proposer, when it is put in the course of transmission (e.g., when the letter is posted); and as against the acceptor, when it comes to the knowledge of the proposer.

2.4 Consideration

Consideration is one of the most essential elements of a contract. An agreement without consideration is generally void. The concept of consideration answers the question – what does each party get in return for his promise?

Definition of Consideration – Section 2(d)

"When, at the desire of the promisor, the promisee or any other person has done or abstained from doing, or does or abstains from doing, or promises to do or to abstain from doing, something, such act or abstinence or promise is called a consideration for the promise."

In simple words, consideration is the price paid by one party for the promise of the other. It is the 'quid pro quo' (something in return) which induces a person to enter into a contract.

Essential Rules Regarding Consideration

(a) Consideration must move at the desire of the promisor: The act or abstinence must be done at the desire or request of the promisor. If it is done voluntarily or at the desire of a third party, it is not a valid consideration. For example, A saves B's property from fire without being asked by B. A cannot demand payment for his services because it was not done at the desire of B.

(b) Consideration may move from the promisee or any other person: Under English law, consideration must move from the promisee only. But under Indian law, consideration may move from the promisee or any other person. This means that a stranger to the consideration can sue on a contract. However, a stranger to the contract (i.e., a person who is not a party to the contract) generally cannot sue on a contract. This is known as the doctrine of privity of contract.

Case: Chinnaya v. Ramayya (1882)

An old lady (A) made a gift of certain property to her daughter (B) with a condition that B would pay an annuity of Rs. 653 to A's brother (C). B agreed. Later, B refused to pay. C sued B. The Court held that the consideration had moved from A (the old lady) and not from C. But under Indian law, consideration may proceed from the promisee or any other person. Therefore, C was entitled to maintain the suit even though he had not personally furnished the consideration.

(c) Consideration may be past, present, or future: Under Indian law, consideration may be past (something already done), present (something done at the time of the promise), or future (something to be done in the future). Under English law, past consideration is generally not valid, but in India, Section 2(d) expressly recognises past consideration by using the words 'has done or abstained from doing.'

(d) Consideration need not be adequate: The law requires that a contract must be supported by consideration, but it does not require that the consideration must be adequate i.e., equal in value. The parties are free to fix their own price. Section 25 (Explanation 2) provides that an agreement to which the consent of the promisor is freely given is not void merely because the consideration is inadequate. However, the inadequacy of consideration may be taken into account by the court to determine whether the consent was freely given.

(e) Consideration must be real and not illusory: Although the consideration need not be adequate, it must be real and not illusory. A promise to do something which the promisor is already legally bound to do is not a valid consideration. Similarly, a promise to perform a public duty is not a valid consideration.

(f) Consideration must not be illegal, immoral or opposed to public policy: If the consideration is unlawful, the agreement is void.

Exceptions to the Rule 'No Consideration, No Contract' – Section 25

The general rule is that an agreement without consideration is void. However, Section 25 provides the following exceptions:

(i) Natural love and affection [Section 25(1)]: An agreement made without consideration is valid if it is made out of natural love and affection between parties standing in a near relation to each other, and it is expressed in writing and registered under the law.

(ii) Compensation for past voluntary services [Section 25(2)]: A promise to compensate, wholly or in part, a person who has already voluntarily done something for the promisor is enforceable without consideration. For example, A finds B's purse and returns it to him. B promises to pay A Rs. 1,000. This promise is valid even though A's act was voluntary.

(iii) Promise to pay a time-barred debt [Section 25(3)]: A promise in writing and signed by the debtor, to pay a debt barred by the Limitation Act, is valid without fresh consideration.

(iv) Gift actually made: Section 25 (Explanation 1) clarifies that the rule 'no consideration, no contract' does not affect the validity of any gift actually made. If a gift has already been given, the absence of consideration does not make it invalid.

(v) Agency [Section 185]: No consideration is necessary to create an agency.

2.5 Capacity to Contract

For a valid contract, the parties must be competent to contract. Section 11 of the Indian Contract Act states that "Every person is competent to contract who is of the age of majority according to the law to which he is subject, and who is of sound mind and is not disqualified from contracting by any law to which he is subject."

From this section, it is clear that the following persons are not competent to contract:

(1) Minors

A minor is a person who has not completed 18 years of age. According to the Indian Majority Act, 1875, a person attains the age of majority on completing 18 years. However, where a guardian has been appointed by the court, the age of majority is 21 years.

The position of a minor's agreement under Indian law was settled by the Privy Council in the following landmark case:

Case: Mohiri Bibi v. Dharmodas Ghose (1903)

Dharmodas Ghose, a minor, executed a mortgage in favour of Brahmo Dutt, a money-lender, to secure a loan of Rs. 20,000. At the time of the mortgage, the money-lender's attorney had knowledge of Dharmodas being a minor. Dharmodas filed a suit for setting aside the mortgage. The Privy Council held that as the mortgage was executed by a minor, it was void ab initio (void from the beginning). An agreement by a minor is absolutely void and not merely voidable.

The important rules relating to minor's agreements are as follows:

(a) An agreement with a minor is void ab initio. It is not merely voidable.

(b) A minor can be a beneficiary or promisee under a contract but cannot be a promisor.

(c) A minor cannot ratify (confirm) an agreement entered into during his minority after attaining majority. Since the agreement is void, there is nothing to ratify.

(d) The doctrine of estoppel does not apply against a minor. If a minor misrepresents his age and enters into a contract, he can still plead minority as a defence.

(e) A minor's property is liable for necessaries supplied to him or to anyone whom he is legally bound to support (Section 68).

(f) A minor cannot be a partner in a partnership firm. However, he may be admitted to the benefits of a partnership with the consent of all partners (Section 30 of the Indian Partnership Act, 1932).

(g) A minor can act as an agent but he cannot be held personally liable to the principal.

(h) A minor's parents or guardians are not liable for contracts entered into by the minor unless the minor is acting as an agent of the parent or guardian.

(2) Persons of Unsound Mind

Section 12 of the Act defines a person of sound mind: "A person is said to be of sound mind for the purpose of making a contract, if, at the time when he makes it, he is capable of understanding it and of forming a rational judgment as to its effect upon his interests."

A person who is usually of unsound mind, but occasionally of sound mind, may make a contract when he is of sound mind. Similarly, a person who is usually of sound mind, but occasionally of unsound mind, may not make a contract when he is of unsound mind. For example, a patient in a lunatic asylum who is at intervals of sound mind may contract during those intervals. A sane man who is delirious from fever or is so drunk that he cannot understand the terms of a contract or form a rational judgment cannot contract while such delirium or drunkenness lasts.

(3) Persons Disqualified by Law

Apart from minors and persons of unsound mind, the following persons are also disqualified from contracting: (a) Alien enemies – A person belonging to a country at war with India cannot enter into a contract with an Indian citizen during the period of war. (b) Foreign sovereigns and ambassadors – They enjoy certain diplomatic immunities and generally cannot be sued in Indian courts without the consent of the Central Government. (c) Convicts – A convict who is undergoing imprisonment cannot enter into a valid contract during the period of his sentence. (d) Insolvents – An insolvent person is disqualified from entering into certain contracts until he obtains a discharge from the court.

2.6 Free Consent

Consent is essential for every contract. Section 13 defines consent as: "Two or more persons are said to consent when they agree upon the same thing in the same sense." This is also called consensus ad idem (meeting of minds).

However, mere consent is not enough. The consent must be free. Section 14 defines free consent as consent which is not caused by – (a) Coercion, (b) Undue Influence, (c) Fraud, (d) Misrepresentation, or (e) Mistake.

When consent is caused by coercion, undue influence, fraud, or misrepresentation, the contract is voidable at the option of the party whose consent was so caused. When consent is caused by mistake, the contract may be void.

(1) Coercion – Section 15

Section 15 defines coercion as the committing, or threatening to commit, any act forbidden by the Indian Penal Code, or the unlawful detaining, or threatening to detain, any property, to the prejudice of any person whatever, with the intention of causing any person to enter into an agreement.

It is not necessary that the coercion should have been exercised by a party to the contract. It may be directed against any person, not necessarily the other party to the contract. Also, it is not necessary that the coercion be exercised at the place where the Indian Penal Code is in force.

Case: Ranganayakamma v. Alwar Setti (1889)

A young widow was prevented from removing the dead body of her husband for cremation until she adopted a boy. The Court held that her consent was obtained by coercion. The adoption was set aside as the agreement was voidable.

(2) Undue Influence – Section 16

A contract is said to be induced by undue influence where the relations subsisting between the parties are such that one of the parties is in a position to dominate the will of the other and uses that position to obtain an unfair advantage over the other.

A person is deemed to be in a position to dominate the will of another when (a) he holds a real or apparent authority over the other (e.g., employer and employee, police officer and accused), or (b) he stands in a fiduciary relationship to the other (e.g., doctor and patient, solicitor and client, parent and child, trustee and beneficiary), or (c) he makes a contract with a person whose mental capacity is temporarily or permanently affected by reason of age, illness, or mental or bodily distress.

Where a person who is in a position to dominate the will of another enters into a contract, and the transaction appears to be unconscionable (unfair), the burden of proving that the contract was not induced by undue influence lies on the person in the dominant position.

(3) Fraud – Section 17

Section 17 defines fraud as any act committed by a party to a contract (or with his connivance or by his agent) with intent to deceive another party or to induce him to enter into the contract. Fraud includes: (a) the suggestion that a fact is true when it is not true and the person making the suggestion does not believe it to be true, (b) active concealment of a fact by one having knowledge or belief of the fact, (c) a promise made without any intention of performing it, (d) any other act fitted to deceive, and (e) any such act or omission as the law specially declares to be fraudulent.

Mere silence as to facts likely to affect the willingness of a person to enter into a contract is not fraud unless there is a duty to speak or unless silence is in itself equivalent to speech. Contracts of insurance are contracts of uberrimae fidei (utmost good faith), where there is a positive duty to disclose all material facts.

Case: Derry v. Peek (1889)

The directors of a tramway company issued a prospectus stating that the company had the right to use steam power. In fact, they had only applied for such right but believed it would be granted. The Board of Trade refused permission. The company was wound up. The House of Lords held that the directors were not liable for fraud because they honestly believed that the statement was true. There was no intent to deceive.

(4) Misrepresentation – Section 18

Misrepresentation means a false statement of fact made innocently (i.e., without any intention to deceive). The person making the statement honestly believes it to be true. The difference between fraud and misrepresentation is the element of intent. In fraud, the false statement is made knowingly or recklessly with an intent to deceive. In misrepresentation, the false statement is made innocently without any intention to deceive.

Section 18 includes: (a) the positive assertion, in a manner not warranted by the information of the person making it, of that which is not true, though he believes it to be true; (b) any breach of duty which, without an intent to deceive, gives an advantage to the person committing it by misleading another; (c) causing, however innocently, a party to an agreement to make a mistake as to the substance of the thing which is the subject of the agreement.

(5) Mistake – Sections 20, 21, 22

A mistake may be of two kinds – mistake of law and mistake of fact.

Mistake of Law: A mistake of Indian law does not make the contract void (Section 21), because everyone is presumed to know the law of his own country ('ignorantia juris non excusat'). However, a mistake of foreign law is treated as a mistake of fact and is excusable.

Mistake of Fact: A mistake of fact may be bilateral (both parties are under a mistake) or unilateral (only one party is under a mistake). Under Section 20, where both the parties to an agreement are under a mistake as to a matter of fact essential to the agreement, the agreement is void. Under Section 22, a contract is not voidable merely because one party was under a mistake as to a matter of fact. A unilateral mistake generally does not affect the validity of a contract.

2.7 Legality of Object and Consideration

It is not enough that the contract has the consent of the parties and is supported by consideration. The consideration and the object of the contract must also be lawful. Section 23 of the Indian Contract Act lays down the circumstances under which the consideration or object of an agreement is unlawful.

According to Section 23, the consideration or object of an agreement is unlawful in the following cases:

(a) If it is forbidden by law – An agreement to do an act which is forbidden by law is void. For example, A promises to obtain for B an employment in the government service and B promises to pay Rs. 1,00,000 to A. The agreement is void because the object is forbidden by law.

(b) If it is of such a nature that, if permitted, it would defeat the provisions of any law – For example, A's estate is sold for arrears of revenue. The law provides that the defaulter is prohibited from purchasing the estate. B purchases the estate for A. This is against the spirit of the law and therefore the agreement is void.

(c) If it is fraudulent – An agreement whose object is to defraud others is void. For example, A, B and C enter into an agreement to divide among themselves the gains acquired by fraud. The agreement is void as the object is unlawful.

(d) If it involves or implies injury to the person or property of another – For example, A promises to pay B Rs. 50,000 if B beats C. The agreement is void because it involves injury to the person of C.

(e) If the court regards it as immoral – An agreement the object of which is immoral is void. For example, a landlord lets a house to a woman of the town knowing that it would be used for immoral purposes. The agreement is void.

(f) If the court regards it as opposed to public policy – Examples of agreements opposed to public policy include: trading with an enemy country, agreements to stifle prosecution, agreements in restraint of marriage, agreements in restraint of trade (except reasonable restraints), agreements in restraint of legal proceedings, agreements for the sale of public offices, and agreements to create monopolies.

Note: If any part of a single consideration for one or more objects, or any one or any part of any one of several considerations for a single object, is unlawful, the agreement is void (Section 24). However, if the legal part can be separated from the illegal part, the legal part may be enforced.

2.8 Void Agreements

Certain agreements have been expressly declared void by the Indian Contract Act. These agreements are void ab initio and cannot be enforced in any court of law. The main void agreements under the Act are as follows:

(1) Agreement by or with a minor or person of unsound mind: As discussed in Section 2.5, a minor's agreement is void ab initio.

(2) Agreement without consideration (Section 25): An agreement made without consideration is void, subject to the exceptions discussed in Section 2.4.

(3) Agreement in restraint of marriage (Section 26): Every agreement in restraint of the marriage of any person, other than a minor, is void. For example, an agreement by A with B that A will not marry anyone other than B is void (unless it amounts to an engagement which is a different thing).

(4) Agreement in restraint of trade (Section 27): Every agreement by which anyone is restrained from exercising a lawful profession, trade, or business of any kind is void to that extent. However, there are some exceptions to this rule. For example, an agreement not to carry on business at a particular place during the sale of goodwill is valid. Also, the Partners Act (Sections 11 and 36) allows for reasonable restraint on partners.

(5) Agreement in restraint of legal proceedings (Section 28): Every agreement by which any party thereto is restricted from enforcing his rights under or in respect of any contract by the usual legal proceedings in the ordinary tribunals is void to that extent. However, an agreement to refer disputes to arbitration is valid under the Arbitration and Conciliation Act, 1996.

(6) Agreement the meaning of which is uncertain (Section 29): Agreements the meaning of which is not certain, or capable of being made certain, are void.

(7) Agreements by way of wager (Section 30): A wagering agreement is an agreement in which two parties, professing to hold opposite views touching the issue of a future uncertain event, mutually agree that one shall pay to the other a sum of money depending on the determination of that event. In simple terms, it is a betting agreement. All wagering agreements are void. However, this section does not render void a subscription or contribution to any plate, prize, or sum of money to be awarded to the winner of any horse race.

(8) Agreement to do impossible act (Section 56): An agreement to do an act impossible in itself is void. For example, A agrees with B to discover treasure by magic. The agreement is void.

2.9 Contingent Contracts – Sections 31 to 36

A contingent contract is a contract to do or not to do something, if some event, collateral to such contract, does or does not happen. In simple words, it is a conditional contract. The performance of such contract depends on the happening or non-happening of a future uncertain event.

Section 31 defines a contingent contract as "A contract to do or not to do something, if some event, collateral to such contract, does or does not happen."

For example, A contracts to pay B Rs. 10,000 if B's house is burnt. This is a contingent contract. The obligation to pay arises only if the house is actually burnt. Contracts of insurance are the most common examples of contingent contracts. Similarly, contracts of indemnity and guarantee are also contingent contracts.

Rules Regarding Contingent Contracts

(a) Section 32: Contingent contracts to do or not to do anything if an uncertain future event happens cannot be enforced by law unless and until that event has happened. If the event becomes impossible, such contracts become void.

(b) Section 33: Contingent contracts to do or not to do anything if an uncertain future event does not happen can be enforced only when the happening of that event becomes impossible.

(c) Section 34: If a contract is contingent upon how a person will act at an unspecified future time, the event shall be considered to become impossible when such person does anything which renders it impossible that he should so act within any definite time or otherwise than under further contingencies.

(d) Section 35: Contingent contracts to do or not to do anything if a specified uncertain event happens within a fixed time become void if, at the expiration of that time, the event has not happened, or if before the time fixed, the event becomes impossible.

(e) Section 36: Contingent agreements to do or not to do anything if an impossible event happens are void, whether the impossibility of the event is known or not to the parties to the agreement at the time when it is made.

2.10 Performance of Contracts

The performance of a contract means carrying out of the obligations arising under the contract by the parties to the contract. Each party must perform or offer to perform his promise. Sections 37 to 67 of the Indian Contract Act deal with the performance of contracts.

Who Must Perform?

(a) Promisor himself (Section 40): If it appears from the nature of the case that the intention of the parties was that the promise should be performed by the promisor himself, then the promisor must perform it personally. For example, if A promises to paint a picture for B, A must paint the picture himself because it involves personal skill.

(b) Agent of the Promisor: If the nature of the contract does not require personal performance, the promisor may employ a competent person to perform it on his behalf.

(c) Legal Representatives (Section 37): In case of death of the promisor, his legal representatives are bound to perform the promise, unless a contrary intention appears from the contract. However, the legal representatives are liable only to the extent of the property of the deceased which has come into their hands.

(d) Joint Promisors (Section 42-44): When two or more persons have made a joint promise, then, unless a contrary intention appears from the contract, all such persons must jointly fulfil the promise during their joint lives, and after the death of any of them, his representative jointly with the survivor or survivors, and after the death of the last survivor, the representatives of all jointly. Any one of the joint promisors may be compelled to perform the whole promise. If one joint promisor performs, he can claim contribution from the other joint promisors.

Rules Regarding Performance

(a) Time and Place of Performance (Section 46-50): Where no time is specified, the contract must be performed within a reasonable time. Where no place is specified, the promisor must apply to the promisee to fix a reasonable place. Where time is specified but no application for performance is to be made, the promisor must perform on the day fixed, during the usual hours of business and at the place where the promise ought to be performed.

(b) Reciprocal Promises (Sections 51-54): Reciprocal promises are promises which form the consideration or part of the consideration for each other. Where the order of performance is expressly fixed, the promisor who is to perform first must perform his part first. If no order is fixed, they must be performed simultaneously.

(c) Appropriation of Payment (Sections 59-61): Where a debtor owes several debts to the same creditor and makes a payment which is not enough to satisfy all the debts, the question arises – which debt shall be deemed to have been paid? Section 59 says that the debtor may indicate the debt to which the payment is to be applied. If the debtor does not indicate, Section 60 gives the creditor the right to apply the payment to any lawful debt. If neither party makes any appropriation, Section 61 says the payment shall be applied in order of time (i.e., earliest debt first).

2.11 Discharge of Contracts

A contract is said to be discharged when the rights and obligations created by it come to an end. In other words, when the parties to a contract are freed from their contractual obligations, the contract is said to be discharged. A contract may be discharged in the following ways:

(1) Discharge by Performance

This is the most natural mode of discharge. When both the parties to a contract fulfil their respective obligations as agreed, the contract is discharged. For example, A agrees to sell goods to B for Rs. 10,000. A delivers the goods and B pays the price. The contract is discharged by performance.

(2) Discharge by Mutual Agreement or Consent

Since a contract is created by agreement, it can also be terminated by agreement. Section 62 provides that if the parties to a contract agree to substitute a new contract for it, or to rescind or alter it, the original contract need not be performed. Discharge by mutual agreement can take the following forms:

(a) Novation – When a new contract is substituted for an existing contract, it is called novation. The parties may be the same or different. (b) Rescission – When all or some of the terms of a contract are cancelled, it is known as rescission. (c) Alteration – When one or more of the terms of a contract are changed by mutual consent, it is called alteration. (d) Remission – Section 63 provides that every promisee may dispense with or remit, wholly or in part, the performance of the promise made to him or may extend the time for such performance. (e) Merger – When an inferior right accruing to a party under a contract merges into a superior right accruing to the same party, the contract is discharged by merger.

(3) Discharge by Impossibility of Performance (Frustration) – Section 56

Section 56 deals with the doctrine of frustration or supervening impossibility. It provides that a contract to do an act which, after the contract is made, becomes impossible or unlawful by reason of some event which the promisor could not prevent, becomes void when the act becomes impossible or unlawful.

Examples of supervening impossibility include: (a) destruction of the subject matter, (b) death or personal incapacity of the promisor, (c) change of law making the performance illegal, (d) outbreak of war, and (e) non-existence or non-occurrence of a particular state of things.

Case: Satyabrata Ghose v. Mugneeram Bangur & Co. (1954)

The Supreme Court of India laid down that the doctrine of frustration is an aspect of the law of discharge of contracts by reason of supervening impossibility or illegality and comes within the purview of Section 56 of the Indian Contract Act. Indian law does not follow the English common law doctrine of frustration in its entirety but applies Section 56 to determine whether a contract is discharged.

It is important to note that Section 56 does not apply in the following cases: (a) difficulty of performance is not impossibility; (b) commercial impossibility or hardship is not an excuse; (c) self-induced impossibility is not covered; (d) strikes, lockouts, and civil disturbances do not generally discharge a contract unless there is a force majeure clause.

(4) Discharge by Lapse of Time

If a contract is not performed within the period of limitation prescribed by the Limitation Act, 1963, the aggrieved party loses his right to sue. The contract is deemed to be discharged by lapse of time. For example, the limitation period for a suit based on a contract is generally 3 years from the date when the right to sue accrues.

(5) Discharge by Operation of Law

A contract may be discharged by operation of law in the following cases: (a) by death of the promisor (in case of personal contracts); (b) by insolvency of the promisor (the rights and liabilities of an insolvent are dealt with by the insolvency law); (c) by merger (as discussed above); (d) by alteration of the document without the consent of the other party – the contract is discharged and the party who altered it cannot sue on it.

(6) Discharge by Breach of Contract

Breach of contract occurs when a party to a contract fails to perform his obligation under the contract. Breach may be actual or anticipatory.

Actual Breach: When a party fails to perform his obligations on the due date or during the performance, it is called actual breach. For example, A agrees to deliver goods to B on 1st March. A fails to deliver on 1st March. This is an actual breach.

Anticipatory Breach (Section 39): When a party repudiates the contract before the time fixed for performance, it is called anticipatory breach. The aggrieved party has two options: (a) treat the contract as at an end and immediately sue for damages; or (b) treat the contract as still subsisting and wait for the time of performance. If he opts for (b), the contract remains alive for the benefit of both parties and the party in default may still perform it if the circumstances change.

Case: Hochster v. De La Tour (1853)

A agreed to employ B as a courier from 1st June. On 11th May, A informed B that his services would not be required. B immediately filed a suit for damages. The Court held that B was entitled to sue at once without waiting till 1st June. This case established the doctrine of anticipatory breach.

2.12 Remedies for Breach of Contract

When a contract is broken by one party, the other party (the aggrieved or injured party) has certain remedies available to him. The purpose of remedies is to put the aggrieved party in the position in which he would have been if the contract had been performed. The main remedies for breach of contract are as follows:

(1) Damages – Sections 73 to 75

Damages means monetary compensation for the loss suffered by the aggrieved party due to the breach of contract. The object of awarding damages is to put the injured party in the same position as he would have been in had the contract been performed.

The following types of damages may be awarded:

(a) Ordinary or General Damages: These are damages which naturally arise in the usual course of things from such breach. Under Section 73, when a contract has been broken, the party who suffers by such breach is entitled to receive compensation for any loss or damage caused to him thereby which naturally arose in the usual course of things from such breach.

(b) Special Damages: These are damages which arise from special circumstances known to both parties at the time of entering into the contract. Section 73 also provides that if the parties knew at the time of making the contract that special loss was likely to result from the breach, the aggrieved party can recover special damages.

Case: Hadley v. Baxendale (1854)

A's mill was stopped due to the breakage of a shaft. A gave the shaft to B (a common carrier) to be sent to a manufacturer for repairs. B delayed the delivery. As a result, A's mill remained idle for a longer period and A lost profits. A sued B for the loss of profits. The Court held that B was not liable for the loss of profits because B did not know that delay in delivery would result in stoppage of the mill. Only those damages can be recovered which were in the contemplation of the parties at the time of entering into the contract. This is the rule of remoteness of damage.

(c) Exemplary or Vindictive Damages: These are awarded not to compensate the aggrieved party but to punish the guilty party. In English law, they are generally not awarded in breach of contract cases except in two situations – (i) breach of a promise to marry, and (ii) wrongful dishonour of a cheque by a banker. In Indian law, the courts have awarded such damages in suitable cases.

(d) Nominal Damages: When a breach of contract has occurred but the aggrieved party has not suffered any actual loss, the court may award a very small amount as nominal damages. This is done to establish the legal right of the aggrieved party.

(e) Liquidated Damages and Penalty (Section 74): Sometimes, the parties themselves fix in advance the amount of compensation payable in case of breach. If the amount so fixed is a genuine pre-estimate of the loss, it is called liquidated damages. If the amount is fixed to terrorise the party into performance and is unreasonably high, it is called a penalty. Under English law, the court awards liquidated damages as agreed but reduces the penalty to a reasonable amount. Under Indian law, Section 74 provides that the court may award reasonable compensation not exceeding the amount fixed, whether it is liquidated damages or penalty. Indian law does not draw a distinction between liquidated damages and penalty.

(f) Damages for Breach by a Party Who Has Received Some Advantage (Section 75): A person who rightfully rescinds a contract is entitled to compensation for any damage which he has sustained through the non-fulfilment of the contract.

(2) Specific Performance

In certain cases, the court may direct the party in breach to carry out his promise as per the terms of the contract. This remedy is called specific performance. It is governed by the Specific Relief Act, 1963. Specific performance is granted when (a) damages are not an adequate remedy, (b) the subject matter of the contract is unique (e.g., a particular piece of land or a rare painting), and (c) the court can supervise the performance.

(3) Injunction

An injunction is an order of the court restraining a person from doing something which he promised not to do. It is a preventive relief. Where a party to a contract is doing something which he has promised not to do, the court may issue an injunction to prevent him from doing so. For example, A, a singer, agrees to sing at B's theatre exclusively for one month. A makes a contract to sing at C's theatre. B can obtain an injunction from the court to restrain A from singing at C's theatre.

(4) Quantum Meruit

The term 'quantum meruit' means 'as much as earned' or 'as much as merited.' When a person has done some work under a contract and the other party repudiates the contract or makes its further performance impossible, the party who has performed is entitled to claim reasonable compensation for the work already done. This is the claim on quantum meruit. For example, A is engaged to write a book of 500 pages. After A writes 300 pages, B (the publisher) repudiates the contract. A can claim quantum meruit for the 300 pages already written.

(5) Rescission of Contract

When a contract is broken by one party, the other party may treat the contract as rescinded (cancelled). He is then absolved from all his obligations under the contract. The aggrieved party may also file a suit for rescission and claim damages for the breach.

Note: The aggrieved party has a duty to mitigate (minimise) the loss arising from the breach. Section 73 provides that compensation cannot be given for any remote and indirect loss or damage sustained by reason of the breach, or for any loss which the party could have avoided by taking reasonable steps.

Chapter 3

Special Contracts

The Indian Contract Act, 1872 does not deal only with the general principles of the law of contract. It also deals with certain special types of contracts which are very commonly used in business and daily life. These special contracts are – (a) Contract of Indemnity and Guarantee, (b) Contract of Bailment and Pledge, and (c) Contract of Agency. These are covered under Sections 124 to 238 of the Indian Contract Act. In this chapter, we shall study each of these special contracts in detail.

3.1 Contract of Indemnity and Guarantee

I. Contract of Indemnity – Sections 124 & 125

In everyday business, a person may suffer a loss due to the conduct of another person or due to the conduct of any other person. In such cases, the person who has suffered the loss may want some protection or security against such loss. The contract of indemnity provides such protection.

Definition – Section 124

"A contract by which one party promises to save the other from loss caused to him by the conduct of the promisor himself, or by the conduct of any other person, is called a contract of indemnity."

The person who promises to make good the loss is called the 'indemnifier' (promisor). The person whose loss is to be made good is called the 'indemnity-holder' or 'indemnified' (promisee).

Illustration: A contracts to indemnify B against the consequences of any proceedings which C may take against B in respect of a certain sum of Rs. 200. This is a contract of indemnity.

It is important to note that Section 124 covers only those cases where the loss is caused by the conduct of the promisor or of any other person. It does not cover loss arising from events like accidents, fire, or other natural calamities. In this sense, the definition under Section 124 is narrower than the definition under English law where indemnity includes loss caused by any event including fire, accident, etc. However, Indian courts have taken a wider view and have held that the provisions of the Act are not exhaustive and contracts of insurance (which cover losses due to fire, accident, etc.) are also contracts of indemnity in the wider sense.

Rights of the Indemnity-Holder – Section 125

Section 125 provides that the promisee in a contract of indemnity, acting within the scope of his authority, is entitled to recover from the promisor –

(a) All damages: which he may be compelled to pay in any suit in respect of any matter to which the promise to indemnify applies.

(b) All costs: which he may be compelled to pay in any such suit, if in bringing or defending it he did not contravene the orders of the promisor and acted as it would have been prudent for him to act in the absence of any contract of indemnity, or if the promisor authorised him to bring or defend the suit.

(c) All sums: which he may have paid under the terms of any compromise of any such suit, if the compromise was not contrary to the orders of the promisor and was one which it would have been prudent for the promisee to make in the absence of any contract of indemnity, or if the promisor authorised him to compromise the suit.

Note: The Indian Contract Act is silent about the rights of the indemnifier. However, it is understood that after the indemnifier has made good the loss, he steps into the shoes of the indemnity-holder and acquires all the rights which the indemnity-holder had against third parties. This is based on the principle of subrogation.

II. Contract of Guarantee – Sections 126 to 147

A contract of guarantee is a very common type of contract in business. When a person takes a loan from a bank, the bank usually asks for a guarantor who will repay the loan if the borrower fails to repay. Similarly, when a person is appointed to a post of trust, another person may guarantee his honesty and fidelity. This is the contract of guarantee.

Definition – Section 126

"A contract of guarantee is a contract to perform the promise, or discharge the liability, of a third person in case of his default."

There are three parties involved in a contract of guarantee:

(i) The Surety (or Guarantor): The person who gives the guarantee, i.e., who promises to pay or perform if the principal debtor fails to do so.

(ii) The Principal Debtor: The person in respect of whose default the guarantee is given, i.e., the person who owes the primary liability.

(iii) The Creditor: The person to whom the guarantee is given, i.e., the person to whom the principal debtor owes the liability.

Illustration: A asks B to lend Rs. 5,000 to C and promises that if C does not repay, he (A) will repay. Here, A is the surety, C is the principal debtor, and B is the creditor. This is a contract of guarantee.

A contract of guarantee may be oral or in writing. Section 126 does not require it to be in writing, unlike English law where the Statute of Frauds, 1677 requires a guarantee to be in writing.

Essential Features of a Contract of Guarantee

(a) Three parties and three contracts: A contract of guarantee involves three separate contracts – (i) a principal contract between the principal debtor and the creditor, (ii) a secondary contract between the surety and the creditor, and (iii) an implied contract between the surety and the principal debtor under which the principal debtor is bound to reimburse the surety if the surety has to pay the creditor.

(b) Existence of a principal debt: There must be an existing liability or a principal debt. If there is no principal debt, there can be no guarantee. A guarantee without a principal debt is a nullity.

(c) Consideration: Section 127 provides that anything done, or any promise made, for the benefit of the principal debtor may be a sufficient consideration to the surety for giving the guarantee. The surety need not receive any direct benefit. The consideration received by the principal debtor is sufficient consideration for the surety's promise.

(d) The surety's liability is secondary: The primary liability is that of the principal debtor. The surety's liability is secondary or conditional – it arises only when the principal debtor makes a default. This is the basic difference between indemnity and guarantee.

(e) Concurrence of three parties: All three parties must agree to the arrangement. The consent of all three parties is necessary, though it is not necessary that they all sign the same document.

Types of Guarantee

(i) Specific Guarantee: A guarantee which is given for a single transaction or a single debt is called a specific guarantee. When the debt is paid or the transaction is completed, the guarantee comes to an end.

(ii) Continuing Guarantee – Section 129: A guarantee which extends to a series of transactions is called a continuing guarantee. For example, A guarantees payment to B, a tea dealer, to the amount of Rs. 5,000 for any tea he may from time to time supply to C. This is a continuing guarantee. The surety remains liable until the guarantee is revoked.

A continuing guarantee may be revoked at any time by the surety as to future transactions by giving notice to the creditor (Section 130). However, the surety remains liable for transactions that have already taken place before the notice of revocation. The death of the surety also operates as revocation of a continuing guarantee as to future transactions, unless there is a contract to the contrary (Section 131).

Rights of the Surety

The Indian Contract Act gives extensive rights to the surety. These rights are classified into three categories:

(A) Rights against the Principal Debtor:

(i) Right of Subrogation – Section 140: Where a guaranteed debt has become due, or default of the principal debtor to perform a guaranteed duty has taken place, the surety, upon payment or performance of all that he is liable for, is invested with all the rights which the creditor had against the principal debtor. In simple words, after paying off the debt, the surety steps into the shoes of the creditor and can recover the amount from the principal debtor.

(ii) Right of Indemnity – Section 145: In every contract of guarantee, there is an implied promise by the principal debtor to indemnify the surety. The surety is entitled to recover from the principal debtor whatever sum he has rightfully paid under the guarantee.

(B) Rights against the Creditor:

(i) Right to Securities – Section 141: A surety is entitled to the benefit of every security which the creditor has against the principal debtor at the time when the contract of suretyship is entered into, whether the surety knows of the existence of such security or not. If the creditor loses or parts with such security without the consent of the surety, the surety is discharged to the extent of the value of the security (Section 141).

(ii) Right to Set-Off: If the creditor sues the surety, the surety may avail of any set-off which the principal debtor could have against the creditor.

(C) Rights against Co-Sureties:

(i) Right of Contribution – Sections 146 & 147: Where two or more persons are co-sureties for the same debt, they are liable to contribute equally to the extent of their respective liabilities. If one co-surety has paid more than his share, he can recover the excess from the other co-sureties. Section 146 deals with equal contribution and Section 147 deals with contribution where co-sureties have agreed to different limits of liability.

Illustration: A, B and C are co-sureties to D for the sum of Rs. 3,000. D makes default. A, B and C are liable to pay Rs. 1,000 each. If A pays the entire Rs. 3,000, he can recover Rs. 1,000 each from B and C.

Discharge of Surety

The surety is discharged (freed from his liability) in the following cases:

(1) By Revocation (Section 130): A continuing guarantee may be revoked as to future transactions by notice to the creditor.

(2) By Death of the Surety (Section 131): The death of the surety operates as revocation of a continuing guarantee as to future transactions, unless there is a contract to the contrary.

(3) By Variance in Terms (Section 133): Any variance (change) made without the surety's consent in the terms of the contract between the principal debtor and the creditor discharges the surety as to transactions subsequent to the variance. Even a slight change in terms, if made without the surety's consent, will discharge the surety.

(4) By Release or Discharge of Principal Debtor (Section 134): The surety is discharged by any contract between the creditor and the principal debtor by which the principal debtor is released, or by any act or omission of the creditor, the legal consequence of which is the discharge of the principal debtor.

(5) By Creditor's Act or Omission Impairing Surety's Remedy (Section 139): If the creditor does any act which is inconsistent with the rights of the surety, or omits to do any act which his duty to the surety requires him to do, and the eventual remedy of the surety himself against the principal debtor is thereby impaired, the surety is discharged.

(6) By Loss of Security (Section 141): If the creditor loses or parts with the security without the consent of the surety, the surety is discharged to the extent of the value of the security.

(7) By Giving Time to the Principal Debtor (Section 135 & 136): If the creditor, without the consent of the surety, makes any contract with the principal debtor for giving time for the performance of the contract, the surety is discharged. However, mere forbearance on the part of the creditor to sue the principal debtor does not discharge the surety (Section 137).

Case: State Bank of India v. Indexport Registered (1992)

The Supreme Court held that where a creditor grants an extension of time for repayment of the loan to the principal debtor without the consent of the surety, the surety stands discharged. The principle is that the surety's right to pay the debt when it falls due and then proceed against the principal debtor is impaired by the granting of time.

Distinction Between Indemnity and Guarantee

Table 3.1: Indemnity vs. Guarantee

Point of Distinction	Contract of Indemnity	Contract of Guarantee
Number of Parties	Two parties – Indemnifier and Indemnity-holder	Three parties – Surety, Principal Debtor and Creditor
Number of Contracts	One contract	Three contracts (principal + secondary + implied)
Nature of Liability	Primary – Indemnifier's liability is independent	Secondary – Surety's liability arises on default of principal debtor
Purpose	To compensate for loss	To give security to the creditor
Existing Debt	There may or may not be an existing debt	There must be an existing or future debt/liability
Right of Subrogation	Not specifically provided in the Act	Surety has right of subrogation (Section 140)
Request of	May be at the request of either party	Usually given at the request of the principal debtor
Section	Sections 124–125	Sections 126–147

3.2 Contract of Bailment and Pledge

I. Contract of Bailment – Sections 148 to 181

In our daily life, we often deliver goods to another person for some specific purpose. For example, we give our clothes to a washerman for washing, we give our watch to a watchmaker for repair, we deposit our luggage at the cloakroom of a railway station, we lend a book to a friend. In all these cases, the possession of the goods is transferred from one person to another for a specific purpose. This is called bailment.

Definition – Section 148

"A bailment is the delivery of goods by one person to another for some purpose, upon a contract that they shall, when the purpose is accomplished, be returned or otherwise disposed of according to the directions of the person delivering them."

The person delivering the goods is called the 'bailor.' The person to whom the goods are delivered is called the 'bailee.'

Illustration: A delivers his car to B, a mechanic, for repair. Here, A is the bailor, B is the bailee, and the car is the subject-matter of bailment. When the repair is done, B must return the car to A.

Essential Features of Bailment

(a) Delivery of goods: There must be a delivery of goods from the bailor to the bailee. The delivery may be actual (physical handing over) or constructive (e.g., handing over the key of a warehouse). The essential point is that the possession of the goods must be transferred from the bailor to the bailee.

(b) Delivery for some purpose: The goods must be delivered for some purpose. If goods are delivered without any purpose, it is not a bailment. The purpose may be for safe custody, for repair, for carriage from one place to another, for use by the bailee, or for any other purpose.

(c) Delivery upon a contract: There must be a contract between the bailor and the bailee. The contract may be express or implied. This means that the delivery must be with the consent of both parties.

(d) Return or disposal of goods: It is an essential condition of bailment that the goods shall be returned to the bailor or disposed of according to his directions after the purpose is accomplished. If the goods are not to be returned but are to be consumed (e.g., food), it is not a bailment. Similarly, if money is deposited in a bank, it is not bailment because the same currency notes are not returned. The bank can use the money and return equivalent amount.

(e) Goods only: Bailment is only of goods. It does not cover immovable property. Section 148 uses the word 'goods' which includes movable property only.

(f) No transfer of ownership: In bailment, only the possession is transferred, not the ownership. The ownership of the goods remains with the bailor throughout the period of bailment. This is the main distinction between bailment and sale.

Kinds of Bailment

Bailment may be classified on different bases:

(i) On the basis of consideration: (a) Gratuitous bailment – where no consideration is involved, i.e., neither the bailor nor the bailee gets any remuneration. For example, lending a book to a friend. (b) Non-gratuitous (or bailment for reward) – where either or both parties get some benefit. For example, hiring a car, giving clothes for dry-cleaning.

(ii) On the basis of benefit: (a) Bailment for the exclusive benefit of the bailor – e.g., A leaves his pet with B (free of charge) while A goes on a trip. (b) Bailment for the exclusive benefit of the bailee – e.g., A lends his bicycle to B free of charge. (c) Bailment for the mutual benefit of both – e.g., A gives his clothes to B for dry-cleaning for a fee.

Duties of the Bailor

(1) Duty to disclose defects – Sections 150 & 152: The bailor is bound to disclose to the bailee any faults in the goods bailed of which the bailor is aware and which materially interfere with the use of them or expose the bailee to extraordinary risks. In case of gratuitous bailment, the bailor is liable for damages only if he was aware of the defects and did not disclose them (Section 150). In case of non-gratuitous bailment (bailment for hire), the bailor is liable for damages even if he was not aware of the defects (Section 150, Explanation). For example, A lends a horse to B, which he (A) knows to be vicious, without disclosing this fact. The horse runs away and B is injured. A is liable for damages.

(2) Duty to bear expenses – Sections 158 & 159: In case of gratuitous bailment, the bailor must repay the bailee all necessary expenses incurred for the purpose of bailment (Section 158). In case of non-gratuitous bailment, the bailor must bear all extraordinary expenses (Section 159).

(3) Duty to indemnify the bailee – Section 164: The bailor is responsible to the bailee for any loss which the bailee may sustain by reason that the bailor was not entitled to make the bailment, or to receive back the goods, or to give directions respecting them. In other words, if the bailor's title to the goods is defective and the bailee suffers any loss on account of this, the bailor must indemnify the bailee.

(4) Duty to receive back the goods – Section 164: The bailor is bound to accept the goods when the bailee returns them after the purpose is accomplished. If the bailor refuses to accept, he must indemnify the bailee for any cost of custody or return.

Duties of the Bailee

(1) Duty to take reasonable care – Section 151: In all cases of bailment, the bailee is bound to take as much care of the goods bailed to him as a man of ordinary prudence would, under similar circumstances, take of his own goods of the same bulk, quality, and value. The standard of care is that of a reasonable man. If the bailee takes such care, he is not liable for any loss, destruction, or deterioration of the goods (Section 152).

(2) Duty not to make unauthorised use of goods – Sections 153 & 154: The bailee must not make any use of the goods bailed which is not authorised by the terms of the bailment. If the bailee makes an unauthorised use, he is liable to the bailor for any damage arising to the goods from or during such unauthorised use. Also, if the goods are damaged by reason of such unauthorised use, the bailee is liable even though he has taken reasonable care.

Illustration: A lends his horse to B for riding. B puts the horse in a cart. The horse is injured. B is liable for the injury because he made an unauthorised use of the horse (for cart instead of riding).

(3) Duty not to mix goods – Sections 155, 156 & 157: The bailee must keep the goods of the bailor separate from his own goods. If the bailee, with the consent of the bailor, mixes the goods with his own, both parties have a proportionate interest in the mixture (Section 155). If the bailee, without the consent of the bailor, mixes the goods with his own, and the goods can be separated, the bailee must bear the cost of separation (Section 156). If the goods cannot be separated, the bailee must compensate the bailor for the loss of his goods (Section 157).

(4) Duty to return the goods – Sections 160 & 161: The bailee is bound to return, or deliver according to the bailor's directions, the goods bailed, without demand, as soon as the time for which they were bailed has expired, or the purpose for which they were bailed has been accomplished (Section 160). If the bailee fails to return the goods at the proper time, he is responsible for any loss, destruction, or deterioration of the goods from that time, even without any negligence on his part (Section 161).

(5) Duty to return any accretion to the goods – Section 163: The bailee must deliver to the bailor any increase or profit which may have accrued from the goods bailed. For example, A leaves a cow in B's care. The cow has a calf. B must deliver the calf as well as the cow to A.

Termination of Bailment

A bailment is terminated in the following cases: (a) When the purpose of bailment is accomplished. (b) When the period of bailment expires. (c) When the bailee acts inconsistently with the terms of bailment (Section 153). (d) When the bailor or bailee dies. (e) A gratuitous bailment may be terminated at any time by the bailor, subject to Section 159 which requires the bailor to indemnify the bailee for any loss caused by premature termination.

Bailee's Lien

Particular Lien – Section 170: A particular lien is the right of the bailee to retain the goods bailed until his charges for services rendered in respect of those particular goods are paid. For example, a tailor can retain the clothes until his tailoring charges are paid. This lien is available only in respect of the particular goods for which services have been rendered and charges are due.

General Lien – Section 171: A general lien is the right to retain any goods belonging to the other party until all dues are paid, not merely the charges in respect of the particular goods. Section 171 gives general lien to bankers, factors, wharfingers, attorneys, and policy brokers. No other person has a right to general lien unless there is an express contract or usage of trade to that effect.

Case: Atul Mehra v. Bank of Maharashtra (2001)

The Court held that a banker has a general lien over all securities and goods deposited by a customer in the ordinary course of banking business. The banker can retain the securities until all dues are cleared. This is different from a particular lien which is limited only to the goods in respect of which the charges are due.

Finder of Goods – Section 71 & Sections 168–169

A person who finds goods belonging to another and takes them into his custody is subject to the same responsibility as a bailee (Section 71). He is bound to take reasonable care of the goods and to try to find the true owner.

Under Section 168, the finder of goods has no right to sue the owner for compensation for trouble and expense voluntarily incurred in preserving the goods and finding the true owner. However, he has a right of lien – he may retain the goods against the owner until he receives such compensation.

Under Section 169, if the owner cannot be found with reasonable diligence, or if the owner refuses to pay the lawful charges, the finder may sell the goods in the following cases: (a) when the thing is in danger of perishing or of losing the greater part of its value, or (b) when the lawful charges of the finder amount to two-thirds of the value of the thing found.

II. Contract of Pledge – Sections 172 to 181

Pledge is a special kind of bailment where goods are bailed as security for the payment of a debt or for the performance of a promise. It is a very common form of secured transaction in business and banking.

Definition – Section 172

"The bailment of goods as security for payment of a debt or performance of a promise is called 'pledge.' The bailor is in this case called the 'pawnor' (or pledgor). The bailee is called the 'pawnee' (or pledgee)."

Illustration: A borrows Rs. 50,000 from B and delivers his gold ornaments to B as security for the repayment of the loan. This is a pledge. A is the pawnor and B is the pawnee.

Essential Features of Pledge

(a) There must be a bailment of goods. (b) The bailment must be by way of security for a debt or performance of a promise. (c) The goods must be delivered to the pawnee. Delivery may be actual or constructive (e.g., delivery of the key of the godown where goods are stored, or delivery of the document of title like a railway receipt or a bill of lading). (d) The ownership of the goods remains with the pawnor. Only possession is transferred to the pawnee. (e) The pawnee has a right to retain the goods until the debt is repaid.

Rights of the Pawnee

(1) Right of Retainer – Section 173: The pawnee may retain the goods pledged not only for payment of the debt or the performance of the promise but also for the interest of the debt and all necessary expenses incurred by him for the preservation of the goods pledged. However, the pawnee cannot retain the goods for any debt or promise other than the one for which the goods were pledged, unless there is a contract to that effect.

(2) Right to Retain for Subsequent Advances – Section 174: The pawnee shall not, in the absence of a contract to that effect, retain the goods pledged for any debt or promise other than the debt or promise for which they are pledged. But the parties may by contract extend the pawnee's right of retainer to subsequent advances also.

(3) Right to Extraordinary Expenses – Section 175: The pawnee is entitled to receive from the pawnor extraordinary expenses incurred by him for the preservation of the goods pledged. However, he has no right to retain the goods for such expenses – he can only sue the pawnor for such expenses.

(4) Right in Case of Default by Pawnor – Section 176: If the pawnor makes default in payment of the debt or performance of the promise, the pawnee may – (a) bring a suit against the pawnor for the debt or promise and retain the goods as collateral security, or (b) sell the goods pledged after giving reasonable notice of the sale to the pawnor. If the sale proceeds exceed the amount of the debt, the pawnee must return the surplus to the pawnor. If the sale proceeds are less than the debt, the pawnor is still liable to pay the deficiency.

Rights of the Pawnor

(1) Right to Redeem – Section 177: If a time is fixed for the payment of the debt, the pawnor may redeem the goods pledged at any time before the actual sale of the goods, on payment of the amount due, together with any expenses that have arisen from his default. This is the pawnor's right of redemption.

(2) Right to be informed before sale: The pawnee must give reasonable notice to the pawnor before selling the goods. If the goods are sold without reasonable notice, the sale is not valid and the pawnor can recover damages.

(3) Right to receive surplus: If the goods are sold and the sale proceeds exceed the amount of debt, the pawnor has the right to receive the surplus.

(4) Right to preservation of goods: The pawnor has the right to expect that the pawnee will take reasonable care of the goods pledged.

Pledge by Non-Owners – Sections 178 & 179

As a general rule, only the owner of goods or a person authorised by the owner can make a valid pledge. However, there are certain exceptions where a pledge by a non-owner is also valid:

(a) Pledge by a mercantile agent (Section 178): A mercantile agent who is in possession of goods or documents of title to goods with the consent of the owner can make a valid pledge of such goods in the ordinary course of business, provided the pawnee acts in good faith and without notice that the agent has no authority to pledge.

(b) Pledge by a person in possession under a voidable contract (Section 178A): When a person has obtained possession of goods under a contract voidable under Sections 19 or 19A, he may make a valid pledge, provided the contract has not been rescinded at the time of the pledge and the pawnee acts in good faith and without notice of the defect in the pawnor's title.

(c) Pledge by seller or buyer in possession: Under Section 30(1) of the Sale of Goods Act, 1930, a seller who is in possession of goods after selling them can make a valid pledge to a person who acts in good faith. Similarly, under Section 30(2), a buyer who has obtained possession with the seller's consent may make a valid pledge.

(d) Pledge by co-owner in possession: A co-owner who is in sole possession of goods with the consent of the other co-owners may make a valid pledge.

(e) Pledge by a person who has a limited interest: A person who has a limited interest in goods may make a valid pledge to the extent of that interest.

Distinction Between Bailment and Pledge

Table 3.2: Bailment vs. Pledge

Point of Distinction	Bailment	Pledge
Definition	Delivery of goods for any purpose	Delivery of goods as security for debt
Purpose	For safe custody, repair, carriage, use, etc.	For security against a loan or promise
Right to Sell	Bailee has no right to sell	Pawnee can sell after notice on default
Right to Use	May or may not use (depends on terms)	Pawnee generally cannot use goods
Scope	Wider – all types of delivery of goods	Narrower – only security for debt/promise
Return of Goods	On accomplishment of purpose	On repayment of debt
Sections	Sections 148–171	Sections 172–181

3.3 Contract of Agency

In the modern business world, it is not always possible for a person to carry out all his business activities himself. He may need the help of others to act on his behalf. For example, a person living in Delhi may need to buy property in Chennai. He cannot personally go to Chennai every time. So, he appoints someone in Chennai to act on his behalf. This relationship between the person who appoints and the person who is appointed is called the relationship of agency. The law relating to agency is contained in Sections 182 to 238 of the Indian Contract Act, 1872.

Definition

Section 182 defines an agent and a principal as follows: "An agent is a person employed to do any act for another or to represent another in dealings with third persons. The person for whom such act is done, or who is so represented, is called the principal."

Thus, an agent acts on behalf of his principal. Whatever the agent does within the scope of his authority binds the principal. The agent is merely an instrument or representative of the principal. The basic principle of agency is expressed in the Latin maxim 'qui facit per alium, facit per se' which means 'he who acts through another is deemed in law to do it himself.'

Essential Features of Agency

(a) Agreement: There must be an agreement between the principal and the agent. The agreement may be express or implied.

(b) Authority: The principal must confer authority on the agent to act on his behalf. The agent derives his power to act from this authority.

(c) Consideration not necessary – Section 185: No consideration is necessary to create an agency. This is an important exception to the general rule that every contract requires consideration. A person may become an agent without receiving any remuneration.

(d) Principal must be competent: Any person who is of the age of majority and is of sound mind may employ an agent (Section 183). In other words, the principal must be competent to contract.

(e) Agent need not be competent: As between the principal and third persons, any person may become an agent (Section 184). This means that even a minor or a person of unsound mind may be appointed as an agent. However, the minor-agent will not be personally liable to the principal.

Creation of Agency

An agency may be created in the following ways:

(1) By Express Agreement: When the principal expressly appoints the agent by words spoken or written, the agency is created by express agreement. An agency created in writing is called a 'power of attorney.'

(2) By Implied Agreement: When the agency is inferred from the conduct of the parties or from the circumstances of the case, it is called implied agency. The following are the types of implied agency:

(a) Agency by Estoppel – Section 237: When a person, by his words or conduct, leads another to believe that a certain person is his agent, he is estopped from denying the agency. For example, A allows B to act as his agent in dealing with C. C believes that B is A's agent. A cannot later deny that B was his agent.

(b) Agency by Holding Out: This is similar to agency by estoppel. When a principal has previously permitted an agent to act on his behalf and later a third party deals with the agent on the basis of this representation, the principal is bound by the agent's acts.

(c) Agency by Necessity: In certain circumstances, a person may act as an agent of another without the express authority of the principal. This arises in situations of emergency where it is not possible to communicate with the principal and immediate action is necessary to protect the interests of the principal. For example, a carrier of perishable goods may sell the goods if they are likely to perish before reaching the owner.

(d) Agency by Ratification – Sections 196–200: When a person acts as agent without the authority of the principal, and the principal subsequently ratifies (approves) the acts of the agent, an agency by ratification is created. Ratification relates back to the date of the act and has the same effect as prior authority. Ratification may be express or implied.

Section 198 provides that ratification must be of the whole act. The principal cannot ratify a part of the act and reject the rest. Section 199 provides that the act ratified must be one which the principal could have lawfully done himself. Section 200 provides that ratification must be made within a reasonable time.

Types of Agents

Agents may be classified into various types depending on the extent of their authority and the nature of work they do:

(a) Special Agent: A special agent is one who is appointed to perform a particular act or represent the principal in a particular transaction. His authority comes to an end as soon as that act is done. For example, an agent appointed to sell a particular car.

(b) General Agent: A general agent is one who has the authority to do all acts connected with a particular trade, business, or employment. For example, a manager of a shop is a general agent of the owner. He can do all acts which are usually done in the management of such business.

(c) Universal Agent: A universal agent is one whose authority is unlimited. He can do all acts which the principal can lawfully do and can delegate them to others. This type of agency is very rare.

(d) Factor: A factor is a mercantile agent who is entrusted with the possession of goods for the purpose of selling them.

(e) Broker: A broker is an agent who negotiates contracts between two parties. He does not have possession of the goods.

(f) Commission Agent: A commission agent is one who buys or sells goods for a commission.

(g) Del Credere Agent: A del credere agent is one who, in consideration of an extra commission (called del credere commission), guarantees to his principal that the third persons with whom he contracts will perform their obligations. He acts as both an agent and a guarantor.

(h) Sub-Agent – Section 191: A sub-agent is a person employed by and acting under the control of the original agent in the business of the agency. An agent cannot generally delegate his authority to another person ('delegatus non potest delegare' – a delegate cannot further delegate). However, Section 190 allows delegation in certain cases – where the custom of trade permits, where the nature of work requires, or where the principal authorises sub-delegation.

Duties of an Agent

(1) Duty to follow the directions of the principal – Sections 211 & 212: An agent is bound to conduct the business of his principal according to the directions given by the principal. When the agent acts otherwise, if any loss is sustained, the agent must make it good. If any profit accrues, the agent must account for it. Where no directions are given, the agent must follow the custom prevailing in the same kind of business at the place where the agent conducts such business.

(2) Duty to carry out work with skill and diligence – Section 212: An agent is bound to conduct the business of the agency with as much skill as is generally possessed by persons engaged in similar business, unless the principal has notice of his want of skill. The agent must act with reasonable diligence and use his best efforts.

(3) Duty to render proper accounts – Section 213: An agent is bound to render proper accounts to his principal on demand.

(4) Duty to communicate – Section 214: An agent must use all reasonable diligence in communicating with his principal in cases of difficulty and must seek and act on the instructions of the principal.

(5) Duty not to deal on his own account – Sections 215 & 216: An agent must not deal on his own account in the business of the agency without the principal's consent. If an agent deals on his own account without informing the principal, the principal may repudiate the transaction.

(6) Duty to pay sums received for the principal – Section 218: An agent is bound to pay to his principal all sums received on his account, after deducting his own legitimate charges and commission.

(7) Duty not to make secret profits: An agent must not make any secret profit from the agency business. If he does, the principal can recover such profit.

(8) Duty on termination – Section 209: When an agency is terminated, the agent is bound to take, on behalf of the principal, all reasonable steps for the protection of the interests entrusted to him.

Rights of an Agent

(1) Right of Retainer – Section 217: An agent may retain, out of any sums received on account of the principal, all moneys due to himself in respect of advances made or expenses properly incurred by him in conducting the business of the agency, and also his remuneration.

(2) Right to Remuneration – Section 219: An agent is entitled to receive the agreed remuneration or, in the absence of agreement, a reasonable remuneration for the services rendered.

(3) Right of Lien – Section 221: In the absence of any contract to the contrary, an agent has a right to retain goods, papers, and other property (movable or immovable) of the principal until the amount due to the agent for commission, disbursements, and services has been paid.

(4) Right to Indemnity – Section 222: The employer of an agent is bound to indemnify him against the consequences of all lawful acts done by such agent in exercise of the authority conferred upon him.

(5) Right to Compensation – Section 225: The agent is entitled to compensation for injury caused to him by the principal's neglect or want of skill.

Duties of the Principal

(a) To pay the agent's remuneration (Section 219). (b) To indemnify the agent for all lawful acts (Section 222). (c) To indemnify the agent against consequences of acts done in good faith (Section 223). (d) To compensate the agent for injury caused by principal's neglect (Section 225). (e) Not to revoke the agency unjustly in case of agency coupled with interest.

Authority of an Agent

The authority of an agent may be express or implied.

Express Authority – Section 187: Express authority is the authority which is given by the principal to the agent in express terms, whether by words spoken or written.

Implied Authority – Section 188: Implied authority is the authority to do every lawful thing which is necessary for the purpose of carrying out the express authority, or which is usually done in the course of conducting such business. For example, an agent employed to sell goods has an implied authority to receive payment and to give receipts.

Apparent (or Ostensible) Authority: This is the authority which the agent appears to have in the eyes of third parties, even if the principal has privately restricted such authority. The principal is bound by the acts of the agent within his apparent authority towards third parties who deal in good faith.

Personal Liability of an Agent

As a general rule, an agent is not personally liable for contracts entered into on behalf of the principal. However, in the following cases, the agent becomes personally liable:

(a) When the agent expressly agrees to be personally liable. (b) When the agent acts for a foreign principal. (c) When the agent acts for an undisclosed principal (the third party can sue either the agent or the principal when the principal is discovered). (d) When the agent acts without authority or exceeds his authority. (e) When the contract is made by the agent in his own name without disclosing the existence of the principal. (f) When the agent receives money by mistake or through fraud.

Termination of Agency – Sections 201 to 210

An agency may be terminated in the following ways:

(1) By revocation by the principal – Section 203: The principal may revoke the authority given to the agent at any time before the authority has been exercised by the agent. However, where the agent has already exercised his authority partly, the principal can revoke only as to the unexercised part.

(2) By renunciation by the agent – Section 206: The agent may renounce the business of the agency by giving reasonable notice to the principal. If the agent renounces without reasonable notice, he must compensate the principal for any damage caused.

(3) By completion of the business of the agency: When the business for which the agency was created is completed, the agency comes to an end.

(4) By death or insanity of the principal or agent – Section 201:

The agency is terminated when the principal or the agent dies or becomes of unsound mind.

(5) By insolvency of the principal – Section 201: The agency is terminated when the principal is adjudicated insolvent.

(6) By expiry of the period of agency: If the agency is for a fixed period, it terminates on the expiry of that period.

(7) By destruction of the subject matter: If the subject matter of the agency is destroyed, the agency comes to an end.

(8) By the principal becoming an alien enemy: If the principal becomes an alien enemy due to the outbreak of war, the agency is terminated.

Irrevocable Agency – Section 202

As a general rule, the principal can revoke the authority of the agent at any time. But in the following cases, the agency becomes irrevocable and the principal cannot revoke it:

(a) Agency Coupled with Interest: Where the agent has himself an interest in the subject matter of the agency, the agency is called 'agency coupled with interest.' Such agency cannot be terminated to the prejudice of the agent's interest. For example, A owes Rs. 10,000 to B. A gives authority to B to sell A's land and to repay himself out of the proceeds. B has an interest in the subject matter of the agency. A cannot revoke this authority.

(b) Authority partly exercised – Section 204: Where the agent has already partly exercised his authority, the principal cannot revoke the agent's authority so far as regards acts already done by the agent.

Note: When an agency is terminated, the agent must stop acting on behalf of the principal. The principal must give reasonable notice of the termination to third parties who have been dealing with the agent. If notice is not given, the principal will be bound by the acts of the agent done after the termination.

Case: Bolton Partners v. Lambert (1889)

An agent, acting without authority, accepted an offer made by a third party on behalf of the principal. The principal later ratified the agent's act. The third party tried to withdraw the offer. The Court held that ratification related back to the date of the original act. Once ratified, the contract was binding from the date the agent accepted the offer. The third party could not withdraw.

Chapter 4

Sale of Goods Act, 1930

The sale of goods is the most common type of commercial transaction in our daily life. We buy and sell goods every day – from buying vegetables in the market to purchasing a car or a house. But what happens when the goods are defective? What if the seller has no right to sell the goods? Who bears the risk if the goods are destroyed during transit? What are the rights of the buyer and the seller? All these questions are answered by the Sale of Goods Act, 1930.

The Sale of Goods Act, 1930 came into force on 1st July, 1930. Before this Act, the law relating to sale of goods was contained in Chapter VII (Sections 76 to 123) of the Indian Contract Act, 1872. These sections were repealed and the Sale of Goods Act was enacted as a separate legislation. The Sale of Goods Act, 1930 is based on the English Sale of Goods Act, 1893 (now replaced by the Sale of Goods Act, 1979 in England). The Act extends to the whole of India except the State of Jammu and Kashmir (now applicable after 2019 reorganisation). It contains 66 sections divided into 7 chapters.

Since the Sale of Goods Act is a special law dealing with sale of goods, it prevails over the Indian Contract Act (which is the general law of contracts) in matters relating to sale of goods. However, the general principles of the Indian Contract Act, such as the rules relating to offer and acceptance, consideration, capacity, free consent, etc., continue to apply to contracts of sale of goods to the extent they are not inconsistent with the Sale of Goods Act (Section 3).

4.1 Definition and Essentials of a Contract of Sale

Definition of a Contract of Sale – Section 4

Section 4(1) of the Sale of Goods Act defines a contract of sale as follows: "A contract of sale of goods is a contract whereby the seller transfers or agrees to transfer the property in goods to the buyer for a price." From this definition, it is clear that a contract of sale may be either a 'sale' or an 'agreement to sell.'

Sale: Where under a contract of sale, the property in the goods is transferred from the seller to the buyer, the contract is called a sale [Section 4(3)]. In a sale, the ownership of the goods passes immediately to the buyer at the time of the contract.

Agreement to Sell: Where under a contract of sale, the transfer of the property in the goods is to take place at a future time or subject to some condition thereafter to be fulfilled, the contract is called an agreement to sell [Section 4(3)]. An agreement to sell becomes a sale when the time elapses or the conditions are fulfilled subject to which the property in the goods is to be transferred [Section 4(4)].

Illustration: A says to B, 'I sell my bicycle to you for Rs. 5,000.' B agrees. The ownership of the bicycle passes from A to B immediately. This is a SALE. But if A says, 'I agree to sell my bicycle to you for Rs. 5,000 next Monday,' B agrees. The ownership will pass next Monday. This is an AGREEMENT TO SELL.

Essential Elements of a Contract of Sale

From the definition of a contract of sale, the following essential elements can be identified:

(1) Two Parties: There must be two distinct parties to a contract of sale – a buyer and a seller. The seller is a person who sells or agrees to sell goods, and the buyer is a person who buys or agrees to buy goods [Section 2(1) and 2(13)]. A person cannot be both a buyer and a seller in the same transaction. However, there is one exception – a part-owner can sell goods to another part-owner [Section 4(1)]. Also, in case of sale by an agent, the agent may buy for himself with the consent of the principal.

(2) Goods: The subject matter of a contract of sale must be 'goods.' Section 2(7) defines goods as "every kind of moveable property other than actionable claims and money; and includes stock and shares, growing crops, grass, and things attached to or forming part of the land which are agreed to be severed before sale or under the contract of sale." Thus, goods include all types of moveable property except actionable claims (like debts) and money. Immovable property like land and buildings is not 'goods' and cannot be the subject of a contract of sale under this Act.

Classification of Goods

Goods may be classified into the following categories:

(a) Existing Goods: These are goods which are owned or possessed by the seller at the time of the contract of sale [Section 6]. Existing goods may be further classified as – (i) Specific goods: goods identified and agreed upon at the time a contract of sale is made [Section 2(14)]. For example, A agrees to sell 'this particular horse' to B. (ii) Ascertained goods: these are goods which are identified and agreed upon after the contract of sale is made. The term is not defined in the Act but is used in Section 18. Ascertained goods are goods which were unascertained at the time of the contract but have since been identified. (iii) Unascertained goods: goods which are not specifically identified but are indicated only by description. For example, A agrees to sell to B '10 bags of wheat from my godown" containing 100 bags. The 10 bags have not been identified yet.

(b) Future Goods: These are goods which the seller does not possess at the time of the contract but which will be manufactured, produced, or acquired by him after the making of the contract of sale [Section 2(6)]. A contract for the sale of future goods can only be an agreement to sell and not a sale, because the ownership cannot be transferred at the time of the contract when the goods do not yet exist.

(c) Contingent Goods: These are a sub-category of future goods. They are goods the acquisition of which by the seller depends upon a contingency which may or may not happen [Section 6(2)]. For example, A agrees to sell to B a specific painting which A expects to acquire at an auction. If A is able to buy the painting at the auction, the contract takes effect. If A cannot acquire it, the contract becomes void.

(3) Price: The consideration for a contract of sale must be money, which is called the 'price.' Section 2(10) defines price as the money consideration for the sale of goods. If goods are exchanged for goods, it is barter and not sale. However, if goods are exchanged partly for goods and partly for money, it is a sale. The price may be fixed in the contract itself, or may be left to be fixed in a manner agreed upon, or may be determined by the course of dealing between the parties [Section 9]. Where the price is not fixed, the buyer must pay a reasonable price [Section 9(2)]. What is a reasonable price depends on the circumstances of each case.

(4) Transfer of Property (Ownership): There must be a transfer or an agreement to transfer the property (i.e., ownership) in goods from the seller to the buyer. The word 'property' in the Sale of Goods Act means the general property (i.e., ownership) and not merely the possession. A mere transfer of possession without transfer of ownership is not a sale but may be a bailment or a hire-purchase agreement.

(5) All Essentials of a Valid Contract: Since a contract of sale is a special type of contract, all the essential elements of a valid contract under the Indian Contract Act, 1872 must also be present. There must be a lawful offer and acceptance, intention to create legal relations, capacity of parties, free consent, lawful consideration, and lawful object. The contract must not be one which is declared void by law.

Distinction Between Sale and Agreement to Sell

Table 4.1: Sale vs. Agreement to Sell

Point of Distinction	Sale	Agreement to Sell
Transfer of property	Property passes immediately to the	Property is to pass at a future date or on

	buyer	fulfilment of condition
Type of contract	It is an executed contract	It is an executory contract
Risk	Risk passes to buyer even if goods are with seller	Risk remains with seller
Consequences of breach	Buyer can sue for price of goods (Section 56)	Seller can only sue for damages (Section 57)
Right to resell	Seller cannot resell; if he does, second buyer gets no title	Seller can resell; second buyer gets good title (if in good faith)
Insolvency of buyer	Seller must deliver goods to official receiver; can claim price only	Seller can refuse to deliver and retain the goods
Insolvency of seller	Buyer can claim the goods from official receiver	Buyer can only claim rateable dividend, not the goods
Nature of right	Buyer gets right in rem (against whole world)	Buyer gets right in personam (against seller only)

Distinction Between Sale and Other Transactions

(A) Sale and Hire-Purchase

In a hire-purchase agreement, goods are delivered to a person on the condition that he will pay the price in instalments. The hirer (buyer) has the option to return the goods at any time before the payment of all instalments. The ownership of the goods remains with the seller until the last instalment is paid. In a sale, the ownership passes immediately to the buyer. The main distinctions are: (a) In sale, the property passes immediately; in hire-purchase, the property passes only on payment of the last instalment. (b) In sale, the buyer cannot return the goods; in hire-purchase, the hirer can return at any time. (c) In sale, the buyer can pass a good title to a third person; in hire-purchase, the hirer cannot pass title until he acquires it. (d) The position of the hirer is that of a bailee until the last instalment is paid. (e) If the hirer becomes insolvent, the goods belong to the owner (seller), not to the hirer's creditors.

Case: Helby v. Matthews (1895)

A person took a piano on hire-purchase agreement. Before paying all the instalments, he pledged it with a third party. The question was whether the third party got a good title. The House of Lords held that the hirer was not a 'buyer in possession' and therefore could not pass a good title. The owner (seller) was entitled to recover the piano from the third party. This case established the important distinction between sale and hire-purchase.

(B) Sale and Bailment

In bailment, only possession is transferred and the goods are to be returned. In sale, the ownership is transferred and the goods are not to be returned. In bailment, there is no price; the consideration (if any) is the service rendered. In sale, the consideration is the price in money.

(C) Sale and Gift

In a gift, the property in goods is transferred without any consideration. In sale, the property is transferred for a price. A gift is not a contract of sale because there is no price. However, both in gift and sale, the ownership is transferred.

(D) Sale and Barter

In barter, goods are exchanged for goods. There is no price involved. In sale, goods are exchanged for money (price). If goods are exchanged partly for goods and partly for money, it depends on the circumstances whether the transaction is a sale or a barter. Generally, if the money element is dominant, it is treated as a sale.

(E) Sale and Contract for Work and Labour

Sometimes it is difficult to determine whether a transaction is a sale of goods or a contract for work and labour (service). If the substance of the contract is the transfer of goods, it is a sale. If the substance is the skill and labour applied and the transfer of goods is only incidental, it is a contract for work and labour.

Case: Robinson v. Graves (1935)

A painter was commissioned to paint a portrait. The question was whether this was a sale of goods or a contract for work and labour. The Court held that this was a contract for work and labour because the essence of the contract was the skill of the painter. The transfer of the canvas and paint was merely incidental.

Note: The distinction between sale and contract for work and labour is important for purposes of taxation. Under GST, the supply of goods is taxed differently from the supply of services. Therefore, this distinction has great practical significance in the Indian context.

4.2 Conditions and Warranties

In every contract of sale, there are certain terms which the parties agree upon. Some of these terms are very important and go to the root of the contract. Some other terms are of lesser importance and are only collateral to the main purpose of the contract. The Sale of Goods Act divides these terms into two categories – conditions and warranties.

Condition – Section 12(2)

Section 12(2) defines a condition as a stipulation essential to the main purpose of the contract, the breach of which gives rise to a right to treat the contract as repudiated. In simple words, a condition is a term which is so important that if it is broken, the other party has the right to cancel the contract altogether and also claim damages.

Illustration: A wants to buy a car which can run at a speed of 150 km/hour. He tells B (the seller) about this requirement. B sells a car to A saying that it can run at 150 km/hour. Later A finds that the car cannot exceed 100 km/hour. Here, the speed was a condition of the contract. A can reject the car and cancel the contract.

Warranty – Section 12(3)

Section 12(3) defines a warranty as a stipulation collateral to the main purpose of the contract, the breach of which gives rise to a claim for damages but not to a right to reject the goods and treat the contract as repudiated. In simple words, a warranty is a less important term. If it is broken, the buyer can claim damages but cannot reject the goods.

Illustration: A buys a bicycle from B. B says that the bicycle has a good carrier. Later, A finds that the carrier is defective. The carrier is not the main purpose of buying the bicycle. It is only collateral. A cannot reject the bicycle but can claim damages for the defective carrier.

Distinction Between Condition and Warranty

Table 4.2: Condition vs. Warranty

Point	Condition	Warranty
Nature	Essential to the main purpose of the contract	Collateral to the main purpose
Effect of breach	Aggrieved party can repudiate the contract + claim damages	Aggrieved party can only claim damages
Treatment	Breach of condition can be treated as breach of warranty	Breach of warranty cannot be treated as breach of condition
Section	Section 12(2)	Section 12(3)

When a Condition is Treated as a Warranty – Section 13

In the following cases, a breach of condition is treated as a breach of warranty (i.e., the buyer loses his right to reject the goods and can only claim damages):

(a) Voluntary waiver by the buyer: Where a contract of sale is subject to any condition to be fulfilled by the seller, the buyer may waive the condition or elect to treat the breach of the condition as a breach of warranty and not as a ground for treating the contract as repudiated [Section 13(1)].

(b) Acceptance of goods by the buyer: Where a contract of sale is not severable and the buyer has accepted the goods or part thereof, the breach of any condition to be fulfilled by the seller can only be treated as a breach of warranty and not as a ground for rejecting the goods [Section 13(2)]. Once the buyer has accepted the goods, he cannot later reject them for breach of condition.

Note: A condition cannot be elevated to the level of something greater. But a warranty cannot be elevated to the level of a condition. In other words, a breach of warranty never gives the right to reject the goods.

Implied Conditions

An implied condition is one which the law reads into the contract even though the parties have not expressly included it. The following are the implied conditions in a contract of sale:

(1) Condition as to Title – Section 14(a): In every contract of sale, unless the circumstances of the contract are such as to show a different intention, there is an implied condition on the part of the seller that – (i) in the case of a sale, he has a right to sell the goods, and (ii) in the case of an agreement to sell, he will have a right to sell the goods at the time when the property is to pass. If the seller has no title to the goods, the buyer can reject the goods and recover the price paid.

Case: Rowland v. Divall (1923)

A bought a car from B and used it for several months. Later, it was found that B had no title to the car as the car was a stolen one. A was compelled to return the car to the true owner. A sued B for the return of the price. The Court held that there was a total failure of consideration because B had no right to sell the car. A was entitled to recover the full price even though he had used the car for several months.

(2) Condition of Sale by Description – Section 15: Where there is a contract for the sale of goods by description, there is an implied condition that the goods shall correspond with the description. If the goods do not match the description, the buyer can reject them. If the sale is by description as well as by sample, the goods must correspond both with the description and the sample.

Illustration: A orders for 'Basmati rice' from B. B supplies 'ordinary rice.' The goods do not correspond with the description. A can reject the goods.

(3) Condition of Sale by Sample – Section 17: Where goods are sold by sample, there are the following implied conditions: (a) that the bulk shall correspond with the sample in quality, (b) that the buyer shall have a reasonable opportunity of comparing the bulk with the sample, and (c) that the goods shall be free from any defect, rendering them unmerchantable, which would not be apparent on reasonable examination of the sample.

(4) Condition of Sale by Sample as Well as by Description – Section 15: If the sale is by sample as well as by description, the goods must correspond both with the sample and with the description. If the goods correspond with the sample but not with the description, the buyer can reject the goods.

(5) Condition as to Quality or Fitness – Section 16(1): As a general rule, there is no implied condition as to the quality or fitness of goods for any particular purpose. This is based on the doctrine of 'caveat emptor' (let the buyer beware). However, Section 16(1) provides an important exception. Where the buyer, expressly or by implication, makes known to the seller the particular purpose for which the goods are required, so as to show that the buyer relies on the seller's skill or judgment, and the goods are of a description which it is in the course of the seller's business to supply, there is an implied condition that the goods shall be reasonably fit for such purpose.

Case: Priest v. Last (1903)

A customer went to a chemist and asked for a hot water bottle. The chemist supplied one. The bottle burst when hot water was put in it and the customer's wife was injured. The Court held that the customer had made known the purpose (to hold hot water) to the seller and had relied on the seller's judgment. There was an implied condition that the bottle should be fit for holding hot water. Since the bottle was not fit for the purpose, the buyer was entitled to damages.

(6) Condition as to Merchantability – Section 16(2): Where goods are bought by description from a seller who deals in goods of that description (whether he is the manufacturer or not), there is an implied condition that the goods shall be of merchantable quality. Merchantable quality means that the goods are of such quality and in such condition that a reasonable man, acting reasonably, would accept them as being of merchantable quality, having regard to the description applied to them and the price. But if the buyer has examined the goods, there shall be no implied condition as regards defects which such examination ought to have revealed.

(7) Condition as to Wholesomeness: In the case of eatables and provisions (foodstuffs), there is an implied condition that the goods shall be wholesome (i.e., fit for human consumption) in addition to being merchantable. This condition is not expressly mentioned in the Act but has been recognised by the courts.

Case: Frost v. Aylesbury Dairy Co. (1905)

A dairy company supplied milk which contained typhoid germs. The wife of the buyer died after consuming the contaminated milk. The Court held that there was an implied condition that the milk would be wholesome. Since the milk was contaminated, the dairy company was liable.

Implied Warranties

The following warranties are implied in a contract of sale, unless the circumstances of the contract show a different intention:

(1) Warranty of Quiet Possession – Section 14(b): The buyer shall have and enjoy quiet possession of the goods. If the buyer is disturbed in the enjoyment of the goods by any person having a superior title, he can sue the seller for breach of this warranty. For example, if A buys a car from B and later C proves that he is the true owner and takes away the car from A, A can sue B for breach of warranty of quiet possession.

(2) Warranty of Freedom from Encumbrances – Section 14(c): The goods shall be free from any charge or encumbrance in favour of any third party not declared or known to the buyer before or at the time when the contract is made. If the buyer has to pay any amount to remove any such charge, he can recover such amount from the seller.

(3) Warranty as to Disclosure of Dangerous Nature of Goods: Where the goods are inherently dangerous or are likely to be dangerous and the buyer is unaware of their dangerous nature, the seller is under a duty to warn the buyer of such danger. Failure to do so amounts to breach of warranty.

Doctrine of Caveat Emptor – Section 16

'Caveat emptor' is a Latin phrase which means 'let the buyer beware.' This is one of the most important principles of the law relating to sale of goods. According to this doctrine, it is the duty of the buyer to be careful while purchasing goods. The seller is under no duty to disclose defects in the goods to the buyer. If the buyer makes a bad choice, he cannot blame the seller for it.

Section 16 embodies this doctrine by stating that "there is no implied warranty or condition as to the quality or fitness for any particular purpose of goods supplied under a contract of sale."

However, the doctrine of caveat emptor is subject to the following exceptions:

(a) Where the buyer makes known the purpose and relies on the seller's skill and judgment (Section 16(1)). (b) Where goods are sold by description and are not of merchantable quality (Section 16(2)). (c) Where there is a usage of trade which annexes an implied condition or warranty (Section 16(4)). (d) Where the seller has made a misrepresentation or has practised fraud and the buyer has relied on such statement. (e) Where the goods are sold by sample and the defect is not apparent on reasonable examination. (f) Where the seller being aware of the defect does not disclose it.

Case: Ward v. Hobbs (1878)

A sold pigs to B by auction. A knew that some of the pigs were suffering from a disease but did not disclose this fact. B's pigs caught the disease and died. B sued A. The House of Lords held that the doctrine of caveat emptor applied. There was no implied warranty that the pigs were free from disease. The buyer should have examined the pigs himself. However, the court observed that if there was fraud or active concealment by the seller, the result would have been different.

4.3 Transfer of Property in Goods

The question 'When does the ownership pass from the seller to the buyer?' is one of the most important questions in the law of sale of goods. This question is significant because the transfer of ownership determines who bears the risk of loss or damage to the goods. The general rule is that risk follows ownership – the person who owns the goods must bear the risk (Section 26).

Section Reference: Section 26: Unless otherwise agreed, the goods remain at the seller's risk until the property therein is transferred to the buyer, but when the property therein is transferred to the buyer, the goods are at the buyer's risk whether delivery has been made or not.

Rules for Transfer of Property in Specific Goods – Sections 19 to 22

Rule 1 – Specific goods in a deliverable state (Section 20): Where there is an unconditional contract for the sale of specific goods in a deliverable state, the property in the goods passes to the buyer when the contract is made, and it is immaterial whether the time of payment or the time of delivery, or both, be postponed. In simple terms, if the goods are identified, ready for delivery, and the contract is unconditional, the ownership passes at the time of the contract itself.

Illustration: A agrees to buy a specific table from B's showroom for Rs. 10,000. The table is ready for delivery. The ownership of the table passes to A at the time of the contract, even though A has not yet paid the price and B has not yet delivered the table.

Rule 2 – Specific goods not in a deliverable state (Section 21): Where there is a contract for the sale of specific goods and the seller is bound to do something to the goods for the purpose of putting them into a deliverable state, the property does not pass until such thing is done and the buyer has notice thereof. The goods are said to be in a deliverable state when they are in such a state that the buyer would, under the contract, be bound to take delivery of them [Section 2(4)].

Illustration: A agrees to sell his old car to B for Rs. 2,00,000. A promises to get the car repainted and serviced before delivery. The ownership of the car will pass to B only when the car is repainted and serviced and B has been informed about it.

Rule 3 – Specific goods in a deliverable state but seller has to do something to ascertain price (Section 22): Where there is a contract for the sale of specific goods in a deliverable state, but the seller is bound to weigh, measure, test, or do some other act or thing with reference to the goods for the purpose of ascertaining the price, the property does not pass until such act or thing is done and the buyer has notice thereof.

Illustration: A agrees to sell potatoes to B at Rs. 30 per kg. The potatoes are in a deliverable state but have not yet been weighed. The property will pass to B only when the potatoes are weighed and B has notice of the weight.

Rules for Transfer of Property in Unascertained Goods – Section 18 & 23

Section 18: Where there is a contract for the sale of unascertained goods, no property in the goods is transferred to the buyer unless and until the goods are ascertained. The goods must be identified and appropriated to the contract before ownership can pass.

Rule 4 – Appropriation of goods (Section 23): Where there is a contract for the sale of unascertained or future goods by description, and goods of that description and in a deliverable state are unconditionally appropriated to the contract, either by the seller with the assent of the buyer or by the buyer with the assent of the seller, the property in the goods thereupon passes to the buyer. Such assent may be express or implied and may be given either before or after the appropriation is made.

Appropriation means setting apart or identifying specific goods for the purpose of the contract. For example, if A agrees to sell 10 bags of wheat to B out of a stock of 100 bags, the property will pass to B only when A separates 10 bags from the stock and communicates this to B.

Delivery to a carrier (e.g., railway or shipping company) for the purpose of transmission to the buyer is deemed to be unconditional appropriation, unless the seller reserves the right of disposal (Section 23(2)).

Rule 5 – Goods Sent on Approval or 'Sale or Return' – Section 24

When goods are delivered to the buyer on approval or 'on sale or return' or other similar terms, the property therein passes to the buyer – (a) when the buyer signifies his approval or acceptance to the seller, or does any other act adopting the transaction, (b) if he does not signify his approval or acceptance but retains the goods without giving notice of rejection, then, if a time has been fixed for return, on the expiration of such time, and if no time has been fixed, on the expiration of a reasonable time.

Reservation of Right of Disposal – Section 25

Section 25 provides that where there is a contract for the sale of specific goods or where goods are subsequently appropriated to the contract, the seller may reserve the right of disposal of the goods until certain conditions are fulfilled. In such a case, the property in the goods does not pass to the buyer until the conditions imposed by the seller are fulfilled. The most common example is where the seller sends goods by railway or shipping and takes the bill of lading or railway receipt in his own name or in the name of his agent. This shows the seller's intention to reserve the right of disposal until the price is paid.

Transfer of Title by Non-Owners – 'Nemo Dat Quod Non Habet'

The general rule of law is that no one can transfer a better title than he himself has. This is expressed by the Latin maxim 'nemo dat quod non habet' which means 'no one can give what he has not got.' Section 27 states: "Where goods are sold by a person who is not the owner thereof and who does not sell them under the authority or with the consent of the owner, the buyer acquires no better title to the goods than the seller had."

However, this rule is subject to the following important exceptions where a buyer may acquire a good title even though the seller had no title or a defective title:

(1) Sale by Estoppel (Section 27, Proviso): If the true owner, by his words or conduct, leads the buyer to believe that the seller has the authority to sell, the owner is estopped from denying the seller's authority. The buyer gets a good title.

(2) Sale by Mercantile Agent (Section 27, Exception): Where a mercantile agent is, with the consent of the owner, in possession of goods or documents of title to goods, any sale made by him in the ordinary course of business of a mercantile agent shall be as valid as if he were expressly authorised by the owner, provided the buyer acts in good faith and without notice.

(3) Sale by Joint Owner (Section 28): If one of the several joint owners of goods is in sole possession thereof with the permission of the co-owners, the property in the goods is transferred to any person who buys them in good faith from such joint owner.

(4) Sale by Person in Possession Under Voidable Contract (Section 29): When the seller of goods has obtained possession under a contract voidable under Section 19 or 19A of the Indian Contract Act (e.g., by fraud), and the contract has not been rescinded at the time of the sale, the buyer acquires a good title, provided he buys in good faith and without notice of the seller's defect of title.

(5) Sale by Seller in Possession After Sale (Section 30(1)): Where a seller, having sold goods, continues in possession of the goods or of the documents of title, any sale by such seller to a second buyer shall have the same effect as if the seller were expressly authorised by the first buyer, provided the second buyer acts in good faith and without notice of the first sale.

(6) Sale by Buyer in Possession (Section 30(2)): Where a buyer, having bought or agreed to buy goods, obtains possession with the consent of the seller, any sale by such buyer to a third person shall have the same effect as if the buyer had the authority of the seller, provided the third person acts in good faith and without notice.

(7) Sale Under Other Laws: Section 27 also saves the provisions of other laws such as sale by a pawnee (Section 176, Indian Contract Act), sale by a finder of goods (Section 169, Indian Contract Act), sale in execution of a court decree, and sale by official liquidator or receiver in insolvency.

Note: The exceptions to the rule of 'nemo dat quod non habet' are designed to protect bona fide (good faith) buyers who have dealt honestly and paid value for the goods. The law seeks to balance the interests of the true owner with the need to protect innocent purchasers in commercial transactions.

4.4 Rights of an Unpaid Seller

The Sale of Goods Act gives special protection to the seller who has not been paid. Such a seller is called an 'unpaid seller.' The Act gives him certain rights even after he has delivered the goods to the buyer.

Who is an Unpaid Seller? – Section 45

Section 45(1) provides that the seller of goods is deemed to be an 'unpaid seller' within the meaning of this Act – (a) when the whole of the price has not been paid or tendered, or (b) when a bill of exchange or other negotiable instrument has been received as conditional payment and the condition on which it was received has not been fulfilled by reason of the dishonour of the instrument or otherwise.

It is important to note that it is not necessary that the seller should be entirely unpaid. Even if a part of the price has been paid and the balance is unpaid, the seller is an unpaid seller to the extent of the unpaid amount.

Rights of an Unpaid Seller

The rights of an unpaid seller are divided into two categories:

(A) Rights against the goods:

Even though the ownership (property) in the goods may have passed to the buyer, the unpaid seller has the following rights against the goods themselves:

(1) Right of Lien – Sections 47 to 49: The unpaid seller who is in possession of the goods is entitled to retain possession of the goods until the full price is paid or tendered. This is called the seller's lien. The unpaid seller can exercise his right of lien in the following cases [Section 47]: (a) where the goods have been sold without any stipulation as to credit, (b) where the goods have been sold on credit but the term of credit has expired, (c) where the buyer becomes insolvent. The seller's lien is a possessory lien. It depends on the possession of the goods. The seller loses his lien in the following cases [Section 49]: (a) when he delivers the goods to a carrier or other bailee for the purpose of transmission to the buyer without reserving the right of disposal, (b) when the buyer or his agent lawfully obtains possession of the goods, (c) by waiver of the lien by the seller. The unpaid seller does not lose his lien merely because he has obtained a decree for the price of the goods [Section 49(2)].

(2) Right of Stoppage in Transit – Sections 50 to 52: When the unpaid seller has parted with the possession of the goods and the buyer becomes insolvent, the seller has the right to stop the goods while they are in transit, resume possession of them, and retain them until the full price is paid. This right is called the right of stoppage in transit.

The conditions for exercising this right are: (a) the seller must be unpaid, (b) the buyer must have become insolvent, and (c) the goods must be in transit (i.e., in the hands of a carrier or other intermediary and not yet received by the buyer).

When are goods deemed to be in transit? [Section 51] The goods are deemed to be in transit from the time they are delivered to a carrier or other bailee for the purpose of transmission to the buyer until the buyer or his agent takes delivery of them. The transit comes to an end when: (a) the buyer or his agent obtains delivery before arrival at the appointed destination, (b) the goods have arrived at the appointed destination and the carrier acknowledges to the buyer that he holds the goods on his behalf, (c) the carrier wrongfully refuses to deliver to the buyer, (d) the buyer obtains delivery by the carrier at a point before the goods reach the destination.

How is the right exercised? [Section 52] The seller may exercise his right of stoppage in transit either by obtaining actual possession of the goods or by giving notice of his claim to the carrier or other bailee. The notice must be given to the principal carrier and not to a servant of the carrier.

(3) Right of Re-Sale – Section 54: The unpaid seller has a right of re-sale in the following cases:

(a) Where the goods are of a perishable nature – the seller may resell the goods without giving any notice to the buyer. (b) Where the seller gives notice to the buyer of his intention to resell and the buyer does not pay within a reasonable time – the seller may resell the goods. (c) Where the seller expressly reserves the right of resale in case the buyer defaults. If the seller resells the goods and realises a profit, he can retain the profit. If the buyer suffers a loss, the buyer has no remedy against the seller if proper notice was given. If the seller suffers a loss on resale, he can claim damages from the buyer.

(B) Rights against the buyer personally:

Apart from rights against the goods, the unpaid seller also has the following rights against the buyer personally:

(1) Suit for Price – Section 55: Where the property in the goods has passed to the buyer and the buyer wrongfully neglects or refuses to pay the price, the seller may sue him for the price. Also, where the price is payable on a certain day irrespective of delivery and the buyer neglects or refuses to pay, the seller may sue for the price although the property in the goods has not passed.

(2) Suit for Damages for Non-Acceptance – Section 56: Where the buyer wrongfully neglects or refuses to accept and pay for the goods, the seller may sue him for damages for non-acceptance. The measure of damages is the estimated loss directly and naturally resulting from the buyer's breach of contract in the ordinary course of events.

(3) Suit for Interest – Section 61: Where there is a specific agreement between the seller and the buyer as to the interest on the price, the seller may recover interest at the agreed rate. In the absence of such agreement, the court may allow interest at such rate as it thinks fit on the amount of the price from the date on which payment was due.

Rights of the Buyer

The Sale of Goods Act also provides certain rights to the buyer. These include:

(1) Suit for Damages for Non-Delivery – Section 57: Where the seller wrongfully neglects or refuses to deliver the goods, the buyer may sue him for damages for non-delivery.

(2) Suit for Specific Performance – Section 58: In a contract for specific or ascertained goods, the court may direct the seller to deliver the goods as per the terms of the contract (specific performance).

(3) Suit for Breach of Warranty – Section 59: Where there is a breach of warranty by the seller, the buyer can (a) set up the breach of warranty in diminution or extinction of the price, or (b) sue the seller for damages for breach of warranty.

(4) Right to Reject – Section 37: Where the seller delivers a quantity greater or less than what was contracted, or mixes the contract goods with goods of a different description, the buyer may accept the goods that are in accordance with the contract and reject the rest, or reject all the goods.

Table 4.3: Summary of Unpaid Seller's Rights

Rights Against Goods	Section	Rights Against Buyer Personally	Section
Right of Lien	47–49	Suit for Price	55
Right of Stoppage in Transit	50–52	Suit for Damages (Non-Acceptance)	56
Right of Re-Sale	54	Suit for Interest	61

PART – II : COMPANIES ACT, 2013 – FORMATION & REGISTRATION

Chapter 5

Introduction to Company Law

When we look around, we see that business in the modern world is mostly carried on by companies. From the neighbourhood grocery store chain to the giant multinational corporations like Reliance, Tata, Infosys, and Wipro – the company form of business organisation dominates the economic landscape. But what exactly is a company? How is it different from a partnership? Why do businessmen prefer to carry on business through a company rather than as individuals or as partners? What are the laws that govern companies in India? This chapter provides answers to these fundamental questions and introduces the student to the fascinating world of company law.

5.1 Historical Background of Company Law in India

The history of company law in India is closely connected with the history of British rule in the country. The concept of the joint stock company was first brought to India by the British traders and merchants. The development of company law in India can be traced through the following stages:

(A) Pre-Independence Period

(i) Joint Stock Companies Act, 1850: This was the first legislation dealing with companies in India. It was based on the English Companies Act of 1844. This Act allowed the formation of companies by registration but did not grant the benefit of limited liability to the members. In other words, the members of a company were personally liable for the debts of the company, just like partners in a partnership firm. Because of this major limitation, the Act did not become very popular.

(ii) Joint Stock Companies Act, 1857: This Act was passed on the pattern of the English Companies Act of 1856. The most important feature of this Act was that it introduced the concept of 'limited liability' for the first time in India. Members of a company were now liable only to the extent of the face value of the shares held by them. This was a revolutionary change and it gave a great boost to the formation of companies in India.

(iii) Indian Companies Act, 1866: This Act was modelled on the English Companies Act of 1862. It consolidated and improved upon the provisions of the earlier Acts. It remained in force for almost 16 years.

(iv) Indian Companies Act, 1882: This Act was based on the English Companies Act of 1880. It continued to govern companies in India until 1913.

(v) Indian Companies Act, 1913: This was a comprehensive legislation which was based on the English Companies (Consolidation) Act of 1908. It introduced the distinction between public companies and private companies for the first time in India. It also made provisions for the audit of accounts, prospectus, and the winding up of companies. This Act, with several amendments, continued to govern Indian companies until 1956.

(B) Post-Independence Period

(i) Companies Act, 1956: After Independence, the Government of India felt the need for a comprehensive and modern company law which would meet the requirements of a developing economy. Accordingly, a Company Law Committee was appointed under the chairmanship of Shri H.C. Bhabha in 1950. On the basis of the recommendations of this Committee, the Companies Act, 1956 was enacted. This Act was a very detailed and elaborate piece of legislation containing 658 sections and 15 schedules. It governed all aspects of the formation, management, and winding up of companies in India.

The Companies Act, 1956 was amended several times to keep pace with the changing economic environment. Some of the major amendments were made in 1960, 1963, 1965, 1969, 1974, 1977, 1985, 1988, 1996, 1999, 2000, and 2002. Despite these numerous amendments, the Act became outdated and complex over time. It was felt that a completely new Act was needed which would be in tune with the changed economic scenario of liberalisation, privatisation, and globalisation.

(ii) Companies Act, 2013: After a long process of deliberation and consultation, the Companies Bill, 2012 was passed by the Lok Sabha on 18th December, 2012 and by the Rajya Sabha on 8th August, 2013. It received the assent of the President on 29th August, 2013 and was published in the Official Gazette on 30th August, 2013. The provisions of the Act were notified in phases. The first set of 98 sections was notified on 12th September, 2013. The remaining sections have been notified subsequently. The Companies Act, 2013 has replaced the Companies Act, 1956 almost entirely.

The Companies Act, 2013 contains 470 sections (compared to 658 sections in the 1956 Act) and 7 schedules (compared to 15 schedules in the 1956 Act). It is more compact and better organised than the earlier Act. However, many of the substantive provisions are contained in the Rules which have been framed under the Act. The Act has been further amended by the Companies (Amendment) Act, 2015, the Companies (Amendment) Act, 2017, and the Companies (Amendment) Act, 2020, among others.

Table 5.1: Historical Development of Company Law in India

Year	Legislation	Key Feature
1850	Joint Stock Companies Act	First company law; no limited liability

1857	Joint Stock Companies Act	Introduced limited liability
1866	Indian Companies Act	Consolidation of earlier laws
1882	Indian Companies Act	Based on English Act of 1880
1913	Indian Companies Act	Public vs. Private company distinction
1956	Companies Act	Comprehensive post-independence Act; 658 sections
2013	Companies Act	Modern Act; 470 sections; replaced 1956 Act

5.2 Companies Act, 2013 – Salient Features

The Companies Act, 2013 brought about several significant changes in the corporate law framework of India. The Act was designed to be in conformity with international best practices and to facilitate ease of doing business while ensuring adequate protection for investors and other stakeholders. The following are the salient features of the Companies Act, 2013:

(1) Introduction of One Person Company (OPC): For the first time in India, the concept of One Person Company has been introduced [Section 2(62)]. An OPC is a company which has only one member. This is a significant departure from the earlier requirement of a minimum of two members for a private company. The OPC concept allows a single entrepreneur to carry on business with the benefits of limited liability and a separate legal entity. This is a great boost for start-ups and small entrepreneurs.

(2) Class Action Suits: Section 245 of the Act introduces the concept of class action suits for the first time in Indian company law. A specified number of members or depositors can file an application before the National Company Law Tribunal (NCLT) if they believe that the management of the company is conducting the affairs in a manner prejudicial to the interests of the company or its members or depositors.

(3) National Company Law Tribunal (NCLT) and Appellate Tribunal (NCLAT): The Act provides for the constitution of the NCLT and the NCLAT [Sections 407–434] to adjudicate all matters relating to companies. The NCLT replaces the Company Law Board and the High Court jurisdiction in company matters. The NCLAT is the appellate body. This brings all company law matters under one single adjudicatory body, ensuring consistency and specialisation.

(4) Corporate Social Responsibility (CSR): Section 135 of the Act introduces mandatory Corporate Social Responsibility for the first time. Every company having a net worth of Rs. 500 crore or more, or a turnover of Rs. 1,000 crore or more, or a net profit of Rs. 5 crore or more during the immediately preceding financial year is required to constitute a CSR Committee and spend at least 2% of the average net profits of the preceding three years on CSR activities as specified in Schedule VII.

(5) Independent Directors: The Act lays great emphasis on the role of independent directors in corporate governance. Section 149(4) requires every listed public company to have at least one-third of the total number of directors as independent directors. The Act specifies the qualifications, duties, and liabilities of independent directors in detail. A separate code for independent directors is given in Schedule IV of the Act.

(6) Woman Director: Section 149(1), read with Rule 3 of the Companies (Appointment and Qualification of Directors) Rules, 2014, requires certain class of companies to appoint at least one woman director. This includes every listed company, every public company having a paid-up share capital of Rs. 100 crore or more, and every public company having a turnover of Rs. 300 crore or more.

(7) Prohibition of Insider Trading: Section 195 of the Act prohibits insider trading. No person, including a director or key managerial personnel, shall enter into insider trading. This provision is in addition to the SEBI (Prohibition of Insider Trading) Regulations.

(8) E-Governance: Section 120 of the Act promotes e-governance in company administration. The Central Government may prescribe that the documents to be filed with the Registrar of Companies may be in electronic form. The filing of annual returns, financial statements, and other documents is now done electronically through the MCA (Ministry of Corporate Affairs) portal.

(9) Registered Valuer: The Act introduces the concept of registered valuers [Section 247]. Any valuation required under the Act must be made by a registered valuer. This is aimed at ensuring proper valuation of assets and liabilities, especially during mergers, amalgamations, and acquisitions.

(10) Fraud and Punishment: The Act takes a very serious view of fraud. Section 447 defines fraud and prescribes severe punishment – imprisonment which shall not be less than 6 months but which may extend to 10 years and a fine which shall not be less than the amount involved in the fraud but which may extend to three times the amount involved. If the fraud involves public interest, the minimum imprisonment is 3 years.

(11) Fast Track Merger: Section 233 provides for a simplified procedure for merger and amalgamation of certain classes of companies (small companies, holding and subsidiary companies, and other prescribed classes) without the need for approval by the NCLT. This is called fast track merger.

(12) Dormant Company: Section 455 introduces the concept of a dormant company. A company which has not been carrying on any business or has not been in operation for the last two consecutive financial years may apply to the Registrar for obtaining the status of a dormant company. This allows companies to maintain their registration without being struck off.

(13) Secretarial Audit: Section 204 mandates secretarial audit for every listed company and every public company having a paid-up share capital of Rs. 50 crore or more, or a turnover of Rs. 250 crore or more. The secretarial audit is to be conducted by a company secretary in practice.

(14) Serious Fraud Investigation Office (SFIO): Section 211 provides for the establishment of the SFIO to investigate serious cases of fraud relating to a company. The SFIO has been given wide powers of investigation and the cases investigated by it are tried by special courts.

(15) Rotation of Auditors: Section 139 provides for the rotation of auditors. An individual auditor cannot be appointed for more than one term of five consecutive years and an audit firm cannot be appointed for more than two terms of five consecutive years. After completion of the maximum term, there is a cooling-off period of five years before reappointment.

Note: The Companies Act, 2013 is a dynamic piece of legislation. The Central Government has been making frequent amendments and issuing notifications and circulars to clarify various provisions. Students are advised to keep themselves updated with the latest amendments and rules.

5.3 Definition and Characteristics of a Company

Definition of Company

The Companies Act, 2013 does not give a comprehensive definition of the word 'company.' Section 2(20) merely states that "'company' means a company incorporated under this Act or under any previous company law." This is a technical and legal definition which tells us that a company is a body incorporated (registered) under the Companies Act.

However, various authors and judges have given more descriptive definitions:

According to Lord Justice Lindley: "A company is an association of many persons who contribute money or money's worth to a common stock and employ it in some trade or business, and who share the profit and loss arising therefrom. The common stock so contributed is denoted in money and is the capital of the company. The persons who contribute it, or to whom it belongs, are members. The proportion of capital to which each member is entitled is his share."

According to Chief Justice Marshall (USA): "A corporation is an artificial being, invisible, intangible, and existing only in the contemplation of law."

According to Professor Haney: "A company is an artificial person created by law, having a separate entity with a perpetual succession and a common seal."

From these definitions, we can understand that a company is essentially a group of persons who come together for a common purpose, contribute capital, and form a separate legal entity which is distinct from its members. The company is created by the process of law (i.e., registration under the Companies Act) and it can do everything that a natural person can do in its own name.

Characteristics of a Company

A company has certain unique features which distinguish it from other forms of business organisation such as sole proprietorship, partnership, and Hindu Undivided Family business. These characteristics are as follows:

(1) Separate Legal Entity: A company has a separate legal existence apart from its members. It is a legal person in the eyes of law. It can own property, enter into contracts, sue and be sued in its own name. The property of the company is not the property of the members and vice versa. The debts of the company are not the debts of the members. This principle was firmly established by the House of Lords in the following landmark case:

Case: Salomon v. Salomon & Co. Ltd. (1897)

Mr. Aron Salomon was a boot and shoe manufacturer. He formed a company called Salomon & Co. Ltd. with himself, his wife, his daughter, and his four sons as the seven members (the minimum required at that time). Salomon sold his business to the company for £39,000. He received £20,000 in debentures (secured by a floating charge on the company's assets), £10,000 in fully paid shares, and the balance in cash. The company soon went into liquidation. The company's assets were not sufficient to pay all the creditors. The unsecured creditors argued that the company was a mere sham and Salomon and the company were the same person, so Salomon should be personally liable. The House of Lords unanimously held that the company was a separate legal entity distinct from its members. Salomon, as a secured creditor (debenture holder), had the first claim on the company's assets. The unsecured creditors had no claim against Salomon personally. Lord Macnaghten said: 'The company is at law a different person altogether from the subscribers to the memorandum.'

(2) Incorporated Body (Created by Law): A company comes into existence only by registration under the Companies Act. It is created by a process of law and can be dissolved only by a process of law. Unlike a partnership which can be created by a mere agreement (oral or written), a company must go through the formal procedure of registration with the Registrar of Companies. The date mentioned in the certificate of incorporation is the date of birth of the company.

(3) Limited Liability: The liability of the members of a company is limited. In a company limited by shares, the liability of each member is limited to the amount unpaid on the shares held by him. For example, if a member holds shares of face value Rs. 100 each and has paid Rs. 75 per share, his liability is only Rs. 25 per share. He cannot be asked to pay anything more even if the company's debts exceed its assets. In a company limited by guarantee, the liability of each member is limited to the amount of guarantee. This feature of limited liability is the greatest advantage of the company form of business and is the main reason for its popularity.

Illustration: A holds 1,000 shares of Rs. 10 each in XYZ Ltd. He has paid Rs. 7 per share. The company goes into liquidation owing Rs. 50 lakhs to its creditors. A's maximum liability is only Rs. 3,000 (i.e., Rs. 3 per share × 1,000 shares). He cannot be asked to pay even one rupee more.

(4) Perpetual Succession: A company has perpetual succession. It continues to exist irrespective of changes in its membership. Members may come and go, but the company goes on forever. The death, insolvency, or retirement of any member does not affect the existence of the company. The company can only be dissolved by the process of law (i.e., winding up). As it is often said, 'members may come and members may go, but the company goes on forever.'

During the First World War, all the members of a private company were killed in an enemy bomb attack. But the company survived because a company does not die with the death of its members. The shares of the deceased members were transmitted to their legal heirs and the company continued to exist.

(5) Common Seal: Under the Companies Act, 1956, every company was required to have a common seal which was the official signature of the company. Since a company is an artificial person, it cannot sign documents like a natural person. The common seal served as a substitute for the personal signature. However, the Companies (Amendment) Act, 2015 has made the common seal optional [Section 9]. A company may or may not have a common seal. If a company does not have a common seal, the documents which were earlier required to be sealed shall now be signed by two directors or by a director and the company secretary.

(6) Transferability of Shares: The shares of a company are freely transferable. Section 44 provides that the shares or debentures or other interests of any member in a company shall be movable property, transferable in the manner provided by the articles of the company. In a public company, the shares are freely transferable and no restriction can be placed on the transfer of fully paid-up shares. In a private company, the articles may restrict the right of transfer of shares [Section 2(68)].

(7) Separate Property: A company, being a separate legal person, can own, enjoy, and dispose of property in its own name. The property of the company is not the property of its members. No member can claim any ownership right over the property of the company during the existence of the company or even during its winding up.

Case: Macaura v. Northern Assurance Co. Ltd. (1925)

Macaura owned a timber estate. He sold the timber to a company of which he was virtually the sole member and the sole creditor. He had insured the timber in his own name. The timber was destroyed by fire. Macaura claimed insurance. The insurance company refused to pay, saying that Macaura had no insurable interest in the timber because the timber belonged to the company, not to Macaura personally. The House of Lords upheld the insurance company's contention. Since the company was a separate legal entity, the timber was the property of the company, not of Macaura. Macaura, as a shareholder, had no insurable interest in the company's property.

(8) Capacity to Sue and Be Sued: A company can sue and be sued in its own name. It can enforce its legal rights through courts and can also be held liable for any wrongs committed by it. All legal proceedings are taken in the name of the company and not in the name of its individual members or directors.

(9) Artificial Legal Person: A company is an artificial person created by law. It has rights and duties like a natural person but it has no body, no soul, and no conscience. It cannot eat, sleep, or think. It acts through its directors and officers who are its agents. A company cannot be imprisoned, but it can be fined. It cannot be guilty of crimes requiring personal intent (mens rea) in many cases, though modern law has increasingly held companies liable for corporate crimes.

(10) Separation of Ownership and Management: In a company, the ownership and management are separated. The shareholders (members) are the owners of the company, but the management is in the hands of the Board of Directors who are elected by the shareholders. The shareholders do not manage the day-to-day affairs of the company. This is different from a partnership where the partners are both owners and managers of the business.

(11) Voluntary Association for Profit: A company is formed by the voluntary association of persons. Its main objective is usually to earn profit, though Section 8 companies are formed for charitable purposes and not for profit. The members join the company voluntarily and can leave by transferring their shares.

5.4 Lifting / Piercing the Corporate Veil

As we have seen, a company has a separate legal personality distinct from its members. This is the fundamental principle of company law established in the Salomon case. The separate legal entity of the company acts as a veil or curtain between the company and its members. The members hide behind this veil and their personal affairs are not affected by the company's affairs. This is called the 'corporate veil' or the 'veil of incorporation.'

However, in certain exceptional circumstances, the courts may disregard the separate legal entity of the company and look behind the corporate veil to identify the persons who are actually controlling the company. When the courts do this, they are said to be 'lifting' or 'piercing' the corporate veil. The purpose is to prevent the misuse of the privilege of limited liability and separate legal entity.

The corporate veil may be lifted in two ways – (a) under the provisions of the statute (i.e., the Companies Act itself), and (b) by the courts under judicial decisions.

(A) Lifting of Corporate Veil Under the Companies Act, 2013

(1) Reduction in Membership (Section 3A): If at any time the number of members of a company is reduced below the statutory minimum (i.e., below two in case of a private company or below seven in case of a public company) and the company carries on business for more than six months while the number is so reduced, every person who is a member of the company during the time that it so carries on business after those six months and is aware of the fact shall be severally liable for the payment of the whole debts of the company contracted during that time.

(2) Misdescription of Name (Section 12): If an officer of a company signs any bill of exchange, promissory note, or cheque on behalf of the company without properly mentioning the company's name, such officer shall be personally liable to the holder of the instrument for the amount due.

(3) Fraudulent Conduct of Business (Section 339): If in the course of winding up of a company it appears that any business has been carried on with intent to defraud creditors of the company or any other person, or for any fraudulent purpose, the Tribunal may declare that any persons who were knowingly parties to the carrying on of the business shall be personally responsible for all or any of the debts or other liabilities of the company.

(4) Fraud (Section 447): Any person who is found to be guilty of fraud as defined in Section 447 shall be punishable with imprisonment and fine. This provision can be used to look behind the corporate entity and hold the real culprits liable.

(5) Holding and Subsidiary Relationship (Section 2(46) & 2(87)): The Act requires that the financial statements of a holding company must include the consolidated financial statements of its subsidiary companies. This is an instance of looking behind the separate entity of each company to see the true financial position of the group.

(6) Investigation of Ownership (Section 216): The Central Government may appoint inspectors to investigate the ownership of a company to find out the true persons who are financially interested in the company and who control or materially influence the policy of the company.

(B) Lifting of Corporate Veil by Courts (Judicial Decisions)

The courts in India and abroad have lifted the corporate veil in the following circumstances:

(1) To determine the character of a company (Enemy character): During wartime, the courts have lifted the corporate veil to determine whether a company is controlled by persons belonging to an enemy country.

Case: Daimler Co. Ltd. v. Continental Tyre and Rubber Co. (Great Britain) Ltd. (1916)

During the First World War, a company was registered in England but its shares were held entirely by German nationals. The company sued for recovery of a trade debt. The House of Lords held that since the company was controlled by enemy aliens, it had an enemy character. The corporate veil was lifted to see who the real controllers of the company were. The suit was dismissed because trading with an enemy was prohibited during wartime.

(2) Where the company is a mere sham or facade: Where the corporate entity is used as a mere cloak or sham to hide the true nature of the transactions or to commit fraud, the courts will lift the corporate veil.

Case: Gilford Motor Company v. Horne (1933)

Horne was an employee of Gilford Motor Company. His contract of employment contained a restraint clause that he would not solicit the customers of the company after leaving the employment. After leaving the company, Horne formed a new company in the name of his wife and started soliciting the old customers through this company. The Court of Appeal held that the new company was a mere sham and was formed to evade the contractual obligation. The corporate veil was lifted and Horne was held personally liable for breach of his covenant.

(3) To prevent fraud or improper conduct: Where the corporate personality is being used as a device to commit fraud or to defeat the provisions of law, the courts will pierce the veil.

(4) Where the company acts as agent of its members: If it can be shown that the company is merely an agent of its members or of another company (the holding company), the principal will be liable for the acts of the company.

(5) To determine the true nature of transactions (Tax evasion): The courts have lifted the corporate veil in cases involving tax evasion to determine the true nature of the transactions.

Case: State of U.P. v. Renusagar Power Co. (1988)

Hindalco Industries Ltd. set up Renusagar Power Co. as a separate company to supply electricity exclusively to Hindalco. The question was whether Renusagar was a separate entity or merely an instrumentality of Hindalco. The Supreme Court of India held that the corporate veil could be lifted to see the real relationship between the two companies. The Court held that since Renusagar was generating and supplying power exclusively to Hindalco, it was in substance the generating unit of Hindalco. The corporate veil was lifted for the purpose of determining the electricity duty liability.

(6) To protect revenue (Tax cases): The courts have pierced the corporate veil in several cases to prevent tax evasion and to protect the revenue of the Government.

(7) Where the company is formed to circumvent the law: If a company is formed for the sole purpose of circumventing or evading a legal obligation, the courts will disregard the separate legal entity.

Case: Life Insurance Corporation of India v. Escorts Ltd. (1986)

The Supreme Court of India observed that the corporate veil may be lifted where the statute itself contemplates lifting the veil, or where there is fraud or improper conduct, or where the company is a mere facade. The Court held that the corporate veil can be pierced in cases of protection of revenue, prevention of fraud, to determine whether a company is an enemy company, and to give effect to welfare legislation.

Note: The doctrine of lifting the corporate veil is an exception to the general rule of separate legal entity. The courts are reluctant to lift the veil and do so only in exceptional circumstances where the ends of justice so require. The general rule established in the Salomon case remains intact and the corporate veil is lifted only as a last resort.

5.5 Company vs. Partnership vs. LLP

To understand the advantages of the company form of business, it is useful to compare it with other forms of business organisation, particularly the partnership firm and the Limited Liability Partnership (LLP).

(A) Distinction Between Company and Partnership

Table 5.2: Company vs. Partnership

Point of Distinction	Company	Partnership Firm
Formation	Formed by registration under the Companies Act	Formed by agreement between partners; registration optional under Partnership Act, 1932
Legal Status	Separate legal entity; a legal person	Not a separate legal entity (except in certain legal contexts)
Liability	Limited liability of members (to the extent of unpaid shares)	Unlimited liability of partners; personally liable for firm's debts
Number of Members	Private Co.: min 2, max 200; Public Co.: min 7, no maximum	Min 2; Max 50 (generally); governed by agreement
Transfer of Interest	Shares freely transferable (in public companies)	Partner cannot transfer interest without consent of all partners
Management	Managed by Board	Managed by partners

	of Directors; separation of ownership and management	themselves; every partner is an agent of the firm
Perpetual Succession	Yes – not affected by death or retirement of members	No – dissolved by death, retirement, or insolvency of a partner (unless agreed)
Property	Company owns its own property; members have no direct ownership	Partnership property belongs to all partners jointly
Governing Law	Companies Act, 2013	Indian Partnership Act, 1932
Statutory Audit	Compulsory audit of accounts	Audit not compulsory (except under tax laws for certain firms)
Dissolution	Only by winding up under the Act or by NCLT order	By agreement, notice, death, insolvency, or court order
Name	Must end with 'Limited' or 'Private Limited'	No such requirement
Common Seal	May have a common seal (optional after 2015 amendment)	No common seal
Annual Filings	Must file annual returns and financial statements with ROC	No such requirement (except tax returns)
Minimum Capital	No minimum paid-up capital required	No minimum capital required

	(since 2015 amendment)	

(B) Distinction Between Company and LLP

The Limited Liability Partnership (LLP) is a relatively new form of business organisation in India. It was introduced by the Limited Liability Partnership Act, 2008. An LLP combines the advantages of a partnership (flexibility of management) with the advantages of a company (limited liability and separate legal entity).

Table 5.3: Company vs. LLP

Point of Distinction	Company	LLP
Governing Law	Companies Act, 2013	Limited Liability Partnership Act, 2008
Legal Status	Separate legal entity	Separate legal entity
Liability	Limited to unpaid amount on shares	Limited to agreed contribution; no personal liability
Members	Called 'shareholders' or 'members'	Called 'partners' or 'designated partners'
Minimum Members	Pvt: 2; Public: 7	Minimum 2 designated partners
Maximum Members	Pvt: 200; Public: unlimited	No maximum limit
Management	Board of Directors	Partners as per LLP agreement
Annual Compliance	Extensive – ROC filings, AGM,	Relatively less – annual return and statement of

	audited accounts	accounts
Statutory Audit	Compulsory for all companies	Required only if turnover exceeds Rs. 40 lakhs or contribution exceeds Rs. 25 lakhs
Ownership of Property	Company owns property	LLP owns property
Transferability	Shares freely transferable (public)	Rights transferable only with consent of other partners
Name	Ends with 'Ltd.' or 'Pvt. Ltd.'	Ends with 'LLP'
Dissolution	By winding up order	By NCLT order or voluntary
Suitability	Large-scale business; public investment	Professional firms; small and medium enterprises

Advantages of Company Form of Business

The following are the main advantages of the company form of business over other forms:

(a) Limited liability of members protects personal assets. (b) Separate legal entity enables the company to own property, enter contracts, and sue in its own name. (c) Perpetual succession ensures continuity of business. (d) Transferability of shares provides liquidity to investment. (e) Large capital can be raised through issue of shares and debentures to the public. (f) Professional management by qualified directors. (g) Greater public confidence and credibility. (h) Tax advantages in certain cases.

Chapter 6

Types of Companies

The Companies Act, 2013 recognises various types of companies. Companies can be classified on different bases such as the mode of incorporation, the extent of liability of members, the number of members, the nature of business, and so on. A thorough understanding of these different types of companies is essential for the study of company law. In this chapter, we shall examine all the important classifications of companies under the Companies Act, 2013.

6.1 Classification on the Basis of Incorporation

On the basis of the manner in which they are formed or incorporated, companies can be classified into three categories:

(A) Chartered Companies

These are companies which are incorporated by a special charter granted by the King or the sovereign. In England, the East India Company and the Bank of England were examples of chartered companies. In India, chartered companies do not exist at present. They are of historical significance only. These companies had very wide powers and could do anything which was not specifically prohibited by their charter.

(B) Statutory Companies

Statutory companies are companies which are created by a special Act of Parliament or State Legislature. They are not registered under the Companies Act. Their powers, duties, and mode of working are defined by the statute which creates them. They do not have a memorandum of association or articles of association. Instead, the Act which creates them serves as their constitution.

Examples: Reserve Bank of India (RBI Act, 1934), Life Insurance Corporation of India (LIC Act, 1956), Food Corporation of India (FCA,

1964), Unit Trust of India (UTI Act, 1963 – now repealed), State Bank of India (SBI Act, 1955), Industrial Finance Corporation of India (IFCI Act, 1948). These companies need not use the word 'Limited' after their name because their constitution is derived from a statute and not from the Companies Act. They enjoy certain exemptions from the provisions of the Companies Act, 2013.

(C) Registered Companies

These are the most common type of companies. They are formed by registration under the Companies Act, 2013 (or any previous company law). The vast majority of companies in India are registered companies. They must have a memorandum of association and articles of association and must comply with all the provisions of the Companies Act. They must use the word 'Limited' (in case of public companies) or 'Private Limited' (in case of private companies) at the end of their name.

All further discussion in this chapter and in the remaining chapters of this book relates to registered companies unless otherwise stated.

6.2 Classification on the Basis of Liability

On the basis of the liability of members, companies can be classified into three types:

(A) Companies Limited by Shares – Section 2(22)

A company limited by shares is a company in which the liability of its members is limited to the amount unpaid on the shares respectively held by them. In other words, no member can be called upon to pay more than the face value of the shares allotted to him. If a member has already paid the full face value of his shares, his liability is nil. This is the most common type of company in India.

Illustration: A holds 500 shares of Rs. 10 each in ABC Ltd. He has paid Rs. 8 per share at the time of allotment. A's total liability is limited to Rs. 1,000 (i.e., Rs. 2 unpaid per share × 500 shares). Even if the company goes into liquidation with debts of Rs. 50 crore, A cannot be asked to pay more than Rs. 1,000.

(B) Companies Limited by Guarantee – Section 2(21)

A company limited by guarantee is a company in which the liability of its members is limited to the amount each member has undertaken to contribute to the assets of the company in the event of its winding up. Each member gives a guarantee (a written undertaking) to pay a fixed amount in case the company is wound up. This amount is called the 'guarantee money.'

Companies limited by guarantee are usually formed for promoting art, science, religion, charity, sports, or similar non-commercial objects. They are not formed for the purpose of earning profits. Trade associations, clubs, and societies are often formed as companies limited by guarantee. Under the Companies Act, 2013, a company limited by guarantee cannot have a share capital [Section 2(21) read with the proviso to Section 4(4)].

Examples: The Associated Chambers of Commerce and Industry of India (ASSOCHAM), Confederation of Indian Industry (CII), various sports bodies, professional bodies, and charitable organisations.

(C) Unlimited Companies – Section 2(92)

An unlimited company is a company in which the liability of its members is unlimited. In other words, the members are personally liable for the debts of the company without any limit. If the assets of the company are not sufficient to pay its debts, the personal property of the members can be used to pay the debts. The liability of the members of an unlimited company is similar to the liability of partners in a partnership firm. Unlimited companies are very rare in India. The main advantage of an unlimited company is that it need not file its financial statements with the Registrar of Companies and hence there is greater secrecy. However, due to the disadvantage of unlimited liability, very few businessmen opt for this form of company.

Note: Under the Companies Act, 2013, a company formed with unlimited liability may subsequently convert itself into a limited company by following the prescribed procedure under Section 18. Similarly, a limited company may also re-register itself as an unlimited company.

Table 6.1: Comparison of Companies Based on Liability

Feature	Limited by Shares	Limited by Guarantee	Unlimited
Liability	Limited to unpaid amount on shares	Limited to guaranteed amount	Unlimited
Share Capital	Must have share capital	Cannot have share capital (2013 Act)	May or may not have share capital
Common Purpose	Trading and profit-making	Charitable, non-profit, professional bodies	Very rare; confidential businesses
Filing of Accounts	Must file with ROC	Must file with ROC	Need not file (exempted)
Section	Section 2(22)	Section 2(21)	Section 2(92)
Use of 'Limited'	Must use 'Ltd.' or 'Pvt. Ltd.'	Must use 'Ltd.' or 'Pvt. Ltd.'	Not required to use 'Ltd.'

6.3 Classification on the Basis of Number of Members

This is the most important classification of companies for practical purposes. On the basis of the number of members and certain restrictions on the transfer of shares, companies are classified into two main categories – Private Company and Public Company.

(A) Private Company – Section 2(68)

Section 2(68) of the Companies Act, 2013 defines a private company as follows: "'Private company' means a company having a minimum paid-up share capital as may be prescribed, and which by its articles – (i) restricts the right to transfer its shares; (ii) except in case of One Person Company, limits the number of its members to two hundred; (iii) prohibits any invitation to the public to subscribe for any securities of the company."

Note: The Companies (Amendment) Act, 2015 has removed the requirement of minimum paid-up share capital. Earlier, a private company was required to have a minimum paid-up share capital of Rs. 1 lakh. Now, there is no minimum paid-up capital requirement.

Essential Characteristics of a Private Company

(1) Restriction on transfer of shares: The articles of a private company must restrict the right to transfer its shares. This means that a member cannot freely sell his shares to any person he likes. The articles usually provide that the shares must first be offered to the existing members (pre-emption right) and the directors have the power to refuse registration of transfer. This restriction ensures that the shares remain within a closed group of persons and outsiders cannot easily gain control of the company.

(2) Limitation on number of members: The number of members of a private company (excluding OPC) is limited to a maximum of 200. The minimum number of members is 2 (or 1 in case of OPC). While counting the number of 200 members, two categories of persons are excluded – (a) persons who are in the employment of the company, and (b) persons who, having been formerly in the employment of the company, were members while in that employment and have continued to be members after the employment ceased. Where two or more persons hold shares jointly, they are treated as a single member.

(3) Prohibition on invitation to public: A private company cannot invite the public to subscribe for its shares or debentures. It cannot issue a prospectus. It can raise capital only from its members, their relatives, and friends, and through private placement. This restriction ensures the private character of the company.

(4) Name: The name of a private company must end with the words 'Private Limited' or the abbreviation 'Pvt. Ltd.'

(5) Minimum members and directors: A private company must have a minimum of 2 members and a minimum of 2 directors [Section 149(1)(a)].

Privileges and Exemptions of a Private Company

A private company enjoys several privileges and exemptions which are not available to a public company. These exemptions are aimed at reducing the regulatory burden on smaller companies. Some of the important privileges are:

(a) It is not required to hold a statutory meeting or file a statutory report. (b) It can commence business immediately after incorporation without obtaining a certificate of commencement of business (Section 10A has been inserted but the requirement is relatively simpler). (c) It needs only 2 members and 2 directors. (d) There is no requirement to appoint independent directors (unless it falls under specified criteria). (e) There are several exemptions from the provisions relating to managerial remuneration. (f) Certain provisions relating to meetings and resolutions are relaxed for private companies. (g) It can give loans to its directors (with certain conditions).

(B) Public Company – Section 2(71)

Section 2(71) defines a public company as follows: "'Public company' means a company which – (a) is not a private company; (b) has a minimum paid-up share capital as may be prescribed."

In other words, a public company is any company which is not a private company. The definition is negative in nature. If a company does not restrict the transfer of shares, does not limit the number of members to 200, and does not prohibit invitation to the public, it is a public company.

Note: The Companies (Amendment) Act, 2015 has removed the requirement of minimum paid-up share capital for public companies also. Earlier, a public company was required to have a minimum paid-up share capital of Rs. 5 lakhs.

Essential Characteristics of a Public Company

(1) No restriction on transfer of shares: The shares of a public company are freely transferable. The company cannot impose any restriction on the transfer of fully paid-up shares. This free transferability is the main feature which makes public companies attractive for investors because they can easily buy and sell shares in the stock market.

(2) No limit on number of members: There is no maximum limit on the number of members in a public company. The minimum number of members is 7. This means that a public company can have thousands or even millions of members (shareholders). Companies like Reliance Industries, TCS, and Infosys have millions of shareholders.

(3) Can invite public subscription: A public company can invite the general public to subscribe for its shares and debentures by issuing a prospectus. It can also get its shares listed on a stock exchange. This enables the company to raise large amounts of capital from the public.

(4) Name: The name of a public company must end with the word 'Limited' or the abbreviation 'Ltd.'

(5) Minimum members and directors: A public company must have a minimum of 7 members and a minimum of 3 directors [Section 149(1)(b)].

(6) Deemed Public Company: Under Section 2(71), a subsidiary of a public company is deemed to be a public company even if it is actually a private company by its articles. This provision is very important because it means that if a private company is a subsidiary of a public company, the private company must comply with all the provisions applicable to public companies.

Distinction Between Private Company and Public Company

Table 6.2: Private Company vs. Public Company

Point of Distinction	Private Company	Public Company
Definition	Section 2(68)	Section 2(71)
Minimum Members	2 (1 for OPC)	7
Maximum Members	200 (excluding employees)	No limit
Minimum Directors	2	3
Transfer of Shares	Restricted by articles	Freely transferable
Public Subscription	Prohibited	Can invite public
Prospectus	Cannot issue	Can issue
Name Suffix	'Private Limited' or 'Pvt. Ltd.'	'Limited' or 'Ltd.'
Statutory Meeting	Not required	Not required under 2013 Act
Independent Directors	Not mandatory (generally)	Mandatory for listed companies
Secretarial Audit	Not required (generally)	Required for specified companies
Annual Return	Director or Company	Director and Company

Signing	Secretary	Secretary
Commencement	Can start business after incorporation	Subject to Section 10A requirements
Listing on Stock Exchange	Cannot list shares	Can list shares
Conversion	Can convert to public company	Can convert to private company

6.4 One Person Company (OPC) – Section 2(62)

The concept of One Person Company is one of the most significant innovations introduced by the Companies Act, 2013. Before this Act, a minimum of two persons were required to form a private company. This meant that a single entrepreneur who wanted to start a business with limited liability had no option but to find at least one more person. The OPC concept removes this barrier.

Definition

Section 2(62) defines a One Person Company as "a company which has only one person as a member." In other words, an OPC is a private company with only one member. It is a hybrid between a sole proprietorship and a company. It gives the single entrepreneur the benefits of limited liability and separate legal entity while allowing him to have complete control over the business.

Key Features and Rules of OPC

(1) Only one member: An OPC has only one member who is the sole shareholder. Only a natural person who is an Indian citizen and resident in India (i.e., has stayed in India for a period of not less than 120 days during the immediately preceding financial year) can incorporate an OPC. A minor cannot be a member or nominee of an OPC. No person can incorporate more than one OPC or become a nominee in more than one OPC.

(2) Nominee – Section 3(1)(c): The memorandum of an OPC must indicate the name of a person who shall, in the event of the death of the sole member or his incapacity to contract, become the member of the company. This person is called the 'nominee.' The nominee must give his prior written consent. The member of an OPC may, at any time, change the name of the nominee by giving notice to the company and the new nominee must also give written consent.

(3) Limited liability: Like other limited companies, the liability of the member of an OPC is limited to the amount unpaid on his shares.

(4) Can only be a private company: An OPC can only be formed as a private company limited by shares. It cannot be incorporated as a company under Section 8 (not-for-profit company) or as a public company.

(5) Director: An OPC must have at least one director. The sole member can also be the sole director. However, an OPC can have a maximum of 15 directors (like any other company).

(6) Relaxations for OPC: The Act provides several relaxations for OPCs: (a) Annual general meeting (AGM) is not required – if a resolution is required to be passed at a general meeting, it is sufficient if the resolution is communicated by the member to the company and entered in the minutes book. (b) The financial statement may not include the cash flow statement. (c) Only one director is required. (d) Several procedural requirements applicable to other companies are relaxed.

(7) Mandatory conversion: An OPC must be converted into a private company or public company if its paid-up share capital exceeds Rs. 50 lakhs or its average annual turnover during the relevant period exceeds Rs. 2 crore. The conversion must be done within six months of the threshold being crossed.

(8) Name: The name of an OPC must end with the words '(OPC) Private Limited.'

Examples: If Mr. Rajesh, a software developer in Indore, wants to start his own IT consulting firm with limited liability, he can form an OPC. He will be the sole member and sole director. He must name a nominee (say, his wife). The company's name would be, for example, 'Rajesh IT Solutions (OPC) Private Limited.'

6.5 Small Company – Section 2(85)

The concept of 'Small Company' has been introduced by the Companies Act, 2013 to reduce the compliance burden on smaller companies. The idea is that small companies should not be burdened with the same level of compliance as large companies.

Definition

Section 2(85) defines a small company as a company, other than a public company, whose – (a) paid-up share capital does not exceed Rs. 4 crore or such higher amount as may be prescribed which shall not be more than Rs. 10 crore, AND (b) turnover as per the profit and loss account for the immediately preceding financial year does not exceed Rs. 40 crore or such higher amount as may be prescribed which shall not be more than Rs. 100 crore.

Note: The thresholds for small company have been revised from time to time. Originally, the limits were Rs. 50 lakhs (capital) and Rs. 2 crore (turnover). They were enhanced to Rs. 2 crore and Rs. 20 crore respectively by the Companies (Amendment) Act, 2017, and further increased to Rs. 4 crore and Rs. 40 crore by notification dated 15th September, 2022. Students should check the latest thresholds applicable at the time of their examination.

However, the following companies are excluded from the definition of a small company: (a) a public company, (b) a holding company or a subsidiary company, (c) a company registered under Section 8, and (d) a company or body corporate governed by any special Act.

Exemptions Available to Small Companies

Small companies enjoy several exemptions and relaxations under the Act and the rules. These include: (a) The annual return of a small company can be signed by a company secretary alone, or where there is no company secretary, by a single director. (b) Cash flow statement is not required to be included in the financial statement. (c) Merger of small companies can be approved by the Regional Director instead of the NCLT (fast track merger under Section 233). (d) Less stringent requirements for Board meetings – the gap between two consecutive Board meetings need not be more than 120 days (instead of the normal requirement). (e) The auditor's report need not include a statement on internal financial controls. (f) Annual return filing procedures are simplified.

6.6 Dormant Company – Section 455

The concept of dormant company is a new introduction under the Companies Act, 2013. Before this Act, companies which were not carrying on any business faced the risk of being struck off by the Registrar of Companies. The dormant company concept allows such companies to maintain their registered status without being struck off.

Definition

Section 455 provides that where a company is formed and registered under this Act for a future project or to hold an asset or intellectual property and has no significant accounting transaction, such a company or an inactive company may make an application to the Registrar for obtaining the status of a dormant company.

An 'inactive company' means a company which has not been carrying on any business or operation, or has not made any significant accounting transaction during the last two financial years, or has not filed financial statements and annual returns during the last two financial years.

A 'significant accounting transaction' means any transaction other than – (a) payment of fees to the Registrar, (b) payments made to fulfil the requirements of the Act, and (c) allotment of shares to subscribers to the memorandum.

Features of Dormant Company

(1) Minimal compliance: A dormant company is required to hold at least one meeting of the Board of Directors in each half of a calendar year and the gap between the two meetings should not be less than 90 days. It is also required to file an annual return.

(2) Status for 5 years: The Registrar shall allow the status of a dormant company for a period of 5 years.

(3) Activation: If a dormant company wants to change its status to 'active', it may apply to the Registrar and the Registrar shall allow the status of an active company.

(4) Striking off: If a dormant company does not comply even with the minimal requirements prescribed for a dormant company, the Registrar may strike off its name from the register of companies.

Examples: A person registers a company to hold a patent which he intends to commercialise in the future. Since the company has no business transactions, he can apply for dormant status. This way, the company remains on the register and the patent continues to be held in the company's name without the burden of full compliance.

6.7 Producer Company – Part IXA (Sections 378A to 378ZU)

The concept of Producer Company was originally introduced in 2002 by the Companies (Amendment) Act, 2002 as Part IXA of the Companies Act, 1956. The purpose was to enable the incorporation of cooperatives as companies. The Companies Act, 2013 has continued the provisions relating to Producer Companies through Section 378A which states that the provisions of Part IXA of the Companies Act, 1956 shall apply to Producer Companies.

Definition

A 'Producer Company' means a body corporate having objects or activities specified in the Act and registered as a Producer Company under the Act. It is essentially a company formed by primary producers (farmers, artisans, craftsmen, weavers, etc.) for the purpose of production, harvesting, procurement, grading, pooling, handling, marketing, selling, export of primary produce of the members, or for import of goods or services for their benefit.

Key Features

(a) It can only be incorporated as a company limited by shares. (b) It must have a minimum of 5 individual producers or 2 producer institutions (or a combination of both, with a minimum of 5 members). (c) The name must end with 'Producer Company Limited.' (d) Only its members can buy its shares. The shares are not freely transferable to non-members. (e) It is managed by a Board of Directors who must be members of the company. (f) It must have a chief executive appointed by the Board. (g) The limited return on share capital is specified in the articles. (h) Profits are distributed to members as patronage bonus based on the volume of business done by each member with the company, not on the basis of shareholding.

Examples: Amul (Gujarat Cooperative Milk Marketing Federation) is a well-known example of a cooperative, though it is registered under the Cooperative Societies Act. Producer Companies under the Companies Act serve a similar function for primary producers.

6.8 Government Company – Section 2(45)

Government companies play a very important role in the Indian economy. Many major industrial and commercial undertakings in India are run by Government companies.

Definition

Section 2(45) defines a Government company as "any company in which not less than fifty-one per cent of the paid-up share capital is held by the Central Government, or by any State Government or Governments, or partly by the Central Government and partly by one or more State Governments, and includes a company which is a subsidiary company of such a Government company."

In simple words, a Government company is a company in which 51% or more of the paid-up share capital is held by the Central or State Government(s). A subsidiary of such a company is also a Government company.

Key Features

(1) Registered under the Companies Act: A Government company is not created by a special statute. It is registered under the Companies Act just like any other company. The only difference is that the Government holds the majority of its shares.

(2) Government control: Since the Government holds 51% or more of the shares, it has effective control over the management and policies of the company. The Government appoints the directors and the key managerial personnel.

(3) Separate legal entity: A Government company is a separate legal entity distinct from the Government. It can sue and be sued in its own name. The employees of a Government company are not Government servants.

(4) Annual Report to Parliament/Legislature – Section 394: The Central Government shall cause an annual report on the working and affairs of each Government company to be prepared and laid before both Houses of Parliament, together with a copy of the audit report and any comments upon or supplement to the report made by the Comptroller and Auditor General (CAG) of India.

(5) Audit by CAG – Section 143(5) to (7): The auditor of a Government company is appointed by the CAG within 180 days from the commencement of the financial year. The CAG may also direct the manner in which the accounts are to be audited and may conduct a supplementary or test audit. The CAG may comment on the audit report.

Examples: Bharat Heavy Electricals Limited (BHEL), Steel Authority of India Limited (SAIL), Oil and Natural Gas Corporation (ONGC), Hindustan Aeronautics Limited (HAL), National Thermal Power Corporation (NTPC), Indian Oil Corporation Limited (IOC), Coal India

Limited (CIL).

6.9 Foreign Company – Section 2(42)

With the liberalisation and globalisation of the Indian economy, many foreign companies have established their presence in India. The Companies Act, 2013 contains provisions to regulate the activities of such foreign companies in India.

Definition

Section 2(42) defines a foreign company as "any company or body corporate incorporated outside India which – (a) has a place of business in India whether by itself or through an agent, physically or through electronic mode; and (b) conducts any business activity in India in any other manner."

Thus, a foreign company is a company which is incorporated outside India but has established a business presence in India. It is not a company incorporated under the Indian Companies Act.

Compliance Requirements – Sections 380 to 393

A foreign company establishing a place of business in India must comply with the following requirements:

(a) It must, within 30 days of the establishment of its place of business in India, deliver to the Registrar for registration certain documents, including a certified copy of the charter, statutes, or memorandum and articles, the full address of the registered or principal office of the company, a list of directors, the name and address of one or more persons resident in India who are authorised to accept service of process on behalf of the company, the full address of the office of the company in India, and a declaration that none of the directors has been convicted or debarred.

(b) It must file with the Registrar an annual return in the prescribed form [Section 384]. (c) It must prepare financial statements of its Indian business operations in accordance with Schedule III and file them with the Registrar [Section 381]. (d) It must display the name of the company and the country of incorporation at the place of business in India. (e) It must comply with the provisions relating to books of accounts, audit, and inspection as applicable.

Note: If a foreign company fails to comply with the above provisions, the company and every officer of the company who is in default shall be liable to a penalty.

6.10 Holding and Subsidiary Companies

In the modern corporate world, it is very common for one company to control another company. When a company controls the composition of the Board of Directors of another company or holds more than half of the total voting power of another company, a parent-child (holding-subsidiary) relationship is created between the two companies.

Definitions

Holding Company – Section 2(46): "'Holding company' in relation to one or more other companies, means a company of which such companies are subsidiary companies." A holding company is also called a 'parent company.'

Subsidiary Company – Section 2(87): "'Subsidiary company' or 'subsidiary', in relation to any other company (that is to say the holding company), means a company in which the holding company – (i) controls the composition of the Board of Directors; or (ii) exercises or controls more than one-half of the total voting power either at its own or together with one or more of its subsidiary companies."

A company is also deemed to be a subsidiary if it is a subsidiary of another company which is itself a subsidiary of a third company. For example, if Company A is a holding company of Company B, and Company B is a holding company of Company C, then Company C is also a subsidiary of Company A. This is called a 'step-down subsidiary' or 'subsidiary of a subsidiary.'

Wholly Owned Subsidiary: Section 2(87)(ii) also provides that a company shall be deemed to be a 'wholly owned subsidiary' of another company if 100% of the share capital is held by the holding company. In a wholly owned subsidiary, the holding company holds all the shares.

Provisions Relating to Holding-Subsidiary Relationship

(a) Consolidated financial statements: The holding company must prepare consolidated financial statements of all its subsidiaries in addition to its own standalone financial statements [Section 129(3)]. (b) A subsidiary of a public company is deemed to be a public company [Section 2(71)]. (c) A company cannot hold shares in its own holding company [Section 19]. This prevents circular holding. (d) The holding company must disclose the number and amount of shares held in the subsidiary and the holding relationship. (e) Layers of subsidiaries are restricted – no company shall have more than 2 layers of subsidiaries (with certain exceptions under Section 2(87)).

Illustration: Tata Sons (holding company) controls Tata Steel, Tata Motors, TCS, Tata Power, Indian Hotels, etc. as its subsidiary and associate companies. This is a classic example of a holding-subsidiary structure in India.

6.11 Associate Company – Section 2(6)

The concept of associate company is relatively new in Indian company law. It was formally introduced by the Companies Act, 2013.

Definition

Section 2(6) defines an 'associate company' as follows: "'Associate company' in relation to another company, means a company in which that other company has a significant influence, but which is not a subsidiary company of the company having such influence and includes a joint venture company."

'Significant influence' means control of at least 20% of the total voting power, or control of or participation in business decisions under an agreement.

Thus, an associate company is one where the other company has significant influence (20% or more voting power) but does not have control as in the case of a subsidiary (where more than 50% voting power is needed). The associate company is a middle ground between a subsidiary and an independent company.

Implications

(a) The holding company must disclose in its financial statements the investment in and profit or loss from associate companies. (b) Transactions between the company and its associate company are treated as related party transactions under Section 188 and are subject to the approval requirements. (c) The concept of associate company is important for accounting purposes because investments in associates are accounted for using the equity method under Indian Accounting Standards (Ind AS 28).

6.12 Nidhi Company – Section 406

Nidhi companies are a special type of company which have been part of Indian corporate law for a long time. They are essentially mutual benefit societies engaged in the business of lending and borrowing money among their own members.

Definition

Section 406(1) provides that the Central Government may, by notification, declare any company as a Nidhi company. A 'Nidhi' or 'Mutual Benefit Society' is a company which has been incorporated with the object of cultivating the habit of thrift and savings amongst its members, receiving deposits from, and lending to, its members only, for their mutual benefit.

Key Features

(1) Must be a public company: A Nidhi company must be a public company. It cannot be a private company.

(2) Members only: A Nidhi company can accept deposits from and lend money only to its members. It cannot deal with non-members.

(3) Net owned funds: A Nidhi company must have net owned funds of Rs. 10 lakh or more as may be prescribed.

(4) Ratio of deposits: The ratio of net owned funds to deposits shall not exceed 1:20.

(5) Minimum members: A Nidhi must have a minimum of 200 members within one year of its incorporation.

(6) Name: The name must contain the word 'Nidhi Limited' at the end.

(7) Exemptions: The Central Government may, by notification, exempt Nidhi companies from certain provisions of the Act. Several provisions relating to public companies are relaxed for Nidhis. The RBI has also exempted Nidhis from the core provisions of the RBI Act relating to NBFCs.

Examples: Nidhi companies are very popular in South India, particularly in Tamil Nadu, Andhra Pradesh, and Kerala. They are known by various names such as 'Nidhi,' 'Permanent Fund,' 'Benefit Fund,' 'Mutual Benefit Fund,' and 'Mutual Benefit Company.'

6.13 Section 8 Company (Not-for-Profit Company)

Section 8 of the Companies Act, 2013 (corresponding to Section 25 of the Companies Act, 1956) provides for the incorporation of companies which are formed for promoting commerce, art, science, sports, education, research, social welfare, religion, charity, protection of environment, or any such other object. These companies do not distribute dividends to their members but apply their profits, if any, or other income in promoting their objects.

Key Features

(1) Objectives: The company must have the objective of promoting commerce, art, science, sports, education, research, social welfare, religion, charity, protection of environment, or any such other useful object. It must intend to apply its profits or other income in promoting its objects.

(2) No distribution of dividends: A Section 8 company must not distribute dividends to its members. All profits must be utilised for the objects of the company.

(3) Licence from the Central Government: The Central Government may grant a licence to such a company directing that it shall be registered as a company with limited liability without the addition of the word 'Limited' or 'Private Limited' to its name [Section 8(1)]. In other words, a Section 8 company need not use the word 'Limited' or 'Private Limited' at the end of its name.

(4) Privileges and exemptions: A Section 8 company enjoys several privileges: (a) No minimum paid-up share capital is required. (b) It need not use the word 'Limited' in its name. (c) Several provisions of the Act relating to AGM, Board meetings, etc. are relaxed. (d) It gets tax benefits under Section 12A of the Income Tax Act, 1961 (if registered as a charitable institution).

(5) Conversion and amalgamation: A Section 8 company cannot convert itself into a company of any other kind. It cannot amalgamate with a company which is not a Section 8 company [Section 8(4)(b)].

(6) Revocation of licence: If the Central Government is satisfied that the affairs of the company are not being conducted in accordance with the objects of the company, or the company has acted against the conditions of the licence, it may revoke the licence [Section 8(6)]. On revocation, the company may be directed to convert itself into a company of any other kind or it may be wound up.

Examples: Infosys Foundation, Tata Trusts (some entities), CII (Confederation of Indian Industry), FICCI (Federation of Indian Chambers of Commerce and Industry), and various educational institutions and charitable bodies are registered as Section 8 companies.

Chapter 7

Formation and Incorporation of a Company

A company does not come into existence overnight. There is a long process involved before a company is born and can start doing business. The formation of a company involves several stages – from the initial idea in the mind of the promoter to the actual registration of the company with the Registrar of Companies and the commencement of business. Each stage has its own legal significance. In this chapter, we shall study the entire process of formation and incorporation of a company in detail.

The formation of a company generally involves the following four stages: (1) Promotion, (2) Incorporation or Registration, (3) Capital Subscription (raising of capital), and (4) Commencement of Business. However, not all stages apply to every company. For a private company, the third stage (capital subscription from the public) is not applicable because a private company cannot invite the public to subscribe for its shares. For a public company which does not intend to issue shares to the public, this stage may also be skipped.

7.1 Stages of Formation – Promotion

The first stage in the formation of a company is the stage of 'promotion.' Every company originates from an idea. Someone conceives the idea of starting a business, explores its feasibility, brings together the necessary resources and persons, and takes the preliminary steps to get the company registered. This process of conceiving a business idea, working out its details, and bringing together the necessary resources for the purpose of forming a company is called 'promotion.'

The term 'promotion' has not been defined in the Companies Act, 2013. However, it has been defined by various judges and authors:

According to Justice Cockburn: "Promotion involves a process of initiation, planning and putting together of the company."

According to Palmer: "Promotion is the preliminary steps taken for the purpose of registration and flotation of a company."

According to Lord Blackburn: "The term promotion is a short and convenient way of designating the persons who set in motion the machinery by which the Act enables them to create an incorporated company."

From the above definitions, we can say that promotion is the process of planning and organizing a new company. It begins when a person first conceives the idea of forming a company and ends when the company is ready to commence business.

Steps Involved in Promotion

The process of promotion generally involves the following steps:

(1) Discovery of a Business Idea: The promotion begins when a person conceives the idea of starting a business. The promoter identifies a business opportunity, analyses the market potential, and decides to set up a company to exploit that opportunity. For example, a person may notice that there is a demand for organic food products in his city and may decide to start a company to manufacture and sell organic food.

(2) Investigation and Feasibility Study: After identifying the business opportunity, the promoter conducts a detailed investigation into the feasibility of the project. This includes studying the market demand, the availability of raw materials, the cost of production, the technology required, the competition, the financial requirements, and the expected returns. In modern practice, this is done through a detailed feasibility report or project report prepared by experts like chartered accountants, management consultants, or technical consultants.

(3) Assembling of Resources: Once the promoter is satisfied that the project is feasible and profitable, he starts assembling the necessary resources. This includes finding suitable persons who are willing to become the first directors and shareholders of the company, arranging for the required land, machinery, technology, licences, and approvals, identifying sources of finance (banks, financial institutions, venture capitalists), and negotiating preliminary contracts for the supply of raw materials, purchase of land, hiring of employees, and so on.

(4) Preparation of Documents: The promoter then arranges for the preparation of the necessary documents for the registration of the company, including the Memorandum of Association, Articles of Association, and other documents required under the Act. He also engages professionals like company secretaries, chartered accountants, and lawyers to assist in the registration process.

(5) Filing for Registration: Finally, the promoter files an application for the registration of the company with the Registrar of Companies along with the required documents and fees. Once the Registrar is satisfied that all requirements have been complied with, he issues the Certificate of Incorporation and the company comes into existence.

(6) Raising Capital: In the case of a public company which intends to raise capital from the public, the promoter also arranges for the issue of a prospectus and the subscription of shares by the public. He enters into agreements with underwriters, bankers, brokers, and stock exchanges for this purpose.

7.2 Promoters – Rights, Duties, and Liabilities

Who is a Promoter?

A promoter is the person who conceives the idea of forming a company, works out the scheme, brings together the subscribers to the memorandum, and sets the company going. He is the person who does the necessary preliminary work to bring the company into existence.

Section Reference: Section 2(69) of the Companies Act, 2013 defines a promoter as – "(a) a person who has been named as such in a prospectus or is identified by the company in the annual return referred to in Section 92; or (b) a person who has control over the affairs of the company, directly or indirectly whether as a shareholder, director, or otherwise; or (c) a person in accordance with whose advice, directions or instructions the Board of Directors of the company is accustomed to act. Provided that sub-clause (c) does not apply to a person who is acting merely in a professional capacity."

It is important to note that a person who merely acts in a professional capacity – such as a solicitor, accountant, architect, or company secretary who provides professional services to the promoter – is not a promoter merely by reason of rendering such professional services.

Position of a Promoter

The legal position of a promoter is unique. He is neither an agent nor a trustee of the company because the company does not exist at the time of promotion. He cannot be an agent of a company which is not yet in existence, and he cannot be a trustee for a company which has not yet been formed. However, the courts have held that a promoter stands in a fiduciary relationship with the company. A fiduciary relationship is a relationship of trust and confidence.

Case: Erlanger v. New Sombrero Phosphate Co. (1878)

Lord Cairns observed that the promoters of a company stand in a fiduciary position towards the company which they are forming. A fiduciary position means a position of trust. The promoters have in their hands the ability and the opportunity of moulding the company to their will. They must, therefore, act with utmost good faith towards the company. They must not make any secret profit at the expense of the company.

Duties of a Promoter

Since the promoter stands in a fiduciary relationship with the company, he owes certain duties to the company. These duties are as follows:

(1) Duty not to make secret profit: The promoter must not make any secret profit at the expense of the company. If he sells his own property to the company, he must disclose this fact and the profit he is making. The disclosure must be made to an independent Board of Directors or to the shareholders of the company. If the promoter makes a secret profit without proper disclosure, the company can compel him to account for and surrender the profit to the company.

Case: Gluckstein v. Barnes (1900)

Certain persons acquired a property and then formed a company to buy the property from them. They made a profit of £20,000 on the sale but disclosed only a part of the profit. The House of Lords held that the promoters were liable to refund the secret profit to the company. The partial disclosure was not sufficient. The promoters were bound to disclose the full profit.

(2) Duty to make full disclosure: The promoter must make full disclosure of all material facts to the company. He must disclose every material fact which may influence the company's decision to enter into a contract. Non-disclosure of material facts amounts to fraud.

(3) Duty of utmost good faith: The promoter must act with utmost good faith (uberrimae fidei) towards the company. He must not place himself in a position where his personal interest conflicts with the interest of the company. He must act honestly and in the best interest of the company at all times.

(4) Duty not to make unfair use of position: The promoter must not take unfair advantage of his position. He must not use the information or opportunity which comes to him in his capacity as promoter for his own personal benefit.

Liabilities of a Promoter

The liabilities of promoters may be discussed under the following heads:

(1) Liability for secret profit: If a promoter makes a secret profit, the company has the following remedies – (a) the company can rescind (cancel) the contract with the promoter, (b) the company can recover the secret profit from the promoter, and (c) the company can sue the promoter for damages for breach of fiduciary duty.

(2) Liability for misstatement in the prospectus – Section 34 & 35: Every promoter is liable for any untrue or misleading statement in the prospectus issued by the company. Section 34 provides that where a prospectus contains any untrue or misleading statement or omits to disclose a material fact, every person who authorised the issue of the prospectus (including the promoter) shall be liable to compensate every person who has sustained any loss or damage by reason of such statement or omission. Section 35 also makes the promoter liable for criminal prosecution for fraud in connection with the issue of the prospectus.

(3) Liability for fraud – Section 447: If a promoter is guilty of fraud as defined in Section 447, he is liable to imprisonment ranging from 6 months to 10 years and a fine not less than the amount involved in the fraud, which may extend to three times the amount.

(4) Liability under SEBI Regulations: In the case of a listed company, the promoter is also subject to the regulations of SEBI (Securities and Exchange Board of India). SEBI (Issue of Capital and Disclosure Requirements) Regulations, SEBI (Listing Obligations and Disclosure Requirements) Regulations, and SEBI (Substantial Acquisition of Shares and Takeovers) Regulations impose various obligations and liabilities on promoters.

Rights and Remuneration of a Promoter

The Companies Act, 2013 does not specifically provide for the remuneration of promoters. However, promoters are entitled to be paid for the services rendered by them in the promotion of the company. The remuneration may be paid in the following forms:

(a) The company may pay a lump sum to the promoter for his services after its incorporation. (b) The company may sell shares to the promoter at a price lower than the market price. (c) The promoter may be allowed to purchase the company's property at a price lower than the market value. (d) The promoter may be given a commission on the shares sold. (e) The promoter may be appointed as a director or managing director of the company and may receive remuneration in that capacity.

Note: The promoter has no right against the company for expenses incurred by him during the promotion unless the company, after incorporation, enters into a contract to pay such expenses. This is because the company was not in existence when the expenses were incurred and a company is not bound by contracts made before its incorporation (pre-incorporation contracts), unless it adopts or ratifies them after incorporation.

Pre-Incorporation Contracts

A pre-incorporation contract is a contract entered into by the promoter on behalf of the company before the company is incorporated. Since the company is not yet in existence, it cannot be a party to the contract. The promoter enters into the contract in his own name but on behalf of the proposed company.

The legal position regarding pre-incorporation contracts is as follows:

(a) The company is not bound: A company cannot be bound by a pre-incorporation contract because it was not in existence when the contract was made. A contract can only bind a party which is in existence at the time of the contract. This is a well-settled principle of law.

Case: Kelner v. Baxter (1866)

Certain promoters entered into a contract for the purchase of stock for a hotel company which was about to be formed. The company was formed and it used the stock but became insolvent without paying for it. The Court held that the company could not be liable on the contract because it was not in existence when the contract was made. The promoters were personally liable because they had signed the contract.

(b) The promoter is personally liable: The promoter who enters into a pre-incorporation contract is personally liable for the contract. Even after the company is incorporated, the promoter's personal liability continues unless the other party agrees to release him (novation).

(c) Ratification by the company: Under the general law of agency, a principal cannot ratify an act done on his behalf before he came into existence. However, Section 15 of the Specific Relief Act, 1963 provides that where a contract is entered into by a promoter on behalf of the company before its incorporation, the company may, after its incorporation, specifically enforce the contract if the company has adopted the contract and communicated such adoption to the other party. Similarly, the other party may also enforce the contract against the company if the company has adopted it.

(d) Section 19(e) of the Specific Relief Act: Section 19(e) provides that a promoter may enforce a pre-incorporation contract specifically if the company has adopted the contract after its incorporation. This provision gives a legal remedy to promoters who enter into contracts for the benefit of the proposed company.

Note: In practice, when a company is formed and starts business, one of its first acts is to pass a resolution adopting the pre-incorporation contracts entered into by the promoters. This is usually done at the first Board meeting after incorporation. However, it is important to remember that adoption (or ratification) of a pre-incorporation contract creates a new contract between the company and the third party and does not validate the original contract.

7.3 Incorporation / Registration of a Company

The second and most important stage in the formation of a company is the stage of incorporation or registration. Incorporation is the process by which a company is registered with the Registrar of Companies and comes into legal existence. A company is born on the date of its incorporation. Before incorporation, the company has no legal existence. It is merely a project or a plan in the mind of the promoter.

The process of incorporation of a company in India is governed by Section 7 of the Companies Act, 2013, read with the Companies (Incorporation) Rules, 2014. The incorporation process has been significantly simplified and streamlined under the 2013 Act, especially with the introduction of online filing through the MCA (Ministry of Corporate Affairs) portal.

Procedure for Incorporation

The following is the step-by-step procedure for incorporating a company under the Companies Act, 2013:

Step 1: Name Approval – Section 4(4) & (5)

The first step is to obtain approval for the proposed name of the company from the Registrar of Companies. The promoter must apply for name reservation through the RUN (Reserve Unique Name) service on the MCA portal or through the SPICe+ form (Simplified Proforma for Incorporating Company Electronically Plus).

The name of the company is very important because it is the identity of the company. The following rules must be followed while selecting a name:

(a) The name must not be identical with or too similar to the name of an existing company or LLP registered in India [Section 4(2)].

(b) The name must not constitute an offence under any law or be undesirable in the opinion of the Central Government [Section 4(2)].

(c) The name of a public company must end with the word 'Limited' and the name of a private company must end with 'Private Limited' [Section 4(1)].

(d) The name must not include words like 'British India,' 'Municipal,' 'Chartered,' 'Imperial,' 'Crown,' 'State,' etc., without the previous approval of the Central Government.

(e) The name must not suggest any connection with or patronage of the Government unless the Government has given its approval.

The approved name is reserved for a period of 20 days from the date of approval. If the application for incorporation is not filed within this period, the name reservation lapses and the promoter will have to apply again.

Practical Tip: Before applying for name approval, it is advisable to check the availability of the proposed name on the MCA portal (www.mca.gov.in). The MCA portal has a 'Check Company Name' facility which allows you to search the database of existing company names. It is recommended to keep at least two or three alternative names ready in case the first choice is not available.

Step 2: Preparation of Documents

The following documents must be prepared and filed with the Registrar of Companies:

(a) Memorandum of Association (MOA): This is the most important document of the company. It contains the fundamental conditions upon which the company is allowed to be incorporated. It defines the name, registered office, objects, liability, and capital of the company. The memorandum must be signed by the subscribers (the first members) and their signatures must be witnessed. The detailed study of the memorandum is covered in Chapter 8.

(b) Articles of Association (AOA): The articles contain the rules and regulations for the internal management of the company. The articles must be signed by the subscribers to the memorandum. The detailed study of the articles is covered in Chapter 9.

(c) Declaration – Section 7(1)(b): A declaration in the prescribed form by an advocate, a chartered accountant, a cost accountant, or a company secretary in practice who is engaged in the formation of the company, and by a person named in the articles as a director, manager, or secretary of the company, that all the requirements of the Act and the rules made thereunder in respect of registration and matters precedent and incidental thereto have been complied with.

(d) Affidavit from Subscribers and First Directors – Section 7(1)(c): An affidavit from each of the subscribers to the memorandum and from persons named as the first directors, stating that he is not convicted of any offence in connection with the promotion, formation, or management of any company, or has not been found guilty of any fraud or misfeasance under this or any previous company law during the preceding five years, and that all the documents filed with the Registrar contain information that is correct and complete and true to the best of his knowledge.

(e) Address of Registered Office: The address of the registered office of the company must be furnished, or a verification of the registered office must be filed within 30 days of incorporation [Section 12].

(f) Particulars of Directors and Subscribers: The particulars of the first directors of the company, including their Director Identification Number (DIN), and the proof of identity and address of the subscribers and first directors must be filed.

(g) Consent of Directors: The consent of each person named as a first director to act in that capacity must be filed [Section 7(1)(e)].

Step 3: Filing with the Registrar – SPICe+ Form

All the above documents are now filed electronically through the SPICe+ (Simplified Proforma for Incorporating Company Electronically Plus) form on the MCA portal. The SPICe+ form is an integrated form which combines several applications into a single form:

(a) Name reservation (Part A of SPICe+). (b) Incorporation of the company (Part B of SPICe+), including the MOA and AOA in the prescribed e-forms (INC-33 for MOA and INC-34 for AOA). (c) Application for allotment of DIN (Director Identification Number) for up to 3 directors. (d) Application for PAN (Permanent Account Number) and TAN (Tax Deduction and Collection Account Number) of the company. (e) Application for GST registration. (f) Application for EPFO (Employees' Provident Fund Organisation) registration. (g) Application for ESIC (Employees' State Insurance Corporation) registration. (h) Application for professional tax registration (in certain states). (i) Opening of bank account for the company.

The filing must be accompanied by the prescribed fees and stamp duty. The fees vary depending on the authorised share capital of the company.

Practical Tip: The SPICe+ form has made the incorporation process much simpler and faster. Earlier, the promoter had to file multiple forms with different authorities (ROC, Income Tax, GST, EPFO, ESIC, etc.). Now, all these registrations are obtained through a single integrated form. This is a significant step towards 'ease of doing business' in India.

Step 4: Verification and Issue of Certificate of Incorporation

After receiving the application, the Registrar of Companies verifies all the documents and the information provided. If the Registrar is satisfied that all the requirements have been complied with, he registers the company and issues the Certificate of Incorporation [Section 7(2)]. The certificate is issued in a prescribed form and bears the Corporate Identity Number (CIN) allotted to the company.

7.4 Documents Required for Registration

Section 7 of the Companies Act, 2013 prescribes the documents and information which must be filed with the Registrar of Companies for the registration (incorporation) of a company. These are summarised in the following table:

Table 7.1: Documents Required for Incorporation

S.No.	Document / Information	Section / Rule
1	Memorandum of Association (MOA) duly signed by subscribers	Section 4, 7(1)(a)
2	Articles of Association (AOA) duly signed by subscribers	Section 5, 7(1)(a)
3	Declaration of compliance by professional (CA/CS/CWA/Advocate)	Section 7(1)(b)
4	Affidavit from each subscriber and first director	Section 7(1)(c)

5	Address of registered office or proof of address	Section 12, 7(1)(d)
6	Particulars of first directors (with DIN)	Section 7(1)(d)
7	Written consent of each first director	Section 7(1)(e)
8	PAN / Passport / Voter ID of subscribers and directors	Rules
9	Address proof of subscribers and directors	Rules
10	NOC from owner of premises (for registered office)	Rules
11	Proof of registered office address (utility bill, etc.)	Rules
12	For OPC: Nominee's consent in Form INC-3	Section 3(1)(c)

Number of Subscribers

Table 7.2: Minimum Subscribers and Directors

Type of Company	Min. Subscribers (Members)	Min. Directors
One Person Company (OPC)	1	1
Private Company	2	2
Public Company	7	3

Each subscriber to the memorandum must take at least one share. The total number of shares taken by the subscribers forms the initial subscribed capital of the company. The subscribers to the memorandum are deemed to have agreed to take the shares indicated against their names and the company must allot these shares to them upon incorporation [Section 10].

7.5 Certificate of Incorporation – Section 7

The Certificate of Incorporation is the most important document in the life of a company. It is the birth certificate of the company. The company comes into existence as a legal person from the date mentioned in the Certificate of Incorporation. Before this date, the company has no legal existence.

Section Reference: Section 7(2): The Registrar on the basis of documents and information filed under sub-section (1), shall register all the documents and information referred to in that sub-section in the register and issue a certificate of incorporation in the prescribed form to the company.

Contents of the Certificate of Incorporation

The Certificate of Incorporation contains the following information: (a) the name of the company, (b) the date of incorporation, (c) the Corporate Identity Number (CIN) – a unique 21-digit alphanumeric code allotted by the MCA, (d) the Permanent Account Number (PAN) allotted by the Income Tax Department, (e) the status of the company (whether public or private), and (f) the state in which the company is registered.

Legal Effects of the Certificate of Incorporation

The issue of the Certificate of Incorporation has the following important legal effects:

(1) Company comes into existence: From the date of incorporation mentioned in the certificate, the subscribers to the memorandum, together with such other persons as may from time to time become members of the company, shall be a body corporate by the name contained in the memorandum [Section 9]. The company becomes a separate legal person with all the attributes of a company – separate legal entity, perpetual succession, common seal (optional), and the power to hold property, enter into contracts, sue and be sued.

(2) Conclusive Evidence: Section 7(4) provides that the certificate of incorporation issued by the Registrar shall be conclusive evidence that all the requirements of the Act in respect of registration and matters precedent and incidental thereto have been complied with and that the company is duly registered under this Act.

Case: Jubilee Cotton Mills Ltd. v. Lewis (1924)

The memorandum of association was signed by the required number of persons. The Registrar issued the Certificate of Incorporation. Later, it was discovered that one of the signatories had died before the certificate was issued. The question was whether the incorporation was valid. The House of Lords held that the certificate of incorporation is conclusive evidence of the validity of the incorporation. Once the certificate is issued, it cannot be challenged on the ground that the requirements of the Act were not complied with. The Court said that the certificate is like a birth certificate – once a child is born, the question of its birth cannot be re-opened.

(3) Members become body corporate: The subscribers to the memorandum and such other persons who become members from time to time become a body corporate capable of exercising all the functions of an incorporated company.

(4) Corporate Identity Number (CIN): Every company is allotted a unique CIN which must be mentioned in all official documents, correspondence, and records of the company.

(5) Name of company: The company acquires the name mentioned in the certificate. The company must paint or affix its name on the outside of every office or place in which its business is carried on [Section 12(3)(a)]. The name must appear on all business letters, bill heads, letter papers, notices, official publications, and other documents.

Can the Certificate of Incorporation be Cancelled?

As a general rule, once the Certificate of Incorporation is issued, it cannot be cancelled or revoked. This is because of the conclusive nature of the certificate. However, under Section 7(7), if it is found that the company has been got incorporated by furnishing any false or incorrect information or representation or by suppressing any material fact or information, the Tribunal (NCLT) may, on an application made to it on being satisfied that the situation so warrants – (a) pass an order for the closure of the company and order the winding up of the affairs of the company; (b) pass such other orders as it may deem fit.

The members of the company shall be jointly and severally liable for all debts and obligations of the company incurred between the date of incorporation and the date of the Tribunal's order. The persons named in the documents filed with the Registrar as officers-in-default shall be liable for all the relevant consequences.

Note: The power to cancel the certificate of incorporation was not available under the Companies Act, 1956. This is a new provision introduced by the 2013 Act to deal with cases of fraudulent incorporation. However, the Tribunal will exercise this power only in extreme cases of fraud or suppression.

7.6 Commencement of Business – Section 10A

Under the Companies Act, 2013, the original Section 11 dealt with commencement of business but was later omitted. The Companies (Amendment) Act, 2018 introduced a new Section 10A which requires certain companies to obtain a declaration of commencement of business before starting their business operations.

Provisions of Section 10A

Section 10A provides that a company incorporated after the commencement of the Companies (Amendment) Act, 2018 and having a share capital shall not commence any business or exercise any borrowing powers unless –

(a) a declaration is filed by a director within a period of 180 days of the date of incorporation of the company in the prescribed form (INC-20A) with the Registrar, verifying that every subscriber to the memorandum has paid the value of the shares agreed to be taken by him on the date of making of such declaration; and

(b) the company has filed with the Registrar a verification of its registered office as provided in Section 12(2).

If a company fails to comply with the provisions of Section 10A and is not able to file the declaration within 180 days of incorporation, the Registrar may, without prejudice to any action under Section 248 (removal of name from register), initiate action for the removal of the name of the company from the register of companies.

Note: In the case of a private company, the company can start business immediately after incorporation, but it must file the declaration under Section 10A within 180 days. In the case of a public company which wants to raise capital from the public, it must first issue a prospectus and receive the minimum subscription before it can commence business. But the minimum subscription requirement is now governed by SEBI regulations rather than the Companies Act.

Summary of Stages of Formation

Table 7.3: Stages of Company Formation at a Glance

Stage	Activities	Applicable To
1. Promotion	Idea conception, feasibility study, assembling resources, engaging professionals	All companies
2. Incorporation	Name approval, filing MOA/AOA and documents, obtaining Certificate of Incorporation	All companies

3. Capital Subscription	Issue of prospectus, raising capital from public, allotment of shares	Public companies (inviting public)
4. Commencement of Business	Filing declaration under Section 10A, verification of registered office	Companies with share capital (post-2018 amendment)

Chapter 8

Memorandum of Association

The Memorandum of Association is the most important document of a company. It is the foundation upon which the entire structure of the company is built. It defines the scope of the company's activities, the extent of its powers, and the limits beyond which the company cannot go. If the company is compared to a building, the Memorandum of Association is its foundation stone. Just as a building cannot stand without a strong foundation, a company cannot exist without a proper memorandum. Every person who deals with the company – whether as a shareholder, creditor, employee, or customer – is presumed to have read the memorandum and to have understood the powers and limitations of the company. This chapter examines the memorandum of association in detail.

8.1 Meaning and Purpose of MOA

Definition

The Companies Act, 2013 does not define the term 'Memorandum of Association' in a descriptive manner. Section 2(56) simply states that "'Memorandum' means the memorandum of association of a company as originally framed or as altered from time to time in pursuance of any previous company law or of this Act."

However, the memorandum has been described by judges and authors in a more meaningful way:

According to Palmer: "The memorandum of association is a document of great importance in relation to the proposed company. It contains the fundamental conditions upon which alone the company is allowed to be incorporated. It is the charter of the company and defines the limitations of the powers of the company."

According to Lord Cairns in Ashbury Railway Carriage and Iron Co. v. Riche (1875): "The memorandum of association of a company is its charter, and defines the limitation of the powers of the company. The memorandum is, as it were, the area beyond which the actions of the company cannot go; inside that area the shareholders may make such regulations for their own government as they think fit."

From the above, we can understand that the Memorandum of Association is the charter or constitution of the company. It defines the company's name, the state in which the registered office is situated, the objects of the company, the liability of its members, and its authorised share capital. It lays down the fundamental conditions and the scope of the company's activities.

Purpose of the Memorandum

The memorandum serves the following important purposes:

(1) It defines the scope and powers of the company: The memorandum clearly states what the company can do and what it cannot do. The company cannot go beyond the powers defined in the memorandum. Any act done beyond the powers of the memorandum is ultra vires (beyond the powers) and void.

(2) It protects the interests of the shareholders: The shareholders invest their money in the company on the basis of the objects stated in the memorandum. The memorandum ensures that the money contributed by the shareholders is used only for the purposes stated therein. The directors cannot use the company's funds for purposes not authorised by the memorandum.

(3) It protects the interests of creditors and third parties: The memorandum is a public document. Any person who deals with the company can inspect the memorandum at the office of the Registrar of Companies. By reading the memorandum, the creditors and third parties can know the extent of the company's powers and the limits of its activities. This protects them from entering into transactions which the company is not authorised to carry out.

(4) It defines the relationship between the company and the outside world: While the Articles of Association govern the internal management of the company, the Memorandum of Association governs the relationship between the company and the outside world. It tells the world about the company's identity, purpose, and limitations.

Form of the Memorandum – Section 4

Section 4(6) provides that the memorandum shall be in the forms specified in the Tables given in Schedule I of the Act. Schedule I provides different forms for different types of companies:

Table	Type of Company	Form
Table A	Company limited by shares	Form of MOA
Table B	Company limited by guarantee and having share capital	Form of MOA
Table C	Company limited by guarantee and not having share capital	Form of MOA
Table D	Unlimited company and having share capital	Form of MOA
Table E	Unlimited company and not having share capital	Form of MOA

The memorandum must be printed, divided into paragraphs numbered consecutively, signed by each subscriber in the presence of at least one witness who shall attest the signature, and dated [Section 4(6)]. The memorandum of a One Person Company must also indicate the name of the nominee [Section 3(1)(c)].

8.2 Contents / Clauses of MOA – Section 4

Section 4 of the Companies Act, 2013 prescribes the matters which must be stated in the memorandum. The memorandum of every company must contain the following six clauses:

(1) Name Clause – Section 4(1)(a)

The first clause of the memorandum must state the name of the company. The name is the identity of the company. It distinguishes one company from another. The following rules must be observed regarding the name of the company:

(a) Suffix: The name of a public limited company must end with the word 'Limited' and the name of a private limited company must end with the words 'Private Limited.' In the case of a One Person Company, the name must end with '(OPC) Private Limited.' A Section 8 company (not-for-profit company) is exempted from using the word 'Limited' or 'Private Limited.'

(b) Prohibition: Section 4(2) provides that no company shall be registered with a name which, in the opinion of the Central Government, is undesirable. A name which is identical with or too nearly resembles the name of an existing company or LLP is not allowed. A name which constitutes an offence under any law is not allowed. Names which suggest patronage of the Government or which include words like 'President,' 'Government,' 'Republic,' etc., require prior approval.

(c) Name displayed: Section 12(3) requires every company to paint or affix its name, along with the address of its registered office, on the outside of every office or place of business. The name must also be printed on all business letters, bill heads, notices, official publications, negotiable instruments, and other official communications.

(d) Rectification of name: If a company has been registered with a name which is identical with or too nearly resembles the name of an existing company, the Registrar may direct the company to change its name within three months [Section 16(1)]. If the company fails to do so, the Registrar may allot a new name to the company.

(e) Change of name: A company may change its name by passing a special resolution and obtaining the approval of the Central Government

[Section 13(2)]. However, if the change involves only the addition or deletion of the word 'Private' consequent on conversion, a special resolution is not needed.

(2) Registered Office Clause – Section 4(1)(b)

The second clause of the memorandum must state the State in which the registered office of the company is to be situated. The memorandum need not give the exact address – it only needs to mention the State (e.g., Madhya Pradesh, Maharashtra, Karnataka, etc.).

However, the company must establish its registered office within 30 days of its incorporation and notify the Registrar within this period [Section 12(2)]. The exact address of the registered office is given in the form filed at the time of incorporation.

The registered office is the official address of the company. It determines the jurisdiction of the Registrar of Companies and the High Court. All communications and notices from the Government, the Registrar, and other authorities are sent to the registered office of the company. The company must keep certain statutory registers and records at its registered office, including the Register of Members, Register of Directors, Register of Charges, and the Minutes Books.

Shifting of Registered Office: The registered office may be shifted from one place to another. The procedure depends on the extent of the shift:

(a) Within the same city, town, or village – A resolution of the Board of Directors is sufficient [Section 12(5)]. (b) From one city/town/village to another within the same State but within the jurisdiction of the same Registrar of Companies – A special resolution of the shareholders is required [Section 12(5)]. (c) From the jurisdiction of one Registrar to another within the same State – A special resolution is required and confirmation of the Regional Director must be obtained [Section 12(5)]. (d) From one State to another State – A special resolution is required and confirmation of the Central Government is required. This involves alteration of the memorandum [Section 13(4)].

(3) Objects Clause – Section 4(1)(c)

The objects clause is the most important clause of the memorandum. It defines the purpose for which the company has been formed and the scope of the company's activities. The objects clause tells the shareholders, creditors, and the world at large what the company is authorised to do.

Section Reference: Section 4(1)(c) provides that the memorandum of a company shall state – "the objects for which the company is proposed to be incorporated and any matter considered necessary in furtherance thereof."

Under the Companies Act, 1956, the objects clause was required to be divided into three sub-clauses – (a) Main Objects, (b) Objects incidental or ancillary to the main objects, and (c) Other Objects. However, under the Companies Act, 2013, this classification has been abolished. Now, the memorandum simply states the objects for which the company is to be incorporated. There is no requirement to divide the objects into sub-clauses.

The objects clause is very important because it defines the legal boundary within which the company must operate. Any act done by the company which is outside the scope of the objects clause is ultra vires (beyond the powers of) the company and is void. This brings us to the important doctrine of ultra vires which is discussed in detail in Section 8.3 of this chapter.

Note: Under the Companies Act, 2013, a company can engage in any lawful activity. Section 4(1)(c) gives greater flexibility to companies in framing their objects clause. Companies can now adopt a wider objects clause to accommodate future business diversification. However, a company engaged in any activity which is not authorised by its objects clause may be penalised and its directors may be held liable

(4) Liability Clause – Section 4(1)(d)

The fourth clause of the memorandum must state the nature of the liability of the members of the company.

(a) In the case of a company limited by shares, the memorandum must state that the liability of its members is limited to the amount unpaid, if any, on the shares respectively held by them. (b) In the case of a company limited by guarantee, the memorandum must state that the liability of its members is limited and that each member undertakes to contribute to the assets of the company in the event of its being wound up while he is a member or within one year after he ceases to be a member, a specified amount not exceeding a specified figure for payment of the debts and liabilities of the company. (c) In the case of an unlimited company, the memorandum must state that the liability of its members is unlimited.

The liability clause protects the members by clearly defining the extent of their liability. In a company limited by shares, no member can be called upon to pay more than the amount unpaid on his shares. This is one of the greatest advantages of the company form of business.

(5) Capital Clause – Section 4(1)(e)

The fifth clause of the memorandum (applicable to companies having a share capital) must state the amount of share capital with which the company is to be registered and the division thereof into shares of a fixed amount.

In other words, this clause states the authorised share capital (also called the 'nominal capital' or 'registered capital') of the company and the number of shares into which it is divided. For example, the memorandum may state: "The authorised share capital of the company is Rs. 50,00,000 (Rupees Fifty Lakhs only) divided into 5,00,000 equity shares of Rs. 10 each."

The authorised share capital is the maximum amount of share capital which the company is authorised to raise by issuing shares. The company cannot issue shares beyond its authorised share capital unless the capital clause is altered by passing a resolution and filing the necessary forms with the Registrar.

Illustration: XYZ Private Limited has an authorised share capital of Rs. 10,00,000 divided into 1,00,000 equity shares of Rs. 10 each. If the company wants to issue more than 1,00,000 shares, it must first increase its authorised share capital by altering the capital clause of the memorandum.

Important Terminology:

(a) Authorised Capital (or Nominal Capital or Registered Capital): The maximum amount of capital which a company is authorised to issue as stated in its memorandum.

(b) Issued Capital: The part of the authorised capital which has actually been offered for subscription (i.e., offered to the public or to private parties).

(c) Subscribed Capital: The part of the issued capital which has been subscribed (taken up) by the subscribers.

(d) Paid-up Capital: The part of the subscribed capital which has actually been paid by the shareholders. If a share of Rs. 10 face value has been issued and the company has called up Rs. 8, and the shareholder has paid Rs. 8, then the paid-up capital per share is Rs. 8. The remaining Rs. 2 per share is the 'uncalled capital.'

(e) Reserve Capital – Section 65: A company limited by shares may, by special resolution, determine that any portion of its uncalled share capital shall not be called up except in the event of, and for the purposes of, the winding up of the company. Such uncalled share capital is called 'reserve capital.' Once a resolution for reserve capital is passed, it cannot be revoked without the permission of the court.

(6) Subscription Clause / Association Clause

The last clause (also called the subscription clause or association clause) contains the declaration of the subscribers. Each subscriber to the memorandum must state:

(a) His name, address, description, and occupation. (b) The number of shares he agrees to take. Each subscriber must take at least one share. (c)

His signature, which must be attested by at least one witness who shall also sign and give his address and occupation.

The subscription clause is the clause by which the subscribers declare that they desire to be formed into a company in pursuance of the memorandum and that they agree to take the number of shares set opposite their respective names. In the case of a One Person Company, there is only one subscriber. In the case of a private company, there must be at least two subscribers, and in the case of a public company, there must be at least seven subscribers.

Table 8.1: Six Clauses of the Memorandum at a Glance

Clause No.	Name of Clause	Contents	Section
1	Name Clause	Name of the company with proper suffix	4(1)(a)
2	Registered Office Clause	State in which registered office is situated	4(1)(b)
3	Objects Clause	Objects for which company is incorporated	4(1)(c)
4	Liability Clause	Nature and extent of liability of members	4(1)(d)
5	Capital Clause	Authorised share capital and its division	4(1)(e)
6	Subscription Clause	Names, addresses, shares taken by subscribers	4(6)

8.3 Doctrine of Ultra Vires

The doctrine of ultra vires is one of the most important doctrines in company law. The term 'ultra vires' is a Latin phrase which means 'beyond the powers.' When a company does any act which is beyond the scope of the powers defined in its memorandum of association, such act is said to be 'ultra vires' the company. An ultra vires act is void ab initio (void from the very beginning) and cannot be ratified even by the unanimous consent of all the shareholders.

The doctrine of ultra vires was established by the House of Lords in the following landmark case:

Case: Ashbury Railway Carriage and Iron Co. v. Riche (1875)

The memorandum of the company stated that its objects were to make, sell, or lend on hire railway carriages and wagons and all kinds of railway plant, fittings, machinery, and rolling stock; to carry on the business of mechanical engineers and general contractors; and to purchase, lease, work, and sell mines and minerals. The company entered into a contract with Riche for the construction of a railway line in Belgium. When the company refused to honour the contract, Riche sued the company. The House of Lords held that the contract for the construction of a railway line was ultra vires the company because the objects clause of the memorandum did not authorise the company to undertake the construction of railway lines. The contract was void and could not be ratified even by the unanimous consent of all the shareholders. Lord Cairns said: 'The memorandum of association is the charter of the company; it defines the limitation of the powers of the company.'

Meaning and Scope of Ultra Vires

The doctrine of ultra vires operates at three levels:

(1) Ultra Vires the Memorandum (Ultra Vires the Company): When an act is beyond the scope of the objects clause of the memorandum, it is ultra vires the company. Such an act is absolutely void and cannot be ratified by the shareholders. No amount of shareholder approval can make an ultra vires act valid. For example, if a company is formed with the object of manufacturing textiles and it enters into a contract to build bridges, the contract is ultra vires the company.

(2) Ultra Vires the Articles but Intra Vires the Memorandum: When an act is within the scope of the memorandum but goes beyond the powers given by the articles of association, the act is ultra vires the articles but intra vires (within the powers of) the memorandum. Such an act is not void. It can be ratified by the shareholders by passing an appropriate resolution. The shareholders can also amend the articles to bring the act within the powers of the articles.

(3) Ultra Vires the Directors but Intra Vires the Company: When an act is within the powers of the company (i.e., within the memorandum and the articles) but has been done by the directors without the required authority, the act is ultra vires the directors. Such an act can be ratified by the shareholders by passing an appropriate resolution. The shareholders can also approve the act retrospectively.

Note: It is very important to understand the distinction between these three levels of ultra vires. Only an act which is ultra vires the memorandum (i.e., ultra vires the company itself) is absolutely void and incapable of ratification. Acts which are ultra vires the articles or ultra vires the directors can be ratified by the shareholders.

Effects / Consequences of Ultra Vires Acts

The following are the important consequences of an ultra vires act:

(1) The act is void ab initio: An ultra vires act is void from the very beginning. It has no legal effect. It is not a voidable act which can be confirmed or ratified – it is an absolute nullity. Even if all the shareholders unanimously agree to ratify the act, it remains void.

(2) No estoppel against the company: The doctrine of estoppel does not apply against a company in respect of an ultra vires act. Even if the company has represented that it has the power to do a particular act, it cannot be estopped from denying the validity of the act if it is ultra vires.

(3) Injunction: Any member of the company can obtain an injunction from the court to restrain the company from doing an act which is ultra vires. This right is available even to a single shareholder.

(4) Personal liability of directors: If the directors enter into an ultra vires transaction, they may be held personally liable for any loss caused to the company. The company can recover damages from the directors who authorised the ultra vires act. The directors may also be liable to account for any profits made from the ultra vires act.

(5) Ultra vires lending: If a company lends money for an ultra vires purpose, the lending is void. However, the company can recover the money if it can be traced into the hands of the borrower. This is based on the equitable principle of restitution.

(6) Ultra vires borrowing: If a company borrows money for an ultra vires purpose, the lender cannot sue the company on the basis of the loan agreement because the agreement is void. However, if the borrowed money has been used to pay off a legitimate debt of the company, the lender is subrogated to the rights of the original creditor (i.e., the lender steps into the shoes of the creditor whose debt has been paid off).

(7) Ultra vires property acquired: If a company acquires property through an ultra vires transaction, the company's right over the property is protected. The company can defend its possession of the property even though it was acquired through an ultra vires act. This is because the ultra vires doctrine protects the company and its shareholders, not the third parties who dealt with the company.

Case: Re Jon Beauforte (London) Ltd. (1953)

A company was formed to manufacture dresses and costumes. The company started manufacturing veneered panels, which was ultra vires its objects. Suppliers who had supplied coke and coal for the manufacture of veneered panels claimed that the company was liable to pay them. The Court held that since the suppliers knew that the company was engaged in an ultra vires business (they had supplied coke and coal, not materials for making dresses), they could not recover the amount. The contracts were ultra vires and void.

Doctrine of Ultra Vires Under the Companies Act, 2013

Under the Companies Act, 2013, the significance of the doctrine of ultra vires has been somewhat reduced. This is because the 2013 Act allows companies to have very broad and general objects clauses. Companies are no longer required to divide their objects into main objects, incidental objects, and other objects (as was required under the 1956 Act). A company can now include very wide and diverse objects in its memorandum, reducing the chances of any act being declared ultra vires. However, the doctrine has not been abolished. If a company does an act which is clearly outside the scope of its objects as stated in the memorandum, the act will still be ultra vires and void. The doctrine continues to serve as an important safeguard for the protection of shareholders and creditors.

Moreover, Section 4(1)(c) requires every company to state its objects. If a company acts beyond its stated objects, any member or creditor can challenge such action. Under Section 245 (class action suit), members can also file an application before the NCLT if the company's affairs are being conducted in a manner prejudicial to the interest of the company or its members.

8.4 Alteration of Memorandum – Section 13

Although the memorandum is the fundamental document of the company, it is not unalterable. The Companies Act, 2013 allows the alteration of the memorandum, but the procedure for alteration depends on which clause is being altered. The conditions for alteration are designed to protect the interests of the shareholders and the public.

(1) Alteration of the Name Clause – Section 13(2) & (3)

A company may change its name by passing a special resolution. However, the change of name is effective only on the issue of a fresh certificate of incorporation by the Registrar [Section 13(3)]. The following situations may arise:

(a) Ordinary change of name: The company must pass a special resolution and obtain the approval of the Central Government. The company must apply to the Registrar for a fresh certificate of incorporation. The Registrar, on being satisfied, will issue a new certificate of incorporation with the changed name.

(b) Change of name ordered by the Registrar – Section 16: If a company has been registered with a name which, in the opinion of the Central Government, is identical with or too nearly resembles the name of an existing company, the Registrar may direct the company to change its name within three months. If the company fails to do so within the specified period, the Registrar may replace the existing name with a new name and issue a fresh certificate of incorporation.

(c) Change involving only 'Private': Where the change of name involves only the addition or deletion of the word 'Private' (as a consequence of conversion from private to public or vice versa), a special resolution is not required. An ordinary resolution is sufficient.

It is important to note that the change of name does not affect the identity of the company. The company remains the same legal entity with the same rights and obligations. All contracts, properties, and legal proceedings continue in the new name of the company.

(2) Alteration of the Registered Office Clause – Section 13(4)

If a company wants to shift its registered office from one State to another, it must alter the registered office clause of the memorandum. The following procedure must be followed:

(a) The company must pass a special resolution approving the change. (b) The application must be filed with the Central Government in the prescribed form along with a copy of the special resolution and other documents. (c) The Central Government may confirm the change if it is satisfied that the change is not opposed to the interests of any creditor or class of creditors and does not adversely affect the public interest. (d) A certified copy of the Central Government's order must be filed with the Registrar of both the States (the State from which the office is being shifted and the State to which it is being shifted). (e) The Registrar of the State to which the office is shifted issues a fresh certificate of incorporation.

Note: The shifting of registered office from one State to another is a significant change because it changes the jurisdiction of the Registrar and the High Court. Therefore, the procedure is more elaborate and requires the approval of the Central Government.

(3) Alteration of the Objects Clause – Section 13(1)

Section 13(1) provides that a company may alter the provisions of its memorandum by passing a special resolution. This general provision covers the alteration of the objects clause. The company must pass a special resolution and file a copy of the altered memorandum with the Registrar within 30 days.

Under the Companies Act, 1956, the alteration of the objects clause was permitted only for certain specified purposes and required the confirmation of the Company Law Board (now NCLT). Under the 2013 Act, the procedure has been simplified. A company can now alter its objects clause by simply passing a special resolution, without the need for confirmation by the NCLT or the Central Government. However, if the company has raised money through a prospectus for a specific object and the money has not been fully utilised, the company must comply with the special procedure under Section 13(8).

Section Reference: Section 13(8): A company which has raised money from public through prospectus and still has any unutilised amount out of the money so raised, shall not change its objects for which it raised the money through prospectus unless a special resolution through postal ballot is passed and the dissenting shareholders are given an exit opportunity by the promoters and shareholders having control.

(4) Alteration of the Liability Clause – Section 13(1)

The liability clause of the memorandum can be altered by passing a special resolution. However, a company cannot increase the liability of its members without their consent. Section 38 provides that no member shall be bound by any alteration made in the memorandum or articles after the date on which he became a member, if such alteration requires him to take or subscribe for more shares than the number held by him at the date of the alteration, or in any way increases his liability as at that date to contribute to the share capital of, or otherwise to pay money to, the company, unless he agrees in writing to be bound by the alteration.

This means that if the company wants to convert from a limited company to an unlimited company (which increases the liability of members), the consent of each member is required. No member can be compelled to accept unlimited liability.

(5) Alteration of the Capital Clause – Section 61

The capital clause can be altered by passing an ordinary resolution in a general meeting, provided the articles of the company authorise such alteration. Section 61 provides that a limited company having a share capital may, if so authorised by its articles, alter the conditions of its memorandum in the following ways:

(a) Increase the authorised share capital: The company may increase its authorised share capital by such amount as it thinks expedient. For example, a company with an authorised capital of Rs. 10 lakhs may increase it to Rs. 50 lakhs.

(b) Consolidation of shares: The company may consolidate and divide all or any of its share capital into shares of larger amount. For example, 10 shares of Rs. 10 each may be consolidated into 1 share of Rs. 100.

(c) Sub-division of shares: The company may sub-divide all or any of its shares into shares of smaller amount. For example, 1 share of Rs. 100 may be sub-divided into 10 shares of Rs. 10 each.

(d) Conversion of shares into stock and vice versa: The company may convert all or any of its fully paid-up shares into stock, and reconvert that stock into fully paid-up shares of any denomination.

(e) Cancellation of unissued shares: The company may cancel shares which have not been taken or agreed to be taken by any person and diminish the amount of its share capital by the amount of the shares so cancelled. This does not amount to reduction of share capital.

Notice of the alteration must be filed with the Registrar within 30 days [Section 64].

Note: It is important to note that the alteration of the capital clause under Section 61 requires only an ordinary resolution (i.e., a simple majority of the members present and voting). This is different from the alteration of other clauses which generally requires a special resolution (i.e., a three-fourths majority). However, the reduction of share capital (which is different from cancellation of unissued shares) requires a special resolution and the confirmation of the NCLT under Section 66.

Table 8.2: Alteration of Memorandum – Summary

Clause	Procedure for Alteration	Section
Name Clause	Special Resolution + Central Government approval + New Certificate	13(2), 13(3)
Registered Office (within same State)	Special Resolution (or Board Resolution for same city)	12(5)
Registered Office (to another State)	Special Resolution + Central Government confirmation + New Certificate	13(4)
Objects Clause	Special Resolution + Filing with ROC within 30 days	13(1)
Objects (with unutilised public money)	Special Resolution by postal ballot + Exit offer to dissenters	13(8)
Liability Clause	Special Resolution + Written consent of each member (if liability increases)	13(1), 38

Capital Clause (increase, consolidation, sub-division, etc.)	Ordinary Resolution (if articles authorise) + Filing with ROC	61, 64
Capital Clause (reduction)	Special Resolution + NCLT confirmation	66

Chapter 9

Articles of Association

In the previous chapter, we studied the Memorandum of Association which is the charter of the company and defines the scope of the company's powers. In this chapter, we shall study the Articles of Association which contain the rules and regulations for the internal management and administration of the company. If the Memorandum of Association is the constitution of the company, the Articles of Association are its bye-laws. The memorandum tells us what the company can do; the articles tell us how the company will do it. Together, the memorandum and the articles form the complete constitution of the company.

9.1 Meaning and Contents of AOA

Definition

Section Reference: Section 2(5) of the Companies Act, 2013 defines 'Articles' as: "'Articles' means the articles of association of a company as originally framed or as altered from time to time or applied in pursuance of any previous company law or of this Act."

This is merely a technical definition. In a more descriptive sense, the Articles of Association may be defined as the document which contains the rules, regulations, and bye-laws for the internal management and administration of the company. The articles govern the relationship between the company and its members, between the members inter se (amongst themselves), and between the company and its directors. They deal with matters such as the issue and allotment of shares, transfer and transmission of shares, forfeiture of shares, meetings and voting, powers and duties of directors, payment of dividends, accounts and audit, borrowing powers, winding up, and other matters relating to the internal affairs of the company.

According to Palmer: "The articles of association are the regulations for the internal management of the affairs of the company, and are binding on the company and its members."

According to Lord Cairns: "The articles of association play a part subsidiary to the memorandum of association. They accept the memorandum of association as the charter of incorporation of the company, and so accepting it, the articles proceed to define the duties, the rights, and the powers of the governing body as between themselves and the company at large, and the mode and form in which the business of the company is to be carried on, and the mode and form in which changes in the internal regulations of the company may from time to time be made."

Contents of Articles of Association

The Articles of Association typically contain regulations relating to the following matters:

(a) Share capital – different classes of shares, rights attached to each class, issue of shares, allotment, calls on shares, lien on shares, forfeiture and surrender of shares. (b) Transfer and transmission of shares – procedure for transfer, right to refuse registration of transfer, transmission on death or insolvency. (c) Alteration of share capital – increase, consolidation, sub-division, and reduction. (d) Conversion of shares into stock and reconversion. (e) General meetings – annual general meeting, extraordinary general meeting, notice, quorum, proxy, voting, resolutions, minutes. (f) Board of Directors – number, appointment, qualifications, disqualifications, remuneration, powers, duties, meetings of Board, rotation of directors. (g) Managing Director, Whole-time Director, and Manager – appointment, powers, remuneration. (h) Borrowing powers. (i) Dividends and reserves. (j) Accounts and audit. (k) Common seal (if the company has one). (l) Indemnity. (m) Winding up.

Form of Articles – Section 5

Section 5(1) provides that the articles of a company shall be in the forms specified in the Tables in Schedule I of the Act as may be applicable to such company.

(a) Table F: Model articles for a company limited by shares. This is the most commonly used form.

(b) Table G: Model articles for a company limited by guarantee and having a share capital.

(c) Table H: Model articles for a company limited by guarantee and not having a share capital.

(d) Table I: Model articles for an unlimited company and having a share capital.

(e) Table J: Model articles for an unlimited company and not having a share capital.

Which Companies Must Have Articles?

Section 5(6) provides that the articles shall be signed by each subscriber of the memorandum, who shall add his name, address, description, and occupation, in the presence of at least one witness who shall attest the signature and likewise add his name, address, description, and occupation. Every company must have its articles of association. However, Section 5(7) provides that a company limited by shares may have its own articles or it may adopt all or any of the regulations contained in the model articles (Table F) given in Schedule I. If a company limited by shares does not register its own articles, the provisions of the model articles in Table F shall apply to that company as if those were its registered articles. However, a company limited by guarantee, an unlimited company, and a One Person Company must have their own articles. They cannot simply rely on the model articles. A private company must include in its articles the three restrictions mentioned in Section 2(68) – restriction on transfer of shares, limitation on number of members to 200, and prohibition of invitation to the public.

Legal Nature of Articles – Section 10

Section 10 of the Companies Act, 2013 provides that the memorandum and articles shall, when registered, bind the company and the members thereof to the same extent as if they respectively had been signed by the company and by each member, and contained covenants on the part of the company and of each member to observe all the provisions of the memorandum and of the articles.

The effect of Section 10 is that the memorandum and articles constitute a contract between the company and its members and between the members inter se. However, this is a contract of a special nature. It is not the same as an ordinary contract. The following are the important aspects of the binding force of the articles:

(1) Articles bind the company to its members: The company is bound to the members by the provisions of the articles. If the company acts in violation of the articles, any member can take legal action against the company to enforce the articles.

Case: Hickman v. Kent or Romney Marsh Sheep Breeders' Association (1915)

The articles of the company provided that any dispute between the company and its members must be referred to arbitration before any legal proceedings are taken. A member filed a lawsuit in court without first referring the dispute to arbitration. The Court held that the articles constituted a contract between the company and its members. Since the articles required arbitration first, the member was bound by this provision. The lawsuit was stayed (suspended) until arbitration was completed.

(2) Articles bind the members to the company: Each member is bound to the company by the provisions of the articles. If a member acts in violation of the articles, the company can take legal action against him. For example, if the articles provide for a lien on shares for any money due from the member to the company, the company can enforce the lien.

(3) Articles bind the members inter se (amongst themselves): The articles constitute a contract between the members themselves. Each member is bound by the articles in his dealings with the other members. If a dispute arises between two members on a matter covered by the articles, the articles will govern the dispute.

Case: Rayfield v. Hands (1958)

The articles of a private company provided that if any member wished to transfer his shares, the directors were bound to take the shares at a fair value. Rayfield, a member, wanted to sell his shares and asked the directors to buy them. The directors refused. The Court held that the articles constituted a binding contract between the members and the directors (who were also members). The directors were bound to buy the shares at a fair value as provided in the articles.

(4) Articles do not bind the company or members to outsiders: The articles do not create any contractual rights in favour of outsiders (i.e., persons who are not members of the company). An outsider cannot sue the company on the basis of the articles even if the articles contain provisions which appear to benefit him.

Case: Eley v. Positive Government Security Life Assurance Co. (1876)

The articles of a company provided that Eley, a solicitor, shall be the company's solicitor for life and shall not be removed except for misconduct. Eley was appointed as the company's solicitor and later became a member of the company. The company then dismissed Eley as its solicitor. Eley sued the company, claiming that the articles gave him a right to be the company's solicitor for life. The Court held that the articles did not create any contractual right in favour of Eley as a solicitor. The articles operated only as a contract between the company and its members in their capacity as members. Eley could not enforce the articles in his capacity as a solicitor (an outsider). He could only enforce rights given to him as a member.

Note: The important principle from the above cases is that the articles operate as a contract only between the company and its members and between the members themselves. Outsiders (non-members) cannot derive any contractual rights from the articles. Even a member cannot enforce a right given to him by the articles in a capacity other than that of a member.

9.2 Relationship Between MOA and AOA

The relationship between the Memorandum of Association and the Articles of Association is a very important topic in company law. Both documents together constitute the constitution of the company, but they have different roles and different legal status. The following points highlight the relationship between them:

(1) MOA is the charter; AOA is the bye-law: The memorandum is the fundamental document which defines the powers and the scope of the company's activities. The articles are subordinate to the memorandum and deal only with the internal management and administration of the company. The memorandum defines what the company can do; the articles define how it shall do it.

(2) MOA is supreme over AOA: If there is any conflict between the provisions of the memorandum and the articles, the provisions of the memorandum shall prevail. The articles cannot override or go beyond the provisions of the memorandum. Any provision in the articles which is inconsistent with the memorandum is void and of no effect.

Case: Ashbury Railway Carriage and Iron Co. v. Riche (1875)

As discussed in Chapter 8, the House of Lords held that the memorandum defines the scope of the company's powers. Even if the articles purport to give wider powers to the company than those contained in the memorandum, the articles cannot enlarge the powers of the company beyond the memorandum. The memorandum is supreme.

(3) AOA is subordinate to the Companies Act: Just as the articles are subordinate to the memorandum, they are also subordinate to the provisions of the Companies Act. Any provision in the articles which is inconsistent with the Act is void. The Act overrides both the memorandum and the articles. For example, even if the articles provide that the company need not hold an annual general meeting, this provision will be void because Section 96 of the Act mandates the holding of an AGM.

(4) AOA can explain ambiguous provisions of MOA: Where the provisions of the memorandum are ambiguous or unclear, the articles may be referred to for the purpose of explaining or interpreting the memorandum. The articles can aid in understanding the true meaning of the memorandum but cannot contradict it.

(5) MOA cannot be altered as easily as AOA: The procedure for altering the memorandum is generally more complex and requires the approval of external authorities (like the Central Government, NCLT, etc.) in certain cases. The articles can be altered by a special resolution of the shareholders without the need for any external approval (subject to certain exceptions).

(6) MOA defines external relations; AOA defines internal relations: The memorandum governs the relationship between the company and the outside world. The articles govern the internal affairs of the company – the relationship between the company and its members, between the members themselves, and between the company and its directors.

Table 9.1: Memorandum vs. Articles

Point of Distinction	Memorandum of Association	Articles of Association
Nature	Charter / Constitution of the company	Bye-laws / Rules for internal management
Purpose	Defines objects, powers,	Defines rules and

	and scope	regulations for management
Relationship	Supreme – prevails over Articles	Subordinate to Memorandum and to the Act
Scope	External affairs (company and outside world)	Internal affairs (company, members, directors)
Compulsory?	Every company must have a MOA	Companies limited by shares may adopt model articles
Alteration	More complex; may require Govt/NCLT approval	Can be altered by special resolution (generally)
Ultra Vires Acts	Ultra vires MOA = absolutely void	Ultra vires AOA = can be ratified by shareholders
Section	Sections 2(56), 4	Sections 2(5), 5
Schedule I	Tables A to E	Tables F to J
Contents	Name, Registered Office, Objects, Liability, Capital, Subscription	Share transfers, meetings, directors, dividends, audit, etc.
Effect of Irregularity	Acts beyond MOA cannot be validated	Acts beyond AOA can be validated by shareholders

9.3 Alteration of AOA – Section 14

One of the advantages of the articles over the memorandum is that the articles can be altered more easily. Section 14 of the Companies Act, 2013 provides the power and the procedure for the alteration of the articles.

Section Reference: Section 14(1): Subject to the provisions of this

Act and the conditions contained in its memorandum, if any, a company may, by special resolution, alter its articles including the alteration in the form of its articles.

Procedure for Alteration

The procedure for altering the articles is as follows:

(1) Special Resolution: The alteration must be approved by a special resolution at a general meeting of the company. A special resolution requires a majority of not less than three-fourths of the members present and entitled to vote (and voting) at the meeting [Section 114(2)]. Alternatively, the resolution may be passed by postal ballot.

(2) Filing with the Registrar: A copy of the altered articles and a copy of the special resolution must be filed with the Registrar within 30 days of the passing of the resolution [Section 14(1)].

(3) Printing and circulation: Every altered article must be printed and copies must be made available to members on request. The company must also furnish a copy of the articles to any member on his request on payment of the prescribed fee [Section 17].

Limitations on the Power of Alteration

Although the company has the power to alter its articles by a special resolution, this power is not absolute. The following limitations apply:

(1) The alteration must not be inconsistent with the Memorandum: Section 14(1) clearly states that the alteration is 'subject to the provisions of this Act and the conditions contained in its memorandum.' The articles cannot be altered in a manner which would conflict with the memorandum. For example, if the memorandum restricts the company to a particular line of business, the articles cannot be altered to authorise the company to carry on a different business.

(2) The alteration must not be inconsistent with thc Companies Act: The articles cannot be altered in a manner which contravenes the provisions of the Companies Act. For example, the articles cannot provide for a quorum of less than the minimum prescribed by the Act.

(3) The alteration must be bona fide and for the benefit of the company as a whole: The alteration must be made in good faith and for the benefit of the company as a whole. It must not be made to benefit the majority at the expense of the minority. However, this does not mean that every member must benefit from the alteration. It is sufficient if the alteration is in the interest of the company considered as a whole.

Case: Allen v. Gold Reefs of West Africa Ltd. (1900)

The articles of the company gave a lien on partly paid shares for debts due from the member. Allen was the only member who held fully paid shares. The articles were altered to extend the company's lien to fully paid shares as well. Allen challenged the alteration on the ground that it was aimed specifically at him. The Court held that the alteration was valid because it was made bona fide for the benefit of the company as a whole. The power to alter articles must be exercised bona fide for the benefit of the company as a whole and not to discriminate against particular members. However, the mere fact that the alteration adversely affects a particular member does not make it invalid if it is otherwise for the benefit of the company.

(4) The alteration must not increase the liability of members without consent: Section 38 provides that no member shall be bound by any alteration made in the articles after the date on which he became a member, if and so far as the alteration requires him to take or subscribe for more shares than the number held by him, or in any way increases his liability to contribute to the share capital or otherwise to pay money to the company, unless he agrees in writing, either before or after the alteration is made, to be bound by the alteration.

(5) The alteration must not constitute a fraud on the minority: The power to alter the articles must not be exercised in a manner which amounts to fraud or oppression of the minority shareholders. If the alteration is designed to expropriate (take away) the property or rights of the minority without reasonable justification, the courts may set it aside.

Case: Brown v. British Abrasive Wheel Co. (1919)

A company needed additional capital. The majority shareholders (holding 98% of the shares) were willing to provide the additional capital only if the minority shareholders (holding 2%) were compelled to sell their shares. The articles were altered to give the majority the power to compulsorily acquire the shares of the minority. The Court held that the alteration was invalid because it was not made bona fide for the benefit of the company as a whole. It was made to benefit the majority shareholders at the expense of the minority.

Case: Sidebottom v. Kershaw, Leese and Co. Ltd. (1920)

The articles of a company were altered to provide that any shareholder who carried on a business competing with the company could be compelled to sell his shares at fair value to the directors. The Court held that the alteration was valid because it was made bona fide for the benefit of the company as a whole. The purpose was to prevent competitors from gaining access to the company's trade secrets through shareholding. Unlike the Brown case, this alteration protected the company's legitimate interests.

(6) The alteration must not violate any order of the NCLT: Where the NCLT has passed any order under Section 242 (oppression and mismanagement) directing the company not to alter the articles without the leave of the Tribunal, the company cannot alter its articles without obtaining such leave.

(7) Conversion of public company into private company: Section 14(1) provides that where a company, being a public company, alters its articles in such a manner that they include the restrictions and limitations prescribed for a private company (Section 2(68)), effectively converting itself into a private company, the company shall not do so unless it gets approval of the Tribunal by an order.

Retrospective Alteration

Can the articles be altered retrospectively, i.e., with effect from a date earlier than the date of the alteration?

The general rule is that the alteration takes effect from the date of the special resolution. However, in certain cases, the courts have allowed retrospective alteration if it is bona fide and for the benefit of the company. It must be noted that even where retrospective alteration is permitted, it cannot take away rights which have already accrued or make valid an act which was invalid when it was done. The alteration operates prospectively (for the future) unless there is a clear intention to make it retrospective, and even then, vested rights cannot be taken away.

Note: The power to alter the articles is a statutory power and not merely a contractual power. It is given by the Act and can be exercised by a special resolution. The court will not interfere with the exercise of this power unless the alteration is contrary to the Act, the memorandum, or the principles of natural justice, or amounts to fraud on the minority.

9.4 Doctrine of Constructive Notice

The doctrine of constructive notice is an important doctrine in company law which arises from the fact that the memorandum and articles of association are public documents. They are filed with the Registrar of Companies and are available for inspection by any member of the public. The doctrine of constructive notice imposes certain obligations on persons dealing with the company.

Meaning of the Doctrine

The doctrine of constructive notice means that every person dealing with a company is deemed to have knowledge of the contents of the memorandum and articles of association of the company, whether he has actually read them or not. Since the memorandum and articles are public documents filed with the Registrar, every person is presumed to have read them and to have understood the powers and limitations of the company. Ignorance of the contents of the memorandum and articles is no excuse.

The doctrine is based on the principle that when a document is required by law to be kept in a public office, every person is deemed to have constructive (implied) notice of the contents of the document. It is the duty of every person dealing with the company to inspect the public documents and ascertain the scope of the company's powers.

Illustration: A enters into a contract with XYZ Ltd. The memorandum of XYZ Ltd. does not authorise the company to enter into such a contract. A did not read the memorandum before entering into the contract. A cannot enforce the contract against the company because he is deemed to have constructive notice of the contents of the memorandum, even though he did not actually read it.

Effects of the Doctrine

(1) Third parties are deemed to know the company's powers: Any person dealing with the company is presumed to know what the company can and cannot do, as stated in the memorandum and articles. If a person enters into a transaction which the company is not authorised to undertake, he cannot claim ignorance of the company's limitations.

(2) Third parties are deemed to know internal regulations: Third parties are also deemed to have knowledge of the articles, including the provisions relating to the powers of directors, quorum for meetings, manner of passing resolutions, and other internal procedures.

(3) Protects the company, not the outsider: The doctrine of constructive notice generally operates in favour of the company and against the outsider. The company can plead that the outsider should have known about the limitations in the memorandum or articles. The outsider cannot plead ignorance.

Criticism of the Doctrine

The doctrine of constructive notice has been criticised on several grounds:

(a) It is harsh on third parties because they may not, in practical life, read the memorandum and articles before entering into every transaction with the company. (b) Even if they read the memorandum and articles, they may not be able to understand the legal implications of the provisions. (c) The doctrine is a legal fiction – it presumes knowledge which may not exist in fact. (d) It gives an unfair advantage to the company because the company can take the benefit of the doctrine even when it has misled the third party about its powers.

Because of these criticisms, the harshness of the doctrine is mitigated by the doctrine of indoor management (discussed in the next section) which protects third parties who deal with the company in good faith.

Note: The doctrine of constructive notice applies only to public documents (i.e., the memorandum and articles filed with the Registrar). It does not apply to internal documents like resolutions of the Board of Directors, minutes of meetings, or agreements between the company and its officers. Third parties are not deemed to have knowledge of such internal matters.

9.5 Doctrine of Indoor Management (Turquand Rule)

The doctrine of indoor management is the counterpart and the antidote to the doctrine of constructive notice. While the doctrine of constructive notice protects the company against outsiders, the doctrine of indoor management protects the outsiders against the company. It is also known as the 'Turquand Rule' or the 'Rule in Royal British Bank v. Turquand.'

Origin and Meaning

The doctrine of indoor management was first laid down in the following landmark case:

Case: Royal British Bank v. Turquand (1856)

The articles of the company provided that the directors could borrow money on behalf of the company only if they were authorised by a resolution passed at a general meeting of the company. The directors borrowed money from Turquand (the Royal British Bank) without obtaining such a resolution. When the company failed to repay the loan, the bank sued the company. The company argued that the borrowing was not authorised because no resolution had been passed. The Court held that the bank was entitled to assume that the internal requirements of the company (i.e., passing of the resolution) had been complied with. The bank was not bound to inquire whether the internal formalities had been observed. The company was bound by the borrowing. This is known as the 'Turquand Rule' or the 'Doctrine of Indoor Management.'

The doctrine means that persons dealing with a company in good faith are entitled to assume that the internal requirements and procedures of the company have been duly complied with. They are not bound to inquire whether the internal management has been done properly. If the act is within the scope of the company's powers (as stated in the memorandum and articles), the outsider can presume that all internal formalities have been observed, even if they have not been.

The justification for this doctrine is that the internal affairs of the company are within the knowledge of the company and its officers, not of the outsiders. An outsider can look at the memorandum and articles to know what the company can do, but he cannot look into the internal proceedings (board meetings, general meetings, resolutions, etc.) to verify whether the proper formalities have been followed. It would be unfair to require outsiders to make such inquiries because they have no access to the internal records of the company.

Application of the Doctrine in India

Indian courts have consistently applied the doctrine of indoor management. The doctrine has been applied in several Indian cases:

Case: Official Liquidator, Manasube & Co. (P) Ltd. v. Commissioner of Police (1966)

The directors of a company transferred certain immovable property of the company without the approval of the general body of shareholders as required by the articles. The transferee (buyer) had acted in good faith. The Madras High Court held that the transferee was protected by the doctrine of indoor management. The transferee was entitled to assume that the internal requirements had been complied with. The transfer was valid.

Case: Lakshmi Ratan Cotton Mills Co. Ltd. v. J.K. Jute Mills Co. Ltd. (1957)

The agent of a company borrowed money from another company without proper authorisation. The Allahabad High Court applied the doctrine of indoor management and held that the lending company was entitled to assume that the agent had the proper authority to borrow. The borrowing company was liable to repay the loan.

Exceptions to the Doctrine of Indoor Management

The doctrine of indoor management is not absolute. It is subject to the following exceptions:

(1) Knowledge of irregularity: The doctrine does not protect a person who has actual knowledge of the irregularity in the internal management. If a person knows that the internal requirements have not been complied with, he cannot claim the protection of the Turquand Rule. For example, if a person who is himself a director of the company knows that no resolution has been passed authorising a particular act, he cannot claim that he was entitled to assume that the resolution had been passed.

Case: Howard v. Patent Ivory Manufacturing Co. (1888)

The articles of a company authorised the directors to borrow up to a certain limit with the approval of the general meeting. The directors themselves lent money to the company in excess of the limit without a resolution of the general meeting. The Court held that the directors could not claim the protection of the Turquand Rule because they knew (or ought to have known) that no resolution had been passed. They had knowledge of the irregularity.

(2) Suspicion of irregularity (Negligence): If the circumstances are such that a reasonable person would have suspected that the internal requirements had not been complied with, the doctrine of indoor management will not apply. A person cannot claim the protection of the Turquand Rule if he did not make reasonable inquiry when the circumstances called for such inquiry. In other words, the doctrine does not protect wilful ignorance or negligence.

(3) Forgery: The doctrine of indoor management does not apply to acts which are forged. A forged document is a nullity in the eyes of law and no right can be acquired through a forged document. If a person relies on a document which turns out to be forged, he cannot claim the protection of the Turquand Rule because a forgery cannot be validated by the doctrine.

Case: Ruben v. Great Fingall Consolidated (1906)

The secretary of a company issued a share certificate with the company's seal affixed thereto and forged the signatures of two directors. A person who obtained the forged certificate and advanced money on the faith of it sought to hold the company liable. The House of Lords held that the company was not liable because the certificate was a forgery. The doctrine of indoor management does not apply to forgeries. A forged document is a nullity and cannot bind the company.

(4) Acts beyond the scope of apparent authority: The doctrine does not protect transactions which are clearly beyond the scope of the officer's authority. If an officer does an act which no reasonable person would believe he was authorised to do, the outsider cannot claim the protection of the Turquand Rule.

(5) No act done at all: The doctrine presumes that internal requirements have been complied with. But it cannot be invoked where there has been no act at all. For example, if a person claims to be a director of the company and enters into a contract on behalf of the company, but he was never appointed as a director, the Turquand Rule may not apply because there was no appointment to begin with.

Table 9.2: Constructive Notice vs. Indoor Management

Point	Doctrine of Constructive Notice	Doctrine of Indoor Management
Nature	Operates against outsiders	Operates in favour of outsiders
Protects	The company	The third parties dealing with the company
Based on	Public documents (MOA and AOA)	Internal proceedings (Board resolutions, etc.)
Presumption	Outsiders are deemed to know public documents	Outsiders can presume internal compliance
Effect	Outsiders cannot claim ignorance of MOA/AOA	Outsiders not bound to verify internal compliance
Origin	General legal principle	Royal British Bank v. Turquand (1856)
Relationship	Creates the problem for outsiders	Provides the remedy for outsiders

Chapter 10

Prospectus

When a public company wants to raise capital from the general public by issuing shares or debentures, it must inform the public about the company, its financial position, its management, the purpose for which the money is being raised, the risks involved, and other relevant facts. This information is provided through a document called the 'Prospectus.' The prospectus is, in effect, an invitation to the public to invest in the company. Since the investing public relies on the information given in the prospectus while making the decision to invest, the law requires that the prospectus must contain truthful and complete information. Any misstatement or concealment of material facts in the prospectus can lead to serious civil and criminal liability. The Companies Act, 2013 contains elaborate provisions regarding the prospectus in Sections 23 to 41.

10.1 Meaning and Definition – Section 2(70)

Definition

Section Reference: Section 2(70) of the Companies Act, 2013 defines 'Prospectus' as: "'Prospectus' means any document described or issued as a prospectus and includes a red herring prospectus referred to in Section 32 or shelf prospectus referred to in Section 31 or any notice, circular, advertisement or other document inviting offers from the public for the subscription or purchase of any securities of a body corporate."

This definition is very wide. It includes not only the document formally called a 'prospectus' but also any notice, circular, advertisement, or other document which invites the public to subscribe for or purchase the securities (shares or debentures) of a company. The intention of the law is to cover every document which is designed to attract public investment, regardless of the name or form of the document.

From the definition, the following essential elements of a prospectus can be identified:

(a) It must be a document: A prospectus must be in the form of a written document. An oral invitation or a verbal statement does not constitute a prospectus. The document may be in printed form or in electronic form.

(b) It must be issued or described as a prospectus: The document must either be described as a prospectus or must be of such a nature that it falls within the definition of a prospectus. Even if a document is not called a prospectus, it may still be treated as a prospectus if it invites the public to subscribe for securities.

(c) It must invite offers from the public: The document must invite the public to subscribe for or purchase the securities of the company. If the invitation is not to the public but to a select group of persons (private placement), it is not a prospectus. The word 'public' is important. It means the general public or any section of the public.

(d) It must relate to securities: The invitation must be for the subscription or purchase of 'securities' of the company. Securities include shares, debentures, and other instruments specified under the Securities Contracts (Regulation) Act, 1956.

When is a Prospectus Not Required?

A prospectus is not required in the following situations:

(a) When a private company raises capital, because a private company cannot invite the public to subscribe for its securities [Section 2(68)]. (b) When shares are offered to existing shareholders under a rights issue [Section 62]. (c) When shares are issued as bonus shares to existing shareholders [Section 63]. (d) When shares are issued through private placement to a select group of persons [Section 42]. (e) When shares are issued under an employee stock option scheme (ESOP). (f) When a company does not offer its securities to the public and issues a document called 'Statement in Lieu of Prospectus' (this concept was present under the 1956 Act; under the 2013 Act, the provisions are different).

Note: Under the Companies Act, 2013, the provisions relating to the prospectus apply primarily to public companies which want to raise capital from the general public. Private companies are not permitted to issue a prospectus. The SEBI (Issue of Capital and Disclosure Requirements) Regulations, 2018 also prescribe detailed disclosure requirements for companies making public issues. Companies must comply with both the Companies Act and the SEBI Regulations.

Deemed Prospectus – Section 25

Section 25 deals with the concept of 'deemed prospectus.' It provides that where a company allots or agrees to allot any securities of the company with a view to all or any of those securities being offered for sale to the public, any document by which the offer for sale to the public is made shall, for all purposes, be deemed to be a prospectus issued by the company.

The purpose of this provision is to prevent companies from evading the requirements of the prospectus provisions by first allotting shares to an intermediary (like an investment bank or a broker) and then getting the intermediary to sell the shares to the public. In such a case, the document used by the intermediary to offer the shares to the public is treated as a prospectus issued by the company, and all the provisions relating to prospectus apply to it.

Illustration: ABC Ltd. allots 1,00,000 shares to XYZ Securities Ltd. (an intermediary) at Rs. 100 per share. XYZ Securities then offers these shares to the general public at Rs. 120 per share. The document used by XYZ Securities to offer the shares to the public is a 'deemed prospectus' and is treated as if it had been issued by ABC Ltd. ABC Ltd. and its directors are liable for any misstatement in this document.

10.2 Contents of Prospectus – Section 26

Section 26 of the Companies Act, 2013 prescribes the matters which must be stated and the reports which must be included in a prospectus. The section requires full disclosure of all material facts and information to enable the public to make an informed decision about whether to invest in the company's securities.

Matters to be Stated in the Prospectus – Section 26(1)

Every prospectus issued by or on behalf of a public company must be dated, and that date shall, unless the contrary is proved, be taken as the date of publication of the prospectus. The prospectus must contain the following information:

(a) Names and addresses: Names and addresses of the registered office of the company, company secretary, Chief Financial Officer, auditors, legal advisers, bankers of the company, trustees (if any), and underwriters (if any).

(b) Dates and details: Dates of the opening and closing of the issue, and declaration about the issue of allotment letters within the prescribed time.

(c) Statement by the Board: A statement by the Board of Directors about the separate bank account for the application money, the allotment of securities to non-resident Indians, and an undertaking that the funds received shall be used only for the purposes stated in the prospectus.

(d) Business and objects: The main objects and present business of the company and its location, information about the promoters, a schedule of material contracts, the time and place at which contracts can be inspected.

(e) Financial information: The amount which the company proposes to raise by the issue, the terms of the issue, the manner of issue (at par, premium, or discount), the purpose for which the money is to be used, the capital structure of the company, the details of directors' and promoters' holdings, financial statements, and auditor's report.

(f) Risk factors: A statement of the risk factors involved in the investment, categorised as those specific to the project, to the company, and to the industry. This is a very important requirement because it helps the investors to understand the risks associated with the investment and to make an informed decision.

(g) Reports: Reports by the auditors of the company for the preceding five financial years relating to profits and losses, assets and liabilities, dividends paid, etc. A report by the auditors of the company relating to the business acquired or to be acquired. Any other reports or information as may be prescribed by the Central Government or SEBI.

Reports to be Set Out in the Prospectus – Section 26(1)(b)

The prospectus must also set out the following reports:

(a) Reports by the auditors of the company with respect to its profits and losses and assets and liabilities and such other matters as may be prescribed, for each of the five financial years immediately preceding the financial year of the prospectus. (b) Reports relating to the profits and losses for each of the five financial years of any business to which the proceeds of the securities are to be applied, directly or indirectly. (c) Reports made by a Registered Valuer in respect of any property or asset, the value of which has a bearing on the prospectus.

Declaration and Signatures

Section 26(4) provides that every prospectus must contain a declaration that the compliance with the provisions of the Act and the rules made thereunder in respect of matters stated in the prospectus has been confirmed. The prospectus must be signed by every person who is named therein as a director or proposed director of the company, or by his agent authorised in writing.

Section 26(5) requires that every prospectus must contain a statement that a copy of the prospectus has been delivered to the Registrar for registration and that it contains the particulars as required by the Act. Section 26(6) provides that no prospectus shall be issued unless on or before the date of its publication, a copy thereof has been delivered to the Registrar for registration.

SEBI Regulations

In addition to the requirements of the Companies Act, 2013, companies making a public issue must also comply with the SEBI (Issue of Capital and Disclosure Requirements) Regulations, 2018 (SEBI ICDR Regulations). These regulations prescribe additional disclosure requirements, including details about the promoters' contribution, lock-in period for promoters' shares, minimum subscription, basis of issue price, risk factors, utilisation of funds, and many other matters. The SEBI regulations are more detailed and specific than the Companies Act and are the primary source of regulation for public issues in India.

Note: Students should note that for listed companies and companies making public issues, the SEBI regulations are equally important as the Companies Act. In practice, the prospectus of a public issue is drafted by merchant bankers (Book Running Lead Managers) in compliance with both the Companies Act and the SEBI ICDR Regulations.

10.3 Red Herring Prospectus – Section 32

The concept of a Red Herring Prospectus was introduced to facilitate the modern method of raising capital through the 'book building' process. Under the book building method, the exact price of the securities is not determined in advance. Instead, a price band (minimum and maximum price) is indicated and the investors bid within this price band. The final price is determined on the basis of the bids received.

Definition – Section 32(1)

Section Reference: Section 32(1): A company proposing to make an offer of securities may issue a red herring prospectus prior to the issue of a prospectus. A red herring prospectus means a prospectus which does not include complete particulars of the quantum or price of the securities included therein.

In simple words, a Red Herring Prospectus is a preliminary prospectus which does not contain the final price of the securities or the exact number of securities being offered. It contains all other information which a regular prospectus must contain. The name 'Red Herring' comes from the traditional practice in the United States where such preliminary prospectuses were printed with a red warning on the cover stating that the registration statement had not yet become effective.

Features of Red Herring Prospectus

(1) Incomplete information: The Red Herring Prospectus does not contain the complete particulars of the quantum (number) or price of the securities. These are determined later through the book building process.

(2) Filed with the Registrar: The Red Herring Prospectus must be filed with the Registrar at least three days before the opening of the subscription list and the offer [Section 32(2)]. It carries the same obligations as are applicable to a regular prospectus.

(3) Variations permitted: Any variation between the Red Herring Prospectus and the final prospectus must be highlighted as variations in the prospectus [Section 32(3)].

(4) Application of funds: Upon the closing of the offer of securities under the Red Herring Prospectus, the prospectus shall state the total capital raised, whether by way of debt or share capital, and the closing price of the securities. Any surplus amount shall be returned to the investors [Section 32(4)].

(5) Same legal obligations: The Red Herring Prospectus is treated as a prospectus for all purposes. The provisions relating to misstatement, liability, and penalties apply to a Red Herring Prospectus in the same manner as they apply to a regular prospectus.

Practical Example: When Zomato Limited came out with its IPO (Initial Public Offering) in July 2021, it issued a Red Herring Prospectus with a price band of Rs. 72-76 per share. Investors bid within this range during the book building period. The final issue price was determined at Rs. 76 per share based on the bids received. This is a typical example of how a Red Herring Prospectus is used in Indian capital markets.

10.4 Shelf Prospectus – Section 31

The concept of Shelf Prospectus has been introduced to facilitate companies which frequently need to raise capital from the public. Instead of issuing a fresh prospectus every time they make a public offer, such companies can issue a single prospectus called a 'Shelf Prospectus' which remains valid for a specified period.

Definition – Section 31(1)

Section Reference: Section 31(1): Any class or classes of companies, as the SEBI may provide by regulations in this behalf, may file a shelf prospectus with the Registrar at the stage of the first offer of securities included therein which shall indicate a period not exceeding one year as the period of validity of such prospectus.

In simple words, a Shelf Prospectus is a prospectus which is issued for one or more issues of securities during a period of up to one year. The company files the shelf prospectus once and can then make multiple offers of securities during the period of its validity without having to file a fresh prospectus each time. The name 'Shelf Prospectus' comes from the idea that the prospectus is kept 'on the shelf' and used whenever needed.

Features of Shelf Prospectus

(1) Valid for up to one year: The Shelf Prospectus is valid for a period not exceeding one year from the date of the first offer made under it. Within this period, the company can make two or more offers without issuing a fresh prospectus.

(2) Information Memorandum: Section 31(2) provides that a company filing a shelf prospectus shall be required to file an information memorandum on all material facts relating to new charges created, changes in the financial position of the company, and such other changes as may be prescribed by SEBI. The information memorandum must be filed with the Registrar before making any subsequent offer.

(3) Filed with the Registrar: The Shelf Prospectus must be filed with the Registrar like any other prospectus.

(4) Updated information: Section 31(3) provides that the information memorandum, together with the shelf prospectus, shall be deemed to be a prospectus. This ensures that the investors always have access to the latest information about the company when they make their investment decision.

(5) Only for specified classes: Only such classes of companies as may be specified by SEBI can issue a shelf prospectus. Typically, this facility is available to banks and other financial institutions which frequently issue bonds and debentures to the public.

Practical Example: Banks like State Bank of India, ICICI Bank, and financial institutions like NABARD, SIDBI, and HUDCO frequently issue bonds and debentures to the public. Instead of preparing a fresh prospectus for each issue, they can file a shelf prospectus once and make multiple offerings during the year, updating the information through information memoranda.

10.5 Abridged Prospectus – Section 33

Definition – Section 2(1)

Section Reference: Section 2(1): 'Abridged Prospectus' means a memorandum containing such salient features of a prospectus as may be specified by the Securities and Exchange Board by making regulations in this behalf.

An Abridged Prospectus is a shorter version of the full prospectus. It contains the salient (important and key) features of the prospectus in a summarised form. The purpose of the abridged prospectus is to make it easier for the general public to understand the basic features of the issue without having to go through the full prospectus which may run into hundreds of pages.

Provisions Relating to Abridged Prospectus

(1) Mandatory attachment: Section 33(1) provides that no form of application for the purchase of any of the securities of a company shall be issued unless such form is accompanied by an abridged prospectus. In other words, every application form for subscribing to a public issue must be accompanied by an abridged prospectus.

(2) Exception: Section 33(2) provides an exception. The requirement of attaching an abridged prospectus does not apply if it is shown that the form of application was issued (a) in connection with a bona fide invitation to a person to enter into an underwriting agreement with respect to the securities, or (b) in relation to shares which were not offered to the public.

(3) Penalty for non-compliance: If a company makes default in complying with the provisions of Section 33, the company and every officer of the company who is in default shall be liable to a penalty which may extend to Rs. 50,000 for each default.

Note: The abridged prospectus is a practical document which helps the common investor to get a quick overview of the issue. In practice, when a person picks up an application form from a bank or broker's office during a public issue, the abridged prospectus is printed on or attached to the application form. The full prospectus is available on the company's website, the SEBI website, and at the offices of the lead managers and registrar to the issue.

10.6 Misstatement in Prospectus – Section 34 & 35

The accuracy and truthfulness of the prospectus is of utmost importance because millions of investors rely on the information given in the prospectus to make their investment decisions. If the prospectus contains false or misleading information, or if it conceals material facts, the investors may be misled into making wrong decisions and may suffer heavy financial losses. To protect the interests of investors, the Companies Act, 2013 contains stringent provisions regarding misstatement in the prospectus.

What Constitutes a Misstatement?

A prospectus is said to contain a 'misstatement' in the following situations:

(a) Untrue statement: A statement included in the prospectus is untrue or misleading in form or context in which it is included.

(b) Omission of material fact: There is an omission from the prospectus of any matter or thing the inclusion of which is required by the Act or the rules made thereunder.

In both cases, the persons responsible for the prospectus may be held liable for compensation and/or criminal punishment.

Civil Liability for Misstatement – Section 35

Section Reference: Section 35(1): Where a person has subscribed for securities of a company acting on any statement included, or the inclusion or omission of any matter, in the prospectus which is misleading and has sustained any loss or damage as a consequence thereof, the company and every person who – (a) is a director of the company at the time of the issue of the prospectus, (b) has authorised himself to be named and is named in the prospectus as a director, or has agreed to become such director, (c) is a promoter of the company, (d) has authorised the issue of the prospectus, (e) is an expert referred to in Section 26(5) – shall, without prejudice to any punishment to which any person may be liable under Section 36, be liable to pay compensation to every person who has sustained such loss or damage.

The following persons are liable to pay compensation:

(a) The company itself. (b) Every director of the company at the time of issue. (c) Every person who has consented to be named as a director. (d) Every promoter of the company. (e) Every person who has authorised the issue of the prospectus. (f) Every expert (such as chartered accountant, valuer, etc.) whose statement is included in the prospectus.

Defences Available – Section 35(2)

The persons liable under Section 35(1) may escape liability if they can prove any of the following defences:

(a) Withdrawal of consent: That he withdrew his consent to the issue of the prospectus before it was issued and it was issued without his authority or consent.

(b) Issue without knowledge: That the prospectus was issued without his knowledge and that on becoming aware of it, he gave reasonable public notice that it was issued without his knowledge or consent.

(c) Reasonable belief: That he had reasonable ground to believe and did, up to the time of the allotment of the securities, believe that the statement was true or that the omission was not misleading. This is called the 'due diligence' defence. If a person can show that he honestly believed, after making proper inquiry, that the statements were true, he can escape liability.

(d) Expert's statement: In respect of a statement made by an expert (like an auditor, valuer, or legal adviser), that the statement was a fair and correct representation of the expert's statement or report, and that the director had reasonable ground to believe that the expert was competent to make the statement.

(e) Official document: That the statement was a correct and fair representation of a statement made by an official person or extracted from a public official document.

Case: Derry v. Peek (1889)

The directors of a tramway company issued a prospectus stating that the company had the right to use steam power for its tramways. In fact, the company had only applied for permission and honestly believed that it would be granted. The permission was refused and the company was wound up. Shareholders sued the directors for fraud. The House of Lords held that the directors were not guilty of fraud because they honestly believed that the statement was true. There was no intention to deceive. However, the Court noted that the directors could still be liable for negligent misrepresentation (though not for fraud).

Case: Peek v. Gurney (1873)

The prospectus of a company contained misrepresentations. Peek, a person who had bought shares in the open market (i.e., from another shareholder and not directly from the company), sued the directors for the loss he suffered. The House of Lords held that Peek could not sue because the prospectus was intended to induce original allottees (those who subscribed directly), not subsequent purchasers. However, this position has been modified in modern law and SEBI regulations now extend protection to all investors, including secondary market purchasers.

10.7 Criminal Liability for Misstatement – Section 34 & 36

In addition to the civil liability (compensation) under Section 35, the persons responsible for the misstatement in the prospectus are also liable to criminal punishment under Sections 34 and 36.

Section 34 – Criminal Liability for Misstatement

Section Reference: Section 34(1): Where a prospectus, issued, circulated, or distributed includes any statement which is untrue or misleading in form or context in which it is included; or where any inclusion or omission of any matter is likely to mislead, every person who authorises the issue of such prospectus shall be liable under Section 447.

Section 447 deals with punishment for fraud. The punishment is imprisonment for a term which shall not be less than 6 months but which may extend to 10 years, and a fine which shall not be less than the amount involved in the fraud but which may extend to three times the amount involved. If the fraud involves public interest, the minimum imprisonment shall not be less than 3 years.

Section 36 – Punishment for Fraudulently Inducing Persons to Invest Money

Section Reference: Section 36(1): Any person who, either knowingly or recklessly, makes any statement, promise, or forecast which is false, deceptive, or misleading, or deliberately conceals any material facts, to induce another person to enter into or offer to enter into – (a) any agreement for, or with a view to, acquiring, disposing of, subscribing for, or underwriting securities; or (b) any agreement, the purpose or the pretended purpose of which is to secure a profit to any of the parties from the yield of securities or by reference to fluctuations in the value of securities; or (c) any agreement for, or with a view to, obtaining credit facilities from any bank or financial institution, shall be liable for action under Section 447. The key elements of Section 36 are: (a) the person must have made a false, deceptive, or misleading statement, promise, or forecast, or must have deliberately concealed material facts; (b) the statement must have been made either knowingly (with full knowledge of its falsity) or recklessly (without caring whether it is true or false); and (c) the purpose must have been to induce another person to invest money or enter into an agreement relating to securities.

Distinction Between Civil and Criminal Liability

Table 10.1: Civil Liability vs. Criminal Liability for Misstatement

Point	Civil Liability (Section 35)	Criminal Liability (Sections 34, 36)
Nature	Compensation for loss suffered	Punishment (imprisonment + fine)
Who can sue?	Person who subscribed on the faith of the prospectus	State / Prosecution agency / SEBI
Intention	No need to prove fraudulent intention; negligence is sufficient	Must prove knowledge or recklessness; fraudulent intent required under Section 36
Remedy	Monetary compensation	Imprisonment (6 months to 10 years) + Fine

Defences	Due diligence, withdrawal of consent, reasonable belief	Truth of the statement; no intent to deceive
Applicable to	Directors, promoters, experts, persons authorising issue	Any person who authorises the issue or makes fraudulent statements
Standard of proof	Balance of probabilities (civil standard)	Beyond reasonable doubt (criminal standard)
Concurrent?	Can be claimed along with criminal liability	Can be imposed along with civil liability

Other Remedies Available to the Investor

Apart from the remedies under the Companies Act, the investor who has been misled by a prospectus has the following additional remedies:

(1) Rescission of the contract of allotment: The investor can rescind (cancel) the contract of allotment and get back his money. However, this right must be exercised within a reasonable time and before the winding up of the company. The investor must also return the shares to the company.

(2) Damages for fraud or deceit: The investor can sue for damages in a civil court under the general law of torts for fraud or deceit. This remedy is available in addition to the remedy under Section 35.

(3) Complaint to SEBI: The investor can file a complaint with SEBI, which has the power to investigate the matter, impose penalties, and take action against the company and its officers under the SEBI Act, 1992 and the SEBI regulations.

(4) Class action suit: Under Section 245 of the Companies Act, 2013, a specified number of members can file a class action suit before the

NCLT if the affairs of the company are being conducted in a manner prejudicial to the interests of the members.

(5) Criminal prosecution: The investor can also file a criminal complaint for fraud and cheating under the Indian Penal Code, 1860 (now Bharatiya Nyaya Sanhita, 2023) in addition to the prosecution under the Companies Act.

Note: In practice, cases of misstatement in the prospectus are usually dealt with by SEBI rather than the courts. SEBI has extensive powers of investigation, enforcement, and adjudication under the SEBI Act. SEBI can impose heavy penalties, ban persons from the securities market, and order companies to refund money to investors. The SEBI Regulations also provide for the concept of 'material misstatement' and 'price sensitive information' which are important in the context of public issues.

Summary of Types of Prospectus

Table 10.2: Types of Prospectus at a Glance

Type	Section	Key Feature	Used For
Regular Prospectus	26	Complete document with all details	Fixed price issues
Red Herring Prospectus	32	Does not contain final price/quantum	Book building IPOs
Shelf Prospectus	31	Valid for multiple issues up to 1 year	Banks and financial institutions
Abridged Prospectus	33	Summary of salient features	Attached to application forms
Deemed Prospectus	25	Document for offer for sale by intermediary	Offer for sale to public

PART – III : SHARE CAPITAL, MEMBERS & DEBENTURES

Chapter 11

Share Capital

Capital is the lifeblood of every business. Without capital, no business can start or survive. In the case of a company, the capital is raised by issuing shares to the public or to a select group of investors. The money collected from the shareholders in return for the shares issued to them constitutes the share capital of the company. The share capital is the foundation of the company's financial structure. The Companies Act, 2013 contains detailed provisions regarding the issue, allotment, transfer, and management of share capital. In this chapter, we shall study all the important aspects of share capital, including the different types of shares, the methods of issuing shares, and the various transactions relating to shares.

11.1 Meaning and Types of Share Capital

What is a Share?

Section Reference: Section 2(84) defines 'share' as: "'Share' means a share in the share capital of a company and includes stock."

A share is the interest of a shareholder in the company, measured by a sum of money, for the purpose of liability in the first place, and of interest in the second. In simple terms, a share represents a unit of ownership in the company. A person who holds shares in a company is called a 'shareholder' or 'member' of the company.

Section 44 provides that the shares or debentures or other interests of any member in a company shall be moveable property, transferable in the manner provided by the articles of the company. This means that shares are not immovable property but moveable property. They can be bought, sold, transferred, pledged, and inherited like any other moveable property.

According to Justice Farwell in Borland's Trustee v. Steel Bros. & Co. Ltd. (1901): "A share is the interest of a shareholder in the company measured by a sum of money, for the purpose of liability in the first place, and of interest in the second, but also consisting of a series of mutual covenants entered into by all the shareholders inter se."

Nature of Shares

A share confers on its holder the following rights: (a) The right to receive dividends when declared by the company. (b) The right to vote at general meetings of the company. (c) The right to receive a share of the surplus assets on winding up. (d) The right to transfer the shares. (e) The right to receive the annual report and other information. (f) The right to attend and participate in general meetings. These rights are subject to the provisions of the Act and the articles of the company.

A share does not give the shareholder any ownership right over the assets of the company. The company's assets belong to the company, not to its shareholders. The shareholder's interest is in the company itself, not in the company's property. This principle was established in the Macaura case (discussed in Chapter 5).

Types of Share Capital

The share capital of a company may be of the following types:

(1) Authorised Capital (or Nominal / Registered Capital): This is the maximum amount of capital which the company is authorised to issue, as stated in its memorandum of association. For example, if the memorandum states that the authorised share capital is Rs. 1 crore divided into 10 lakh equity shares of Rs. 10 each, the company cannot issue shares exceeding this amount without first increasing the authorised capital.

(2) Issued Capital: This is the part of the authorised capital which has been actually offered for subscription. The company need not issue the entire authorised capital at one time. It may issue the shares in stages as and when the need for capital arises.

(3) Subscribed Capital: This is the part of the issued capital which has been actually subscribed (applied for and allotted) by the shareholders. Sometimes, the entire issued capital may not be subscribed. The unsubscribed portion remains with the company for future allotment.

(4) Called-up Capital: This is the part of the subscribed capital which the company has asked the shareholders to pay. The company may not call up the entire subscribed capital at once. It may call up the amount in instalments (application money, allotment money, first call, second call, etc.).

(5) Paid-up Capital: This is the part of the called-up capital which has been actually paid by the shareholders. If a shareholder fails to pay a call, the unpaid amount is called 'calls in arrears.'

(6) Uncalled Capital: This is the part of the subscribed capital which has not yet been called up by the company. The company may call it up at any time in the future.

(7) Reserve Capital – Section 65: This is that portion of the uncalled capital which the company has resolved, by a special resolution, not to call up except in the event of the company being wound up. Reserve capital can only be called up for the purpose of winding up.

Illustration: ABC Ltd. has an authorised capital of Rs. 50,00,000 divided into 5,00,000 shares of Rs. 10 each. It has issued 3,00,000 shares. Out of these, 2,80,000 shares have been subscribed. The company has called up Rs. 8 per share and shareholders have paid Rs. 7 per share. Here: Authorised Capital = Rs. 50,00,000; Issued Capital = Rs. 30,00,000; Subscribed Capital = Rs. 28,00,000; Called-up Capital = Rs. 22,40,000; Paid-up Capital = Rs. 19,60,000; Calls in Arrears = Rs. 2,80,000; Uncalled Capital = Rs. 5,60,000.

11.2 Equity Shares – Section 43

Section Reference: Section 43 provides that the share capital of a company limited by shares shall be of two kinds only: (a) equity share capital, and (b) preference share capital.

Section 43(a) defines equity share capital as all share capital which is not preference share capital. In other words, equity shares are the residual shares – shares which do not carry any preferential rights as to dividend or repayment of capital.

Features of Equity Shares

(1) No fixed rate of dividend: Equity shareholders do not have the right to a fixed rate of dividend. The dividend on equity shares depends on the profits of the company and the decision of the Board of Directors. In a good year, the dividend may be high; in a bad year, there may be no dividend at all.

(2) Voting rights: Equity shareholders have the right to vote on every resolution placed before the company at a general meeting. Every equity shareholder has one vote per share on a poll [Section 47(2)]. They are the real owners and controllers of the company.

(3) Residual claim on assets: On winding up, equity shareholders receive their share of the surplus assets only after the claims of creditors and preference shareholders have been fully satisfied. They bear the highest risk.

(4) Participation in surplus profits: After paying the fixed dividend to preference shareholders, the entire remaining profit is available for distribution to equity shareholders. If the company is highly profitable, equity shareholders benefit the most.

(5) Right to participate in management: Equity shareholders elect the directors and thereby participate in the management of the company. They have the power to appoint and remove directors at general meetings.

Equity Shares with Differential Voting Rights (DVR) – Section 43(a)(ii)

Section 43(a)(ii) provides that equity share capital may include equity shares with differential rights as to dividend, voting, or otherwise in accordance with the prescribed rules. This means that a company can issue equity shares which carry different voting rights from the ordinary equity shares.

The Companies (Share Capital and Debentures) Rules, 2014 prescribe the following conditions for issue of DVR shares: (a) The company must have a consistent track record of distributable profits for the last three years. (b) The company must not have been convicted of any offence under the Act or SEBI Act in the last three years. (c) The issue must be authorised by the articles of the company. (d) The issue must be authorised by an ordinary resolution at a general meeting. (e) The voting rights on such shares shall not exceed 74:26 ratio (74% voting rights cannot hold more than 26% of the total post-issue paid-up equity share capital of the company, or vice versa). (f) The company must have completed three years of existence since the date of its incorporation.

Example: Tata Motors Limited issued DVR (Differential Voting Rights) shares in 2008. These shares carried one-tenth of the voting rights of ordinary equity shares but were entitled to a higher dividend (5% more than ordinary shares). This was one of the first DVR share issues in India. However, Tata Motors later decided to convert all DVR shares into ordinary equity shares in 2023.

11.3 Preference Shares – Section 43(b) & Section 55

Preference shares are shares which carry certain preferential rights over equity shares. These preferential rights relate to the payment of dividend and the repayment of capital on winding up.

Section Reference: Section 43(b) defines preference share capital as that part of the share capital which fulfils both the following requirements: (i) with respect to dividends, it carries a preferential right to be paid a fixed amount or an amount calculated at a fixed rate; AND (ii) with respect to capital, it carries the preferential right to the repayment of a fixed amount or an amount calculated at a fixed rate on winding up or repayment of capital.

Features of Preference Shares

(1) Fixed dividend: Preference shareholders are entitled to receive a dividend at a fixed rate before any dividend is paid to equity shareholders. For example, 10% preference shares of Rs. 100 each would entitle the holder to a dividend of Rs. 10 per share per year.

(2) Priority in repayment of capital: On winding up, preference shareholders are entitled to receive back their capital before anything is paid to equity shareholders.

(3) Limited voting rights: Under Section 47(2), preference shareholders have a right to vote only on resolutions which directly affect the rights attached to their preference shares. However, if the dividend on preference shares has remained unpaid for two years or more, the preference shareholders get the right to vote on all resolutions.

(4) Mandatory redemption: Under Section 55(1), a company limited by shares can issue preference shares which are liable to be redeemed within a period not exceeding 20 years from the date of their issue. The Companies Act, 2013 does not allow the issue of irredeemable preference shares. All preference shares must be redeemable.

Types of Preference Shares

(a) Cumulative Preference Shares: If the company is unable to pay dividend in any year, the unpaid dividend accumulates and is carried forward to the next year. The accumulated arrears of dividend must be paid before any dividend is paid on equity shares. Unless otherwise stated in the articles, all preference shares are presumed to be cumulative.

(b) Non-Cumulative Preference Shares: If the company does not declare a dividend in a particular year, the preference shareholders lose their right to dividend for that year. The unpaid dividend does not accumulate or carry forward.

(c) Participating Preference Shares: These shares carry the right to participate in the surplus profits (after paying dividend to equity shareholders) and in the surplus assets on winding up (after repayment of equity capital). These are rare in practice.

(d) Non-Participating Preference Shares: These shares are entitled only to the fixed dividend and the fixed repayment of capital. They do not participate in any surplus profits or surplus assets. Unless expressly stated otherwise, preference shares are presumed to be non-participating.

(e) Convertible Preference Shares: These shares can be converted into equity shares at the option of the holder or the company, as per the terms of issue.

(f) Non-Convertible Preference Shares: These shares cannot be converted into equity shares. They must be redeemed at the end of their term.

Redemption of Preference Shares – Section 55

Section 55 contains the detailed provisions for the redemption of preference shares. The following conditions must be satisfied:

(a) No preference shares can be redeemed unless they are fully paid up [Section 55(2)(a)]. (b) Preference shares may be redeemed out of the profits of the company which would otherwise be available for dividend, or out of the proceeds of a fresh issue of shares made for the purpose of such redemption [Section 55(2)(b)]. (c) If preference shares are redeemed out of profits, a sum equal to the nominal amount of the shares redeemed must be transferred to a reserve called the 'Capital Redemption Reserve Account.' This reserve can be used only for issuing fully paid bonus shares [Section 55(2)(c)]. (d) The premium, if any, payable on redemption must be provided out of the profits of the company or out of the company's securities premium account, before such shares are redeemed [Section 55(2)(d)].

(e) Where a company is not in a position to redeem preference shares in accordance with the terms of issue or is unable to pay dividend on such shares, it may issue further redeemable preference shares equal to the amount due (including dividend thereon), with the consent of 75% of the holders of such preference shares [Section 55(3)]. (f) The maximum redemption period is 20 years from the date of issue. However, for infrastructure projects, the period may be extended to 30 years with the approval of the members by a special resolution [Section 55(1), proviso].

Note: The Companies Act, 2013 prohibits the issue of irredeemable preference shares. Under the 1956 Act, irredeemable preference shares (i.e., shares which never needed to be redeemed) were permitted. The 2013 Act has mandated that all preference shares must be redeemed within the prescribed time period.

Point	Equity Shares	Preference Shares
Dividend	No fixed rate; depends on profits	Fixed rate; paid before equity dividend
Voting Rights	Full voting rights on all matters	Limited; only on resolutions affecting their rights
Repayment on Winding Up	After preference shareholders	Before equity shareholders
Risk	Higher risk, higher return potential	Lower risk, fixed return
Participation in Management	Active – elect directors	Passive – limited role
Accumulation of Dividend	No accumulation	Cumulative (unless stated otherwise)
Redeemable?	Generally not redeemable (except buy-back)	Must be redeemed within 20 years
Section	43(a)	43(b), 55

11.4 Sweat Equity Shares – Section 54

The concept of sweat equity shares recognises the contribution of directors and employees who add value to the company through their intellectual property, expertise, or efforts (often called 'sweat'). These shares are issued at a discount or for consideration other than cash.

Section Reference: Section 54(1): A company may issue sweat equity shares of a class of shares already issued, if the following conditions are fulfilled: (a) the issue is authorised by a special resolution passed by the company; (b) the resolution specifies the number of shares, the current market price, consideration if any, and the class of directors or employees to whom such equity shares are to be issued; (c) not less than one year has elapsed since the date on which the company had commenced business; and (d) the sweat equity shares of a company listed on a recognised stock exchange are issued in accordance with the regulations made by SEBI in this behalf.

Sweat equity shares are equity shares issued by a company to its directors or employees at a discount to the market price or for consideration other than cash, for providing their know-how, creating intellectual property rights, or adding value to the company in any manner. The shares must be of a class already issued by the company.

The shares issued must be valued by a registered valuer and the consideration for the sweat equity must also be valued by a registered valuer. The company must maintain a Register of Sweat Equity Shares. These shares are subject to a lock-in period of 3 years from the date of allotment. The total sweat equity shares issued in a year shall not exceed 15% of the total paid-up equity share capital of the company or Rs. 5 crore, whichever is higher. The total sweat equity shares issued shall not exceed 25% of the paid-up equity capital of the company at any time.

11.5 Issue of Shares at Premium – Section 52

When a company issues shares at a price higher than their face value (or nominal value), the shares are said to be issued at a premium. The difference between the issue price and the face value is called the 'share premium.'

Illustration: If ABC Ltd. issues shares of face value Rs. 10 at Rs. 25 per share, the premium is Rs. 15 per share (Rs. 25 – Rs. 10 = Rs. 15). The face value (Rs. 10) is credited to the Share Capital Account and the premium (Rs. 15) is credited to the Securities Premium Account.

Section 52(1) provides that where a company issues shares at a premium, whether for cash or otherwise, a sum equal to the aggregate amount of the premium received on those shares shall be transferred to an account called the 'Securities Premium Account.' This account is treated almost like share capital.

Utilisation of Securities Premium Account – Section 52(2)

The Securities Premium Account can be utilised only for the following purposes:

(a) To issue fully paid bonus shares to the members. (b) To write off the preliminary expenses of the company. (c) To write off the expenses of, or the commission paid or discount allowed on, any issue of shares or debentures of the company. (d) To provide for the premium payable on the redemption of any redeemable preference shares or of any debentures of the company. (e) For the purchase of its own shares (buy-back) under Section 68.

The Securities Premium Account cannot be used for payment of dividends or for any other purpose not specified above. This restriction ensures that the premium collected from shareholders is used for the benefit of the company and is not distributed to the shareholders as dividend.

Note: The Companies Act, 2013 does not impose any restriction on the amount of premium that a company can charge. The premium is decided by the company based on the market conditions, the financial performance of the company, the demand for shares, and other relevant factors. In the case of listed companies, the issue price (including premium) is determined through the book building process regulated by SEBI.

11.6 Issue of Shares at Discount – Section 53

When shares are issued at a price lower than their face value, they are said to be issued at a discount. For example, if a share of face value Rs. 10 is issued at Rs. 8, the discount is Rs. 2 per share.

Section Reference: Section 53(1): Except as provided in Section 54, a company shall not issue shares at a discount. Any share issued by a company at a discounted price shall be void.

This is a very important provision. Under the Companies Act, 2013, the issue of shares at a discount is completely prohibited (except in the case of sweat equity shares under Section 54). This is a significant change from the Companies Act, 1956 which permitted the issue of shares at a discount subject to certain conditions (under the old Section 79).

Section 53(2) provides that where any company contravenes the provisions of Section 53(1), the company shall be punishable with a fine which shall not be less than Rs. 1 lakh but which may extend to Rs. 5 lakhs, and every officer who is in default shall be punishable with imprisonment for a term which may extend to 6 months or with a fine which shall not be less than Rs. 1 lakh but which may extend to Rs. 5 lakhs, or with both.

Section 53(3) provides that any share issued at a discount shall be treated as having been issued at the face value. The amount of the discount shall be recoverable from the allottee as if it were a debt due from him. In other words, even if shares are illegally issued at a discount, the allottee must pay the full face value.

Note: It is important to distinguish between 'issue of shares at a discount' (which is prohibited) and 'issue of shares at below market price' (which may be permitted in certain cases, e.g., sweat equity shares or rights issue). The prohibition under Section 53 relates to the face value, not the market value. A company can issue shares at a price lower than the market value as long as the issue price is not below the face value.

11.7 Bonus Shares – Section 63

Bonus shares are additional shares issued by the company to its existing shareholders free of cost. They are issued out of the company's reserves (accumulated profits) or the securities premium account. Bonus shares are also called 'capitalisation shares' because they represent the capitalisation of the company's profits.

When a company has accumulated large reserves and free reserves over the years, it may decide to distribute a part of these reserves to the shareholders in the form of bonus shares. The shareholders do not pay anything for these shares. The issue of bonus shares increases the number of shares held by each shareholder but does not change the percentage of their shareholding.

Illustration: XYZ Ltd. has 10 lakh equity shares of Rs. 10 each. It declares a bonus issue of 1:2 (one bonus share for every two shares held). Mr. A, who holds 200 shares, will receive 100 bonus shares free of cost. After the bonus issue, A will hold 300 shares. The total number of shares of the company will increase to 15 lakh.

Conditions for Issue of Bonus Shares – Section 63(1)

Section 63(1) prescribes the following conditions for the issue of bonus shares:

(a) Authorised by articles: The issue must be authorised by the articles of the company.

(b) Authorised by ordinary resolution: The issue must be approved by an ordinary resolution at a general meeting on the recommendation of the Board of Directors.

(c) Not issued out of capitalisation of reserves created by revaluation of assets: Bonus shares cannot be issued by capitalising reserves created by the revaluation of assets. The issue must be made out of free reserves, the securities premium account, or the capital redemption reserve account [Section 63(1)(a) to (c)].

(d) Not issued in lieu of dividend: The company shall not issue bonus shares in lieu of dividend.

(e) Fully paid-up: The company must not have any default in the payment of interest or principal on its fixed deposits or debt securities, or in the payment of statutory dues to employees. Also, partly paid-up shares must be made fully paid-up before issuing bonus shares.

(f) Once announced, cannot be withdrawn: Section 63(2) provides that the bonus shares shall not be issued in lieu of dividend, and once the Board of Directors has approved the bonus issue, it cannot be withdrawn.

11.8 Calls on Shares and Forfeiture

Calls on Shares

When a company issues shares, it may not require the shareholders to pay the entire face value at once. The company may call up the money in instalments. Each demand for payment by the company is called a 'call.' The provisions relating to calls are usually contained in the articles of association. The general rules regarding calls are: (a) A call must be made by a resolution of the Board of Directors. (b) Due notice of the call must be given to the shareholders specifying the amount to be paid, the time and place of payment. (c) A call must not exceed one-fourth of the face value of the share, unless the articles provide otherwise. (d) There must be a minimum interval of one month between two successive calls. (e) All shareholders must be treated equally in the matter of calls. (f) If a shareholder fails to pay the call money, he is liable to pay interest on the unpaid amount from the due date.

The stages of payment usually are: (i) Application money – paid at the time of application, (ii) Allotment money – paid on allotment, (iii) First call, Second call, and so on, (iv) Final call – the last instalment. Under

SEBI regulations, for a public issue, the company must call up at least 25% of the face value at the time of application.

Forfeiture of Shares

If a shareholder fails to pay the call money even after proper notice, the company has the power to forfeit his shares. Forfeiture means the cancellation of the allotment of shares and the termination of the shareholder's membership. The shares are taken back by the company. The amount already paid by the shareholder is not returned to him.

The power to forfeit shares is not given by the Companies Act directly. It is derived from the articles of association. The articles usually provide the procedure for forfeiture, which includes giving notice to the defaulting shareholder and allowing him a reasonable time to make the payment before the shares are actually forfeited.

The procedure for forfeiture is: (a) The Board of Directors must pass a resolution for forfeiture. (b) A notice must be served on the defaulting shareholder giving him at least 14 days' time to pay the due amount with interest. (c) The notice must state that if the amount is not paid within the specified time, the shares will be forfeited. (d) If the shareholder still fails to pay, the Board may forfeit the shares by a resolution. (e) After forfeiture, the shares become the property of the company. (f) The forfeited shares may be reissued to another person at any price, but the amount collected on the original issue plus the amount collected on reissue must not be less than the face value of the shares.

The effect of forfeiture is that the shareholder ceases to be a member of the company from the date of forfeiture. However, he remains liable to pay the company any amount which was unpaid at the time of forfeiture. The company may also cancel the forfeiture and restore the shares to the member if he pays the arrears before the shares are reissued.

11.9 Transfer and Transmission of Shares

Transfer of Shares – Section 56

Transfer of shares means the voluntary transfer of shares by one person (the transferor) to another person (the transferee) by means of a proper instrument of transfer. It is a bilateral act involving the consent of both the transferor and the transferee.

Section 56(1) provides that a company shall not register a transfer of securities of the company unless a proper instrument of transfer, duly stamped, dated, and executed by or on behalf of the transferor and the transferee, has been delivered to the company along with the certificate relating to the securities, or if no such certificate is in existence, the letter of allotment of securities, within a period of 60 days from the date of execution of the instrument.

The procedure for transfer is: (a) The transferor and transferee must execute an instrument of transfer (Form SH-4). (b) The instrument must be duly stamped under the Indian Stamp Act. (c) The instrument along with the share certificate must be delivered to the company within 60 days. (d) The company must register the transfer within one month from the date of receipt of the instrument [Section 56(4)(a)] or send notice of refusal within 30 days stating the reasons [Section 56(4)(b)]. (e) In case of refusal, the aggrieved party may appeal to the Tribunal (NCLT) within 30 days.

In a public company, the shares are freely transferable and the company cannot refuse to register the transfer of fully paid-up shares. In a private company, the articles usually restrict the right of transfer by giving the Board of Directors the power to refuse registration.

For listed companies, shares are held and transferred in dematerialised (electronic) form through depositories (NSDL and CDSL). Physical transfer of shares has been virtually eliminated for listed companies under SEBI regulations. Transfer of dematerialised shares is effected through the depository system and does not require an instrument of transfer.

Transmission of Shares

Transmission of shares means the transfer of shares by operation of law, as distinguished from a voluntary transfer. Transmission occurs in the following situations: (a) On the death of a shareholder – the shares are transmitted to the legal heirs or legal representative of the deceased. (b) On the insolvency of a shareholder – the shares vest in the Official Receiver or the Official Assignee. (c) On the lunacy of a shareholder – the shares may be transmitted to the guardian appointed by the court.

In the case of transmission, no instrument of transfer is needed. The legal heir must produce the death certificate, succession certificate, probate, or letters of administration (as applicable) along with the share certificate. The company then registers the shares in the name of the legal heir or representative.

Point	Transfer	Transmission
Nature	Voluntary act of the parties	By operation of law
Cause	Sale, gift, exchange	Death, insolvency, lunacy
Instrument	Instrument of transfer required	No instrument required
Stamp Duty	Stamp duty payable	No stamp duty
Parties	Transferor and transferee	Legal heir, official receiver, or guardian
Consideration	Usually involves consideration	No consideration
Section	Section 56	Section 56

11.10 Buy-Back of Shares – Section 68

Buy-back means the purchase by a company of its own shares. Under the general rule, a company is not allowed to purchase its own shares because it would amount to reduction of capital and would affect the interests of creditors. However, Section 68 permits a company to buy-back its own shares subject to certain conditions.

Conditions for Buy-Back – Section 68(2)

The buy-back must comply with the following conditions:

(a) The buy-back must be authorised by the articles of the company. (b) A special resolution must be passed at a general meeting. However, if the buy-back is 10% or less of the total paid-up equity capital and free reserves, a Board resolution is sufficient [Section 68(2)(b)]. (c) The buy-back must not exceed 25% of the aggregate of the paid-up capital and free reserves of the company. (d) The ratio of secured and unsecured debts owed by the company after buy-back shall not be more than twice the paid-up capital and its free reserves (i.e., the debt-equity ratio must not exceed 2:1). (e) All the shares for buy-back must be fully paid-up. (f) The buy-back must be completed within one year from the date of the special resolution or the Board resolution, as the case may be. (g) The company must not make any further issue of the same kind of securities within six months of the buy-back (except bonus shares or discharge of obligations).

Sources of Buy-Back – Section 68(1)

A company may purchase its own shares or other specified securities out of: (a) its free reserves, (b) the securities premium account, or (c) the proceeds of the issue of any shares or other specified securities (but not from the proceeds of an earlier issue of the same kind of shares or securities).

Purposes of Buy-Back

Companies buy-back their shares for various reasons: (a) To return surplus cash to shareholders. (b) To improve earnings per share (EPS) by reducing the number of shares. (c) To support the share price in the market. (d) To prevent hostile takeovers by reducing the number of shares available in the market. (e) To consolidate the promoters' holding.

(f) To provide an exit opportunity to shareholders.

After the buy-back, the company must extinguish and physically destroy the securities bought back within seven days of the last date of completion of buy-back [Section 69(2)]. The company must also transfer a sum equal to the nominal value of the shares bought back to the Capital Redemption Reserve Account [Section 69(1)]. The company cannot issue the same kind of shares within six months after the buy-back [Section 68(8)].

Example: Infosys, TCS, Wipro, and other large IT companies have frequently undertaken buy-back of shares to return surplus cash to shareholders and to improve earnings per share. In 2023-24, several Indian companies undertook buy-backs valued at thousands of crores of rupees

11.11 Reduction of Share Capital – Section 66

Reduction of share capital is a more drastic step than buy-back. While buy-back involves the company purchasing its own shares in the market or from the shareholders, reduction of capital involves a formal alteration of the capital clause of the memorandum.

Section Reference: Section 66(1): Subject to confirmation by the Tribunal on an application by the company, a company limited by shares or limited by guarantee and having a share capital may, by special resolution, reduce the share capital in any manner.

The reduction may take any of the following forms: (a) Reducing the liability of the members on account of share capital not paid up. For example, if shares of Rs. 100 are Rs. 75 paid-up, the company may reduce them to Rs. 75 paid-up so that the members are no longer liable for the remaining Rs. 25. (b) Cancelling any paid-up capital which is lost or is unrepresented by available assets. For example, if the company has suffered heavy losses, it may write off the accumulated losses by reducing the share capital. (c) Paying off any paid-up share capital which is in excess of the wants (needs) of the company. For example, if the company has surplus capital, it may return the excess to the shareholders.

The procedure for reduction is: (a) The company must pass a special resolution. (b) An application must be filed with the NCLT. (c) The NCLT shall give notice to the creditors of the company. The creditors may object if their debts are not secured or adequately provided for. (d) If the NCLT is satisfied that the reduction is just and equitable and that the creditors' interests are protected, it may confirm the reduction. (e) A certified copy of the Tribunal's order and the minutes of reduction must be filed with the Registrar. (f) The Registrar shall register the order and the minutes. The reduction takes effect from the date of registration.

Section 66(3) provides that the NCLT shall not confirm the reduction unless it is satisfied that the accounting treatment proposed by the company is in conformity with the accounting standards specified under Section 133 or any other provision of the Act. The Auditor's certificate must be filed confirming that the accounting treatment is correct.

Note: The reduction of capital must be distinguished from the buy-back of shares. In buy-back, the company purchases its own shares from the market or from shareholders through a tender offer. In reduction, the capital is reduced through a formal process approved by the NCLT. Both result in a decrease in the company's share capital, but the procedure and legal requirements are different.

Chapter 12

Members and Membership

A company is an association of persons who come together for a common purpose. These persons are called the 'members' of the company. Without members, a company cannot exist. The members are the backbone of the company – they provide the capital, they elect the directors, they approve the major decisions of the company, and they bear the ultimate risk of the business. In this chapter, we shall study who is a member, how membership is acquired and lost, what rights and liabilities a member has, and how the register of members is maintained.

12.1 Who is a Member? – Section 2(55)

Definition

Section Reference: Section 2(55) of the Companies Act, 2013 defines 'member' as follows: "'Member' in relation to a company, means – (i) the subscriber to the memorandum of the company who shall be deemed to have agreed to become a member of the company, and on its registration, shall be entered as a member in its register of members; (ii) every other person who agrees in writing to become a member of the company and whose name is entered in the register of members of the company; (iii) every person holding shares of the company and whose name is entered as a beneficial owner in the records of a depository."

From this definition, it is clear that there are three categories of persons who can become members of a company:

(A) Subscribers to the Memorandum

The subscribers to the memorandum are the persons who sign the memorandum at the time of the incorporation of the company. They are deemed to have agreed to become members of the company. They become members from the date of incorporation, i.e., from the date on which the certificate of incorporation is issued. Their names are entered in the register of members without any application or allotment. In the case of a public company, there must be at least 7 subscribers; in the case of a private company, at least 2; and in the case of an OPC, only 1 subscriber.

The subscribers are the first members of the company. Even if their names are not entered in the register of members, they are still members by virtue of having signed the memorandum. This is because Section 2(55)(i) says that they 'shall be deemed to have agreed' to become members. It is a legal presumption which cannot be rebutted.

(B) Persons Who Agree in Writing and Whose Names are Entered in the Register

Any person (other than a subscriber) who agrees in writing to become a member of the company and whose name is entered in the register of members becomes a member. This covers persons who acquire shares through allotment (either in an initial issue or in a subsequent issue), through transfer from an existing member, or through transmission (on the death or insolvency of an existing member). Two conditions must be satisfied simultaneously: (i) the person must agree in writing to become a member, and (ii) his name must be entered in the register of members. If either condition is not fulfilled, the person does not become a member.

Illustration: A applies for and is allotted 500 shares in XYZ Ltd. A's application for shares constitutes his agreement in writing to become a member. When the company enters A's name in the register of members, A becomes a member. If the company fails to enter A's name in the register (due to negligence or any other reason), A can compel the company to do so through the Tribunal (NCLT) under Section 59.

(C) Beneficial Owners in a Depository

In the case of shares held in dematerialised (electronic) form, the person whose name appears as the beneficial owner in the records of the depository (NSDL or CDSL) is treated as the member of the company. This provision was necessary because in the depository system, the shares are held in the name of the depository (which is the registered owner), but the actual owner is the person in whose demat account the shares are credited. Section 2(55)(iii) ensures that the beneficial owner (not the depository) is treated as the member for all purposes.

Member vs. Shareholder

The terms 'member' and 'shareholder' are often used interchangeably, but there is a subtle legal distinction between them. A shareholder is a person who holds shares in the company. A member is a person whose name is entered in the register of members. In most cases, a shareholder and a member are the same person. However, there are some situations where the two terms do not overlap:

(a) A subscriber to the memorandum is a member even before shares are allotted to him. He becomes a member on the date of incorporation, but the shares may be allotted to him later. So, he is a member but may not yet be a shareholder in the technical sense.

(b) A person who has transferred all his shares is still a member until the transfer is registered and his name is removed from the register. He is no longer a shareholder (because he has no shares) but he is still a member (because his name is on the register).

(c) A company limited by guarantee does not have share capital. Its members are persons who have agreed to contribute a guaranteed amount on winding up. They are members but not shareholders because there are no shares.

Note: In practice, for companies limited by shares (which are the vast majority of companies), the terms 'member' and 'shareholder' are used synonymously. The legal distinction matters mainly in examination questions and in specific legal situations.

Who Can Become a Member?

The following persons can become members of a company:

(1) Any individual: Any natural person who is of the age of majority (18 years) and of sound mind can become a member. A minor cannot become a member because he is not competent to contract. However, shares can be held by a guardian on behalf of a minor. If shares are allotted to a minor, the allotment is void, and the minor can repudiate the transaction and recover any money paid.

Case: Mohiri Bibi v. Dharmodas Ghose (1903)

As discussed in Chapter 2, the Privy Council held that an agreement with a minor is void ab initio. Following this principle, if a minor is allotted shares in a company, the allotment is void. The minor's name cannot be placed on the register of members and he is not liable for calls. However, in practice, shares are sometimes held in the name of the guardian 'on behalf of' the minor.

(2) Any company or body corporate: A company can become a member of another company by purchasing its shares. For example, Tata Sons Ltd. holds shares in TCS, Tata Motors, and other Tata group companies, making Tata Sons a member of each of those companies. However, a company cannot be a member of its own holding company (Section 19).

(3) Hindu Undivided Family (HUF): An HUF can become a member through its karta (head of the family). The shares are registered in the name of the karta, who holds them as a representative of the HUF.

(4) Partnership Firm: A partnership firm is not a legal person under Indian law, so it cannot hold shares in its own name. However, the partners can hold shares jointly on behalf of the firm, and the shares are registered in the names of the partners.

(5) Trust: A trust can hold shares through its trustee(s). The shares are registered in the name of the trustee(s) who hold them on behalf of the trust.

(6) Foreign nationals and NRIs: Foreign nationals and Non-Resident Indians can become members of Indian companies, subject to the provisions of the Foreign Exchange Management Act (FEMA), 1999 and the regulations of the Reserve Bank of India. FEMA prescribes the limits and conditions under which foreign investment in Indian companies is permitted.

(7) Government: Both the Central Government and State Governments can become members of companies. In Government companies, the Government holds 51% or more of the paid-up share capital.

Modes of Acquiring Membership

Membership in a company can be acquired in the following ways:

(a) By subscribing to the memorandum: The subscribers become members on incorporation.

(b) By allotment of shares: A person who applies for shares and is allotted shares becomes a member when his name is entered in the register.

(c) By transfer: A person who acquires shares by transfer from an existing member becomes a member when the transfer is registered and his name is entered in the register.

(d) By transmission: The legal heir or legal representative of a deceased member acquires membership by transmission when his name is entered in the register.

(e) By estoppel or acquiescence: If a person, though not formally a member, allows his name to remain on the register of members without objection, he may be treated as a member by estoppel and may be held liable for unpaid calls.

(f) By holding shares in a depository: A person whose name appears as beneficial owner in the records of the depository becomes a member.

Minimum and Maximum Number of Members

Type of Company	Minimum Members	Maximum Members
One Person Company (OPC)	1	1
Private Company	2	200 (excluding employees)

Public Company	7	No maximum limit

If the number of members falls below the statutory minimum and the company carries on business for more than six months while the number is so reduced, every person who is a member during that time and who is aware of this fact shall be severally liable for the debts of the company contracted during that period [Section 3A]. This is one of the situations where the corporate veil is lifted (as discussed in Chapter 5).

12.2 Register of Members – Section 88

Every company is required to maintain a register of its members. The register of members is one of the most important statutory registers which a company must keep. It is the authoritative record of who the members of the company are.

Section Reference: Section 88(1): Every company shall maintain a register of members indicating separately for each class of equity and preference shares held by each member residing in or outside India, and enter therein the following particulars, namely: (a) the name, address, and occupation, if any, of each member, the address of his registered email, and the date on which each person was entered in the register as a member; (b) the number of shares held by each member and the distinctive numbers of such shares (if any); (c) the date on which any person ceased to be a member.

Contents of the Register

The register of members must contain the following information for each member:

(a) Name, address, occupation, and email address. (b) Date on which the person was entered as a member. (c) Date on which the person ceased to be a member. (d) Number of shares held, with distinctive numbers (for physical shares). (e) The amount paid or agreed to be considered as paid on the shares. (f) In the case of a company having share capital, whether a preference shareholder or an equity shareholder, and the class of shares held. (g) The amount of any lien on the shares. (h) Particulars of joint holders, if any.

Place of Keeping the Register – Section 88(2)

The register of members must be kept at the registered office of the company. However, the company may, by passing a special resolution, keep the register at any other place in India in which more than one-tenth of the total number of members reside. If the register is kept at any place other than the registered office, the company must file with the Registrar a notice of the address at which it is kept within 15 days.

Index of Members – Section 88(3)

Every company having more than fifty members must maintain an index of the names of the members. The index must be kept at the same place as the register. The entries in the index must be consistent with the entries in the register. Any alteration in the register must be made in the index within 14 days.

Inspection and Copies – Section 94

Section 94 provides that the register of members, the index of members, and the register of debenture-holders must be open for inspection during business hours by any member of the company without charge and by any other person on payment of a prescribed fee not exceeding Rs. 50 for each inspection. Any member or debenture-holder of the company is entitled to obtain copies of any part of the register on payment of the prescribed fee.

The right of inspection is an important right because it enables members and creditors to ascertain who the other members of the company are, what shares they hold, and whether there has been any irregularity in the maintenance of the register. If the company refuses inspection or fails to furnish copies, the company and every officer who is in default shall be liable to a penalty.

Foreign Register – Section 88(4)

Section 88(4) allows a company having a share capital to maintain a register of members residing outside India, which is called the 'foreign register.' The foreign register is considered a part of the register of members. It is kept at the registered office of the company or at any office of the company in the country where the foreign members reside. The foreign register must be open for inspection and copies must be made available in the same manner as the main register.

Rectification of Register – Section 59

Section 59 provides for the rectification of the register of members in the following cases:

(a) Name not entered: If the name of any person is, without sufficient cause, entered in the register of members of a company, or if the name of a member is, without sufficient cause or unnecessary delay, omitted from the register, or if default is made or unnecessary delay takes place in entering the fact of any person having become or ceased to be a member, the aggrieved person, or any member of the company, or the company, may apply to the Tribunal (NCLT) for rectification of the register.

(b) Order of the Tribunal: On receiving such an application, the Tribunal may, after hearing the parties, order the rectification of the register and may also order the company to pay damages to the aggrieved party.

(c) Power of the Tribunal: The Tribunal has wide powers. It can order the company to enter a name in the register, to remove a name from the register, or to correct any error in the register. The Tribunal may also decide any question relating to the title of any person who is a party to the application, whether the question arises between members or between the company and its members.

If there is a default in complying with the provisions relating to the register of members, the company and every officer who is in default shall be liable to a penalty not less than Rs. 50,000 which may extend to

Rs. 5,00,000, and where the default is a continuing one, with a further penalty of Rs. 1,000 for every day during which the default continues.

Case: Re Sussex Brick Co. (1904)

The Court held that the register of members is prima facie evidence (but not conclusive evidence) of the facts stated therein. If any entry in the register is wrong, it can be rectified by the court on application. The register is important, but it can be challenged if there is evidence that the entry was made incorrectly or fraudulently.

Note: Under the Depositories Act, 1996, for shares held in dematerialised form, the register of beneficial owners maintained by the depository is treated as the register of members for all purposes of the Companies Act. The company must update its register based on the information received from the depository.

12.3 Rights and Liabilities of Members

Rights of Members

The members of a company have the following important rights:

(1) Right to receive dividends: When a dividend is declared by the company, every member is entitled to receive his share of the dividend in proportion to the shares held by him. However, it is important to note that the members have no right to demand a dividend. The declaration of dividend is within the discretion of the Board of Directors, subject to the approval of the shareholders at the AGM. The shareholders can approve a dividend at a rate equal to or lower than the rate recommended by the Board, but they cannot increase the rate.

(2) Right to vote: Every member of a company limited by shares has the right to vote at the meetings of the company. The voting right is proportionate to the shareholding. On a poll, every member has one vote for every share held by him [Section 47]. Equity shareholders have the right to vote on every resolution. Preference shareholders have the right to vote only on resolutions directly affecting them, but they get full voting rights if their dividend has remained unpaid for two or more consecutive years.

(3) Right to attend meetings: Every member has the right to attend the general meetings of the company, to speak at such meetings, and to participate in the discussions. The company cannot deprive a member of this right by any provision in the articles.

(4) Right to appoint proxy: A member who is unable to attend a general meeting in person has the right to appoint another person as his proxy to attend and vote on his behalf [Section 105]. A proxy need not be a member of the company.

(5) Right to receive annual reports: Every member has the right to receive a copy of the annual report of the company, including the Board's report, the auditor's report, and the financial statements (balance sheet, profit and loss account, and cash flow statement) before the AGM [Section 136].

(6) Right to inspect registers and records: Members have the right to inspect certain statutory registers and records of the company, including the register of members, the register of directors, the minutes of general meetings, and other documents [Section 94, Section 119, Section 170].

(7) Right to transfer shares: Every member has the right to transfer his shares. In a public company, the right to transfer fully paid-up shares is unrestricted. In a private company, the transfer may be restricted by the articles.

(8) Right to share in surplus on winding up: On the winding up of the company, after all creditors and preference shareholders have been paid, the equity shareholders are entitled to a proportionate share of the surplus assets of the company.

(9) Right to apply for relief in case of oppression and mismanagement: If the affairs of the company are being conducted in a manner prejudicial to the interests of the company or its members, the members may apply to the NCLT for relief under Sections 241 and 242.

The eligible members are those who hold at least one-tenth of the issued share capital or at least 100 members (whichever is less) in the case of a company having a share capital.

(10) Right to file a class action suit: Under Section 245, a specified number of members may file a class action suit before the NCLT if they believe that the management or conduct of the affairs of the company is being done in a manner prejudicial to the interests of the company or its members.

(11) Right to requisition a meeting: Members holding not less than one-tenth of the paid-up share capital of the company (carrying the right of voting) can requisition the Board to call an extraordinary general meeting [Section 100].

(12) Right to copies of memorandum and articles: Every member is entitled to receive a copy of the memorandum and articles of the company on payment of the prescribed fee [Section 17].

Liabilities of Members

The liabilities of the members of a company are generally limited. The following are the main liabilities:

(1) Liability to pay for shares: The primary liability of a member is to pay the company the amount due on the shares held by him. In the case of a company limited by shares, the liability is limited to the amount unpaid on the shares. If the shares are fully paid, the member has no further liability. If the shares are partly paid, the member is liable to pay the unpaid amount when the company makes a call.

(2) Liability as contributory in winding up: On the winding up of a company, a member may be required to contribute to the assets of the company as a 'contributory.' Section 2(26) defines a 'contributory' as every person liable to contribute to the assets of a company in the event of its being wound up. The liability of a contributory is limited to the amount unpaid on his shares (in the case of a company limited by shares) or to the amount he has guaranteed (in the case of a company limited by guarantee).

(3) Liability for unpaid calls: If a member fails to pay the call money within the stipulated time, he is liable to pay interest on the unpaid amount. If the default continues, the company may forfeit his shares.

(4) Liability under Section 3A: If the number of members falls below the statutory minimum and the company carries on business for more than six months with the number so reduced, every member who knows of this fact shall be personally liable for the debts of the company contracted during that period.

(5) No liability beyond the shares: A very important point is that the personal property of a member cannot be used to pay the debts of the company. The member's liability is limited to the amount unpaid on his shares. This is the principle of limited liability which is one of the most important features of the company form of business.

Illustration: A holds 1,000 shares of Rs. 10 each in XYZ Ltd. He has paid Rs. 8 per share. The company goes into liquidation with debts of Rs. 10 crore. A's maximum liability is Rs. 2,000 (i.e., Rs. 2 × 1,000 shares). His house, car, and other personal properties are completely safe. The creditors of the company cannot touch A's personal property.

12.4 Cessation of Membership

Membership in a company is not permanent. A member may cease to be a member in the following ways:

(1) By transfer of shares: When a member transfers all his shares to another person and the transfer is registered by the company, the transferor ceases to be a member and the transferee becomes the new member. The membership ends when the name of the transferor is removed from the register and the name of the transferee is entered.

(2) By transmission of shares: On the death of a member, the shares are transmitted to his legal heirs or legal representatives. The deceased member's name is removed from the register and the legal heir's name is entered. The membership of the deceased terminates at the time of his death (though the formal removal from the register may take place later).

(3) By forfeiture of shares: If a member fails to pay the call money and the company forfeits his shares in accordance with the procedure laid down in the articles, the member ceases to be a member from the date of forfeiture. However, he remains liable to pay the unpaid amount.

(4) By surrender of shares: Surrender of shares means the voluntary return of shares by a member to the company. Surrender is not expressly provided for in the Companies Act. It is permitted only if the articles authorise it and it is done in cases where the company could have otherwise forfeited the shares. It is treated as a short cut to forfeiture. Surrender for any other purpose amounts to purchase of its own shares by the company, which is prohibited under Section 67 (except by way of buy-back under Section 68).

(5) By sale of shares under the company's lien: If the articles give the company a lien on shares for any amount due from the member, the company may, after giving proper notice, sell the shares to realise the amount due. The member ceases to be a member when the shares are sold.

(6) By redemption of redeemable preference shares: When the company redeems the redeemable preference shares, the preference shareholders cease to be members to the extent of the shares redeemed.

(7) By buy-back of shares: When the company buys back its shares under Section 68, the members whose shares are bought back cease to be members.

(8) By operation of law: In the following circumstances, membership may cease by operation of law: (a) On adjudication of the member as insolvent – the shares vest in the Official Receiver or Assignee. (b) When the member becomes of unsound mind and a court appoints a guardian who may sell the shares. (c) When a body corporate which is a member is dissolved or wound up.

(9) By winding up of the company: When the company is wound up and dissolved, the membership of all members automatically terminates.

(10) By rescission of the contract of allotment: If the allotment of shares was obtained by fraud, misrepresentation, or mistake, the member may get the allotment rescinded (cancelled) by the court. In that case, the membership terminates and the member's name is removed from the register.

Table 12.1: Modes of Cessation of Membership

S.No.	Mode	Voluntary or Involuntary
1	Transfer of shares	Voluntary
2	Transmission (death/insolvency)	Involuntary (by law)
3	Forfeiture of shares	Involuntary (by company)
4	Surrender of shares	Voluntary
5	Sale under company's lien	Involuntary (by company)
6	Redemption of preference shares	As per terms of issue
7	Buy-back of shares	Voluntary (acceptance of offer)
8	Operation of law (insolvency, etc.)	Involuntary (by law)
9	Winding up of the company	Involuntary (by law)
10	Rescission of allotment	By court order

12.5 Depository System and Dematerialisation

In the traditional system, shares of a company were represented by physical share certificates. The share certificate was the documentary evidence of the member's ownership of shares. All transfers of shares required the physical delivery of the share certificate along with a duly stamped transfer deed. This system was slow, cumbersome, and prone to problems like theft, forgery, and delays in transfer. To overcome these problems, India adopted the depository system in the mid-1990s.

What is Dematerialisation?

Dematerialisation (commonly called 'demat') is the process of converting physical share certificates into electronic form. When shares are dematerialised, the physical certificates are cancelled and the equivalent number of shares is credited to the member's demat account maintained with a Depository Participant (DP). After dematerialisation, the shares exist only in electronic form in the records of the depository. There is no physical certificate.

The Depository System

The depository system in India is governed by the Depositories Act, 1996 and the regulations framed by SEBI. The key players in the depository system are:

(1) Depository: A depository is an institution which holds securities in dematerialised form and provides services related to the holding, transfer, and settlement of securities. In India, there are two depositories – (a) National Securities Depository Limited (NSDL), established in 1996, and (b) Central Depository Services (India) Limited (CDSL), established in 1999. Both are registered with SEBI.

(2) Depository Participant (DP): A depository participant is an agent of the depository. It is the intermediary between the depository and the investor. Banks, stockbrokers, custodians, and financial institutions may act as DPs. The investor opens a demat account with a DP, similar to opening a bank account. The DP maintains the investor's demat account.

(3) Issuer Company: The company whose securities are held in the depository system. The company enters into an agreement with the depository for the dematerialisation of its securities.

(4) Registrar and Transfer Agent (RTA): The RTA is appointed by the company to maintain the register of members and to process transfers and other corporate actions. Major RTAs in India include KFin Technologies (formerly Karvy) and Link Intime India Pvt. Ltd.

Process of Dematerialisation

The process of converting physical shares into electronic form involves the following steps: (a) The investor opens a demat account with a Depository Participant (DP). (b) The investor fills up a Dematerialisation Request Form (DRF) and submits it to the DP along with the physical share certificate(s). The investor must deface the physical certificate by writing 'Surrendered for Dematerialisation' on the face of the certificate. (c) The DP forwards the request to the depository and also sends the physical certificate to the company or its RTA for verification. (d) The company or RTA verifies the certificate and confirms the dematerialisation to the depository. (e) The depository credits the equivalent number of shares to the investor's demat account. (f) The physical share certificate is destroyed after dematerialisation.

Rematerialisation

Rematerialisation is the reverse process – converting dematerialised shares back into physical form. The investor fills a Rematerialisation Request Form (RRF) and submits it to the DP. The depository debits the shares from the investor's demat account and the company issues physical share certificates to the investor. However, rematerialisation is now very rare because SEBI has mandated that all transfers of shares of listed companies must be in dematerialised form only.

Advantages of the Depository System

The depository system has brought several benefits: (a) Elimination of paperwork and physical handling of certificates. (b) Instant transfer of shares – settlement is done on T+1 basis (transaction plus one day). (c) Elimination of risks like theft, forgery, loss, and damage of physical certificates. (d) No stamp duty on transfer of shares in dematerialised form. (e) Lower transaction costs. (f) Easy pledging of shares for loans.

(g) Automatic credit of dividends, bonus shares, and rights shares to the demat account. (h) Reduction in disputes and litigation. (i) Greater transparency and efficiency in the securities market.

Legal Framework

Section 2(55)(iii) of the Companies Act recognises the beneficial owner in the records of a depository as a member. Section 56(6) provides that the transfer of securities held in a depository shall be by means of entries in the records of the depository. Section 89 requires the declaration and disclosure of beneficial interest in shares. SEBI has mandated the dematerialisation of shares of all listed companies and of companies which intend to list their shares.

Practical Point: From April 2019, SEBI has made it mandatory for transfer of securities of listed companies to be in dematerialised form only. Physical transfer is no longer permitted for listed companies. This means that if you hold physical shares of a listed company and want to sell them, you must first get them dematerialised and then sell them through the stock exchange.

Note: SEBI has also mandated that all unlisted public companies must issue securities in dematerialised form only (w.e.f. 2nd October, 2018). Private companies are not covered by this mandate, but many private companies voluntarily maintain shares in demat form for convenience.

Chapter 13

Debentures

Companies need funds not only in the form of share capital but also in the form of borrowed capital. While shares represent ownership capital, debentures represent borrowed capital (i.e., debt capital). When a company needs money for expansion, modernisation, or working capital, it may issue debentures to the public or to a select group of investors instead of (or in addition to) issuing shares. Debentures are one of the most commonly used instruments of corporate borrowing. The Companies Act, 2013 contains detailed provisions regarding the issue, redemption, and regulation of debentures in Section 71 and the Companies (Share Capital and Debentures) Rules, 2014.

13.1 Meaning, Definition & Types of Debentures

Definition

Section Reference: Section 2(30) of the Companies Act, 2013 defines 'debenture' as follows: "'Debenture' includes debenture stock, bonds, and any other instrument of a company evidencing a debt, whether constituting a charge on the assets of the company or not."

This definition is very broad. It includes not only the traditional debenture but also debenture stock, bonds, and any other instrument which evidences a debt of the company. The key feature of a debenture is that it is an acknowledgement of a debt. The company which issues debentures is the borrower, and the person who holds the debentures is the lender (creditor).

In the words of Justice Chitty in Levy v. Abercorris Slate and Slab Co. (1887), "A debenture means a document which either creates a debt or acknowledges it, and any document which fulfils either of these conditions is a debenture."

In simple language, a debenture is a written instrument issued by a company under its common seal (or signed by authorised officers) acknowledging a debt and containing a promise to repay the debt on a specified date and to pay interest at a fixed rate until the debt is repaid. It is a loan certificate issued by the company.

Essential Features of a Debenture

(1) It is a debt instrument: A debenture represents a loan taken by the company. The debenture holder is a creditor of the company, not an owner. Unlike a shareholder who has an ownership stake in the company, a debenture holder has only a creditor's claim against the company.

(2) Fixed rate of interest: Debentures carry a fixed rate of interest which is payable periodically (usually half-yearly or annually) irrespective of whether the company earns a profit or not. Interest on debentures is a charge on the profits of the company and must be paid before any dividend is declared on shares.

(3) Repayment of principal: The principal amount of the debenture must be repaid on the maturity date specified in the terms of issue. Unlike equity shares which are permanent capital, debentures are temporary capital – they must be repaid after a specified period.

(4) May or may not be secured: Debentures may be secured by a charge on the assets of the company, or they may be unsecured. Secured debentures give the holder a right to the assets of the company in case the company fails to repay. Unsecured debentures (also called 'naked debentures') have no such security.

(5) Issued under the seal of the company: Traditionally, debentures were issued under the common seal of the company. Under the 2013 Act, since the common seal is optional, debentures may be issued under the signature of authorised officers.

(6) Moveable property: Like shares, debentures are moveable property and can be transferred from one person to another. Bearer debentures can be transferred by mere delivery. Registered debentures require an instrument of transfer.

(7) Issued in series: Debentures are usually issued in a series, with each debenture having a distinctive number. All debentures of the same series carry the same terms and conditions.

Illustration: ABC Ltd. issues 10,000 debentures of Rs. 1,000 each carrying interest at 10% per annum, redeemable after 5 years, secured by a floating charge on the assets of the company. The total debt raised is Rs. 1 crore. The company must pay Rs. 10 lakh as interest every year and must repay the principal of Rs. 1 crore at the end of 5 years.

Types of Debentures

Debentures can be classified on various bases:

(A) On the Basis of Security

(i) Secured Debentures (or Mortgage Debentures): These are debentures which are secured by a charge on the assets of the company. The charge may be a fixed charge on specific assets (such as land, building, machinery) or a floating charge on the general assets of the company. If the company fails to repay, the debenture holders can sell the charged assets and recover their money. Under Section 71(3) of the Companies Act, 2013, secured debentures must be secured by a charge on any property or assets of the company having a sufficient value.

(ii) Unsecured Debentures (or Naked Debentures or Simple Debentures): These are debentures which are not secured by any charge on the assets of the company. The debenture holders are ordinary unsecured creditors. In the event of winding up, they have no priority over other unsecured creditors. Under the Companies Act, 2013, Section 71(3) read with Rule 18(1)(a) of the Companies (Share Capital and Debentures) Rules, 2014, a company cannot issue unsecured debentures to the public. All debentures issued to thc public must be secured.

(B) On the Basis of Redeemability

(i) Redeemable Debentures: These are debentures which are to be repaid after a specified period or on the occurrence of a specified event.

The terms of issue specify the date of redemption and the method of redemption (e.g., at par, at premium, by conversion into shares, or by instalments). Most debentures issued by companies are redeemable debentures.

(ii) Irredeemable (or Perpetual) Debentures: These are debentures which are not redeemable during the lifetime of the company. They are repaid only when the company is wound up. They are also called 'perpetual debentures' because they continue in existence for an indefinite period. However, under the Companies Act, 2013, the issue of irredeemable debentures is effectively prohibited. Section 71(1) read with Rule 18(7) provides that debentures must be redeemed in accordance with the terms of issue and within a period not exceeding 10 years from the date of issue (or 30 years in the case of infrastructure companies). Therefore, all debentures must now be redeemable.

(C) On the Basis of Convertibility

(i) Convertible Debentures: These are debentures which can be converted into equity shares of the company after a specified period at the option of the holder or the company, as per the terms of issue. These are further divided into:

(a) Fully Convertible Debentures (FCDs): The entire face value of the debenture is converted into equity shares. After conversion, the debenture ceases to exist and the holder becomes an equity shareholder.

(b) Partly Convertible Debentures (PCDs): Only a part of the face value is converted into equity shares. The remaining part continues as a debenture and is redeemed on the maturity date.

(ii) Non-Convertible Debentures (NCDs): These are debentures which cannot be converted into equity shares. They must be redeemed in cash on the maturity date. Most corporate bonds issued in India today are non-convertible debentures.

Note: Under the Companies Act, 2013, Section 71(1) expressly states that a company may issue debentures with an option to convert such debentures into shares, either wholly or partly, at the time of redemption.

However, the voting rights on such debentures are available only when they are actually converted into shares.

(D) On the Basis of Registration

(i) Registered Debentures: These are debentures which are registered in the name of the holder in the company's register of debenture holders. The interest is paid to the registered holder. Transfer of registered debentures requires an instrument of transfer, just like the transfer of shares. Most debentures issued in India are registered debentures.

(ii) Bearer Debentures: These are debentures which are payable to the bearer. They are not registered in the name of any particular person. They are transferred by mere delivery, like currency notes. Interest coupons are attached to the debenture and the bearer can collect the interest by presenting the coupon. Bearer debentures are rare in India.

(E) On the Basis of Priority of Payment

(i) First Debentures (or First Mortgage Debentures): These are debentures which carry a first charge on the assets of the company. In the event of winding up, they are repaid first, before any payment is made to the holders of second debentures.

(ii) Second Debentures (or Second Mortgage Debentures): These are debentures which carry a second charge on the assets of the company. They are repaid only after the first debenture holders have been paid in full. Because of the higher risk, they usually carry a higher rate of interest.

Table 13.1: Types of Debentures at a Glance

Basis	Type	Key Feature
Security	Secured (Mortgage)	Charge on company's assets
Security	Unsecured (Naked)	No charge; ordinary creditor status

Redeemability	Redeemable	Repaid on maturity date
Redeemability	Irredeemable (Perpetual)	Not redeemable; now effectively prohibited
Convertibility	Fully Convertible (FCD)	Entire value converts to equity shares
Convertibility	Partly Convertible (PCD)	Part converts to shares; rest redeemed
Convertibility	Non-Convertible (NCD)	Cannot convert; redeemed in cash
Registration	Registered	In holder's name; transfer by deed
Registration	Bearer	Payable to bearer; transfer by delivery
Priority	First Mortgage	First charge; paid first
Priority	Second Mortgage	Second charge; paid after first debenture holders

13.2 Issue of Debentures – Section 71

Section 71 is the principal section dealing with the issue of debentures. It lays down the conditions and requirements which must be complied with when a company issues debentures.

Power to Issue Debentures

Section Reference: Section 71(1): A company may issue debentures with an option to convert such debentures into shares, either wholly or partly at the time of redemption. Provided that the issue of debentures with an option to convert such debentures into shares, wholly or partly, shall be approved by a special resolution passed at a general meeting.

Thus, any company can issue debentures. However, if the debentures carry an option to convert into shares (wholly or partly), the issue must be approved by a special resolution. Non-convertible debentures can be issued with a Board resolution.

Conditions for Issue of Debentures

(1) Secured Debentures – Section 71(3): Where a company issues debentures secured by a charge on its assets, the company must create a charge on its properties or assets of adequate value for the amount due on the debentures. The charge must be created before the issue of the debentures or within such time as specified by SEBI. The secured debentures shall be redeemable in accordance with the terms of their issue.

(2) Debenture Redemption Reserve – Section 71(4): The company shall create a Debenture Redemption Reserve (DRR) account out of the profits of the company available for payment of dividend. The company must transfer an adequate amount to the DRR before the debentures are redeemed. The DRR can be used only for the purpose of redemption of debentures. Rule 18(7) of the Companies (Share Capital and Debentures) Rules, 2014 prescribes the amount of DRR as 10% of the outstanding debentures (for listed companies and certain other companies). However, certain categories of companies are exempt from creating DRR, including banking companies, NBFCs, housing finance companies, and companies issuing debentures under a shelf prospectus.

(3) Trust Deed – Section 71(5) & (6): The company must execute a debenture trust deed within 60 days of allotment of debentures [Section 71(5)]. The company must appoint a debenture trustee before the issue of the debentures [Section 71(6)]. These provisions are discussed in detail in Section 13.4 of this chapter.

(4) No Issue at Discount: Like shares, debentures cannot be issued at a discount to their face value. However, they can be issued at a premium or at par. They can also be redeemed at a premium (the premium on redemption must be provided for out of profits or out of the securities premium account).

(5) Allotment and Listing: Debentures issued to the public must comply with the SEBI (Issue and Listing of Non-Convertible Securities) Regulations, 2021. Listed debentures must be listed on a recognised stock exchange. The allotment must be made within the prescribed time, and the allotment letter must be issued to the debenture holders.

(6) Register of Debenture Holders – Section 88: The company must maintain a register of debenture holders, similar to the register of members. The register must contain the name, address, and other details of each debenture holder, the number and amount of debentures held, the date of allotment, and the date of redemption.

(7) Voting Rights: Debenture holders do not have voting rights at the general meetings of the company. They are creditors, not members. However, holders of convertible debentures will get voting rights when (and if) their debentures are converted into equity shares.

Remedies of Debenture Holders in Case of Non-Payment

If a company fails to pay the interest on debentures or fails to redeem the debentures on the due date, the debenture holders have the following remedies:

(a) Sue the company: The debenture holder can file a suit against the company for recovery of the principal amount and interest due.

(b) Enforce the charge: If the debentures are secured by a charge on the company's assets, the debenture holder (through the debenture trustee) can enforce the charge by selling the charged assets and recovering the amount due.

(c) Appoint a receiver: The debenture trust deed usually empowers the debenture trustee to appoint a receiver to take over the management of the charged assets and to sell them for the benefit of the debenture holders.

(d) File a winding up petition: Under the Insolvency and Bankruptcy Code, 2016, the debenture holders can file an application for the initiation of corporate insolvency resolution process against the company if the default exceeds Rs. 1 crore.

(e) Apply to the NCLT: Under Section 71(10), any debenture holder may file an application before the NCLT to claim any such loss or damage or any action against the company.

Section Reference: Section 71(10): If a company fails to redeem the debentures on the date of their maturity or fails to pay interest on the debentures when it is due, the Tribunal may, on the application of any or all of the debenture holders, or debenture trustee, after hearing the parties, direct the company to redeem the debentures forthwith or on such conditions as it deems fit, by the payment of principal and interest due thereon.

Note: Section 71(11) provides that where a company fails to redeem debentures as per the order of the Tribunal, the officers in default shall be punishable with imprisonment up to 3 years or with fine which shall not be less than Rs. 2 lakhs but which may extend to Rs. 5 lakhs, or with both.

13.3 Distinction Between Shares and Debentures

The distinction between shares and debentures is one of the most fundamental distinctions in company law. Both are instruments for raising capital, but they differ in their nature, rights, and legal status. The following table summarises the key differences:

Table 13.2: Shares vs. Debentures

Point of Distinction	Shares	Debentures
Nature	Ownership capital (equity)	Borrowed capital (debt)
Holder's Status	Shareholder is a member (owner)	Debenture holder is a creditor (lender)
Return	Dividend (not	Interest (fixed rate; must

	guaranteed; depends on profits)	be paid even in loss)
Voting Rights	Equity shareholders have full voting rights	No voting rights (unless debenture trust deed provides)
Security	Not secured by any charge	May or may not be secured by a charge on assets
Repayment	Shares are not repaid (except buy-back/reduction)	Debentures must be repaid on maturity
Risk	Higher risk – no guaranteed return	Lower risk – fixed interest and secured (if secured)
Priority in Winding Up	Paid last, after all creditors and preference holders	Paid before shareholders; secured debentures paid first
Issue at Discount	Prohibited (Section 53)	Also prohibited
Conversion	Shares cannot be converted into debentures	Debentures can be converted into shares
Tax Treatment	Dividend is not tax-deductible for company	Interest is tax-deductible for company
Trust Deed	Not required	Required for secured debentures
Control	Shareholders control the company	Debenture holders have no control
Section	Sections 43–68	Section 71

From the above comparison, it is clear that shares and debentures serve different purposes and carry different rights and risks. Shares give ownership and control but carry higher risk. Debentures give fixed income and security but no ownership or control. A prudent investor will maintain a balanced portfolio of both shares and debentures depending on his risk appetite, investment horizon, and financial goals.

Case: Borland's Trustee v. Steel Bros. & Co. Ltd. (1901)

Justice Farwell explained the distinction between a share and a debenture. He said that a share is the interest of a shareholder in the company measured by a sum of money, for the purpose of liability in the first place and of interest in the second. A debenture, on the other hand, is merely a creditor's claim for a debt due to him. The shareholder is an owner; the debenture holder is a creditor. The rights and obligations of the two are fundamentally different.

13.4 Debenture Trust Deed

When a company issues secured debentures to the public, it is practically impossible for each individual debenture holder to monitor the company's compliance with the terms of issue and to enforce the charge on the company's assets. Therefore, the law requires the appointment of a 'debenture trustee' who acts on behalf of all the debenture holders collectively. The terms and conditions of the debenture trust and the rights and duties of the trustee are contained in a document called the 'Debenture Trust Deed.'

Appointment of Debenture Trustee – Section 71(5) & (6)

Section 71(5) provides that the company must appoint a debenture trustee before the issue of a prospectus or letter of offer for subscription of its debentures. The debenture trustee must be registered with SEBI [SEBI (Debenture Trustees) Regulations, 1993]. The trustee must give a written consent before being appointed. No person shall be appointed as a debenture trustee if he is a beneficiary of the debentures, has any pecuniary interest in the company, or is personally interested in any transaction of the company.

Execution of Trust Deed – Section 71(7)

Section Reference: Section 71(7): The company shall pay interest and redeem the debentures in accordance with the terms and conditions of their issue. The trust deed shall contain such clauses as may be prescribed.

The debenture trust deed must be executed by the company within 60 days of the allotment of debentures. Rule 18(4) of the Companies (Share Capital and Debentures) Rules, 2014 prescribes the matters which must be included in the trust deed. These include:

(a) A provision for the appointment of a new trustee in case the existing trustee ceases to hold office. (b) The number of debentures authorised to be issued. (c) The amount of debentures and the rate of interest. (d) The time and mode of redemption. (e) The assets on which the charge is created and the nature and extent of the charge. (f) The rights and duties of the debenture trustee. (g) The powers of the trustee to appoint a receiver or to sell the charged assets. (h) Provisions for the creation and maintenance of the Debenture Redemption Reserve. (i) The conditions under which the company may modify the terms of the debentures.

Duties of the Debenture Trustee – Section 71(8)

Section 71(8) provides that the debenture trustee shall take steps to protect the interests of the debenture holders and redress their grievances in accordance with the trust deed and the provisions of the Act. The trust deed shall provide for the following:

(a) The debenture trustee shall satisfy himself that the assets of the company issuing debentures are sufficient to discharge the principal amount at all times.

(b) The debenture trustee shall see that the terms of the debentures or the trust deed are not prejudicial to the interest of the debenture holders.

(c) The debenture trustee shall call a meeting of the debenture holders whenever required.

(d) The debenture trustee shall ensure that the company does not commit any breach of the terms of the debentures or the trust deed.

(e) The debenture trustee shall take appropriate measures to protect the interest of the debenture holders as and when any breach of the trust deed or the terms of the debentures occurs.

Section 71(9) provides that if at any time the debenture trustee comes to a conclusion that the assets of the company are not sufficient to discharge the principal amount as and when it becomes due, the debenture trustee may file a petition before the Tribunal (NCLT) and the Tribunal may, after hearing the company, order the company to take necessary steps to protect the interest of the debenture holders.

Note: The debenture trustee plays a very important role in protecting the interests of the debenture holders. He is the custodian of the rights of the debenture holders. SEBI has framed detailed regulations – SEBI (Debenture Trustees) Regulations, 1993 – which prescribe the qualifications, duties, and responsibilities of debenture trustees. Only entities registered with SEBI can act as debenture trustees.

13.5 Charge on Assets – Registration of Charges

As we have seen, secured debentures are secured by a charge on the assets of the company. The concept of 'charge' is very important in the context of debentures and corporate borrowing. A charge gives the debenture holder (or any other secured creditor) a right to the assets of the company in priority over other unsecured creditors.

What is a Charge?

A charge is a security interest created by the company in favour of its creditors over the assets of the company. It gives the creditor a right to the assets in case the company fails to repay the debt. The company retains ownership and possession of the assets but the assets are 'encumbered' (burdened) by the charge. The creditor can sell the charged assets and recover his money if the company defaults.

Types of Charges

(1) Fixed Charge (or Specific Charge): A fixed charge is a charge on a specific, identified asset of the company. For example, a charge on a particular piece of land, a particular building, a particular machinery, or a particular patent. The company cannot deal with the charged asset (sell, transfer, or further mortgage) without the consent of the charge holder. The asset is identified and earmarked for the security of the creditor.

(2) Floating Charge: A floating charge is a charge on the general assets of the company which are not specifically identified. It 'floats' over the assets and does not attach to any specific asset until the charge 'crystallises' (becomes fixed). Until crystallisation, the company is free to deal with the assets in the ordinary course of business – it can buy, sell, replace, or use the assets without the consent of the charge holder. The charge crystallises when: (a) the company goes into liquidation, (b) the company ceases to carry on business, (c) the creditor or receiver intervenes to enforce the charge, or (d) an event specified in the debenture deed occurs.

Case: Illingworth v. Houldsworth (1904)

Lord Macnaghten explained the distinction between a fixed charge and a floating charge. He said: 'A specific (fixed) charge is one that without more fastens on ascertained and definite property or property capable of being ascertained and defined; a floating charge, on the other hand, is ambulatory and shifting in its nature, hovering over and so to speak floating with the property which it is intended to affect until some event occurs or some act is done which causes it to settle and fasten on the subject of the charge within its reach and grasp.'

Table 13.3: Fixed Charge vs. Floating Charge

Point	Fixed Charge	Floating Charge
Attaches to	Specific, identified	General assets – not

	assets	specifically identified
Company's right to deal	Cannot sell or deal without consent	Free to deal in ordinary course of business
Nature	Static – attached from the start	Dynamic – floats until crystallisation
Crystallisation	Not required – already attached	Occurs on liquidation, default, or intervention
Priority	Has priority over floating charge	Ranks after fixed charge
Examples	Charge on land, building, specific machinery	Charge on stock-in-trade, book debts, all assets
Risk to creditor	Lower risk – specific asset secured	Higher risk – assets may change

Registration of Charges – Sections 77 to 87

The Companies Act, 2013 requires that certain charges must be registered with the Registrar of Companies. Registration is mandatory to protect the interests of creditors and the public.

Section Reference: Section 77(1): It shall be the duty of every company creating a charge within or outside India, on its property or assets or any of its undertakings, whether tangible or otherwise, and situated in or outside India, to register the particulars of the charge signed by the company and the charge holder together with the instruments, if any, creating such charge in such form, on payment of such fees and in such manner as may be prescribed, with the Registrar within a period of 30 days of its creation.

Time Limit for Registration

The charge must be registered within 30 days of its creation [Section

77(1)]. However, the Registrar may allow registration within a period of 300 days of creation of the charge on payment of additional fees as prescribed [proviso to Section 77(1)]. If the charge is still not registered within 300 days, the company may apply to the Central Government for extension of time, and the Central Government may allow such registration on such terms and conditions as it may deem fit.

Effect of Non-Registration – Section 77(3)

If a charge is not registered within the prescribed time, the charge becomes void against the liquidator and any other creditor of the company [Section 77(3)]. This means that if the company goes into liquidation and the charge has not been registered, the charge holder loses his priority over other creditors. The charged assets become available to all creditors equally. However, the money secured by the charge becomes immediately payable by the company.

This is a very important consequence. Non-registration does not make the debt void – the company still owes the money. But it makes the security (i.e., the charge) void against other creditors and the liquidator. This means that the creditor loses his preferential right to the charged assets and becomes an ordinary unsecured creditor.

Register of Charges – Section 85

Section 85 requires every company to keep at its registered office a register of charges. The register must contain the following information: (a) a description of the property charged, (b) the amount of the charge, (c) the name of the person entitled to the charge, (d) the date of creation of the charge, and (e) the date of modification or satisfaction of the charge. The register must be open for inspection by any member or creditor of the company free of charge, and by any other person on payment of the prescribed fee.

Modification and Satisfaction of Charges – Section 79 & 82

If the terms of a charge are modified (changed), the company must file the particulars of the modification with the Registrar within 30 days [Section 79]. When a charge is fully satisfied (i.e., the debt is fully repaid), the company must file a notice of satisfaction with the Registrar [Section 82]. On receipt of the notice, the Registrar shall enter a memorandum of satisfaction on the register of charges. If the company fails to file the notice of satisfaction, the charge holder or any other interested person may apply to the Registrar for the entry of satisfaction.

Practical Example: When a company takes a loan from a bank and creates a charge on its assets, the bank's charge is registered with the ROC. When the company repays the loan in full, the company files a notice of satisfaction (Form CHG-4) with the ROC. The ROC then enters a memorandum of satisfaction, and the charge is removed from the register. The assets are then free from encumbrance.

Note: The provisions relating to registration of charges have been substantially simplified under the Companies Act, 2013 as compared to the 1956 Act. Under the 2013 Act, all charges (whether specific or floating) must be registered. The distinction between charges which required registration and those which did not (which existed under the 1956 Act) has been abolished. Now, every charge created by the company must be registered with the ROC within the prescribed time.

PART – IV : MANAGEMENT & ADMINISTRATION

Chapter 14

Directors

A company is an artificial person. It cannot think, act, or make decisions by itself. It must act through human beings. The persons who are entrusted with the management of the company's affairs are called 'Directors.' They are the brain and the hands of the company. They formulate the policies, take the decisions, and manage the day-to-day operations of the company. The Board of Directors is the supreme governing body of a company. The law relating to directors is one of the most important and frequently tested areas of company law. The Companies Act, 2013 contains elaborate provisions regarding the appointment, qualification, disqualification, duties, powers, removal, and resignation of directors in Sections 149 to 172.

14.1 Meaning and Definition of Director

Section Reference: Section 2(34) of the Companies Act, 2013 defines 'director' as: "'Director' means a director appointed to the Board of a company."

This is a very simple and circular definition. It does not explain the nature, role, or position of a director. However, various judicial pronouncements and authors have provided more meaningful descriptions.

According to Palmer: "Directors are persons duly appointed by the company to direct and manage the business of the company. They are the brain of the company which is the body. The company can and does act only through them and therefore they are called directors."

The position of a director is a unique one. He is neither a master nor a servant of the company. He is not an agent in the ordinary sense, nor is he a trustee in the strict legal sense. However, the law has borrowed from all these concepts to define the position of a director. A director occupies a fiduciary position in relation to the company – he must act in good faith and in the best interests of the company.

Legal Position of a Director

(1) Director as Agent: A director is an agent of the company. He acts on behalf of the company and his acts, when done within the scope of his authority, bind the company. The company acts through its directors and the directors represent the company in its dealings with third parties. However, a director is not an agent in the strict sense because he has his own discretion and is not bound to follow the instructions of any individual shareholder.

(2) Director as Trustee: A director holds a position of trust. He is in charge of the company's money, assets, and affairs. He must use the company's property only for the purposes of the company and must not make any secret profit. However, he is not a trustee in the strict legal sense because he does not hold the company's property in trust – the company itself owns its property.

Case: City Equitable Fire Insurance Co. Ltd. (1925)

Justice Romer explained the position of directors and said that directors are not trustees in the strict sense of the term. They do not hold the company's property in trust. But they are in a fiduciary position towards the company and must exercise their powers honestly and in good faith for the benefit of the company as a whole. They must exercise the degree of care and skill which a reasonably prudent businessman would exercise in his own affairs.

(3) Director as Managing Partner: In some ways, the directors of a company are similar to the managing partners of a partnership firm. They control the management and affairs of the company, just as managing partners control the affairs of the firm. However, directors are elected by the shareholders and are accountable to them, unlike partners who may be owners and managers simultaneously.

(4) Director as Officer: Section 2(59) defines 'officer' to include a director. Therefore, a director is an officer of the company and is subject to all the duties and liabilities imposed on officers by the Act.

14.2 Types of Directors (Independent, Woman, etc.)

The Companies Act, 2013 recognises several types of directors. Each type has a different role, different qualifications, and different responsibilities.

(1) Executive Director (Whole-time Director / Managing Director)

An executive director is a director who is involved in the day-to-day management of the company. He may be designated as the Managing Director or Whole-time Director. He is a full-time employee of the company and receives remuneration. The terms 'Managing Director' and 'Whole-time Director' are separately defined and are studied in detail in Chapter 15.

(2) Non-Executive Director

A non-executive director is a director who is not involved in the day-to-day management of the company. He attends Board meetings, participates in decision-making, provides guidance and oversight, but does not have any executive role. He may or may not receive sitting fees for attending Board meetings. Most directors of listed companies are non-executive directors.

(3) Independent Director – Section 149(6)

The concept of independent directors is one of the most important innovations of modern corporate governance. Independent directors are non-executive directors who are independent of the management and the promoters of the company. Their primary role is to bring an independent and unbiased perspective to the Board's deliberations and to protect the interests of minority shareholders and other stakeholders.

Section Reference: Section 149(6) defines an independent director as a director other than a managing director or a whole-time director or a nominee director, who – (a) in the opinion of the Board, is a person of integrity and possesses relevant expertise and experience; (b) is not or was not a promoter of the company or its holding, subsidiary, or associate company, and is not related to promoters or directors; (c) has or had no pecuniary relationship with the company, its holding, subsidiary, or associate company, or their promoters, or directors, during the two immediately preceding financial years or during the current financial year; (d) none of whose relatives has or had any pecuniary relationship or transaction with the company amounting to 2% or more of its gross turnover or total income, or Rs. 50 lakhs, whichever is lower, during the two immediately preceding financial years; (e) who, neither himself nor any of his relatives, holds or has held the position of a key managerial personnel or is or has been employee of the company in any of the three financial years immediately preceding; (f) is not a non-independent director of another company where any non-independent director of the company is an independent director; (g) is not a material supplier, service provider, or customer of the company; (h) is not less than 21 years of age.

Appointment of Independent Directors

(a) Mandatory appointment: Section 149(4) requires every listed public company to have at least one-third of the total number of directors as independent directors. The Central Government may prescribe the minimum number of independent directors for any class of companies.

(b) Tenure: An independent director can hold office for a term of up to 5 consecutive years on the Board of a company [Section 149(10)]. He is eligible for reappointment for a second term of 5 years by passing a special resolution [Section 149(10)]. After two consecutive terms, he is not eligible for reappointment as an independent director unless a cooling-off period of 3 years has elapsed [Section 149(11)].

(c) Code of Conduct: Schedule IV of the Companies Act, 2013 contains the Code for Independent Directors. This code lays down the guidelines for professional conduct, the role and functions, and the duties of independent directors.

(d) Liability: Section 149(12) provides that an independent director shall be held liable only in respect of such acts of omission or commission by a company which had occurred with his knowledge, attributable through Board processes, and with his consent or connivance or where he had not acted diligently.

(4) Woman Director – Section 149(1)

Section 149(1) read with Rule 3 of the Companies (Appointment and Qualification of Directors) Rules, 2014 requires certain classes of companies to have at least one woman director on their Board. The following companies must appoint at least one woman director: (a) every listed company, (b) every public company having a paid-up share capital of Rs. 100 crore or more, and (c) every public company having a turnover of Rs. 300 crore or more.

If a company fails to appoint a woman director within the prescribed time, the company and every officer of the company who is in default shall be liable to a penalty as prescribed by the Act.

(5) Nominee Director

A nominee director is a director nominated by a financial institution, bank, Government, or any other body as per the provisions of any law or agreement. For example, when a company takes a loan from a financial institution, the institution may have the right to nominate a director on the Board of the company to protect its interests. A nominee director represents the interests of the person or institution which has nominated him.

(6) Additional Director – Section 161(1)

The articles of a company may confer on the Board of Directors the power to appoint additional directors. An additional director holds office up to the date of the next annual general meeting or the last date on which the annual general meeting should have been held, whichever is earlier. If the articles do not confer this power, the Board cannot appoint additional directors.

(7) Alternate Director – Section 161(2)

The Board of Directors of a company may appoint an alternate director to act in place of a director who is absent from India for a period of not less than three months. The alternate director vacates office when the original director returns to India. An alternate director must not hold office as an alternate director for more than one director in the same company at the same time.

(8) Small Shareholders' Director – Section 151

A listed company may have one director elected by small shareholders. Small shareholders are those who hold shares of nominal value of not more than Rs. 20,000 or such other sum as may be prescribed. The small shareholders' director is appointed by a postal ballot. He holds office for three years and is not eligible for reappointment. He is treated as an independent director.

(9) Resident Director – Section 149(3)

Every company must have at least one director who has stayed in India for a total period of not less than 182 days during the financial year [Section 149(3)]. This ensures that at least one director is available in India for the purposes of the company.

Type of Director	Key Feature	Section
Executive (MD/WTD)	Full-time; manages daily affairs	2(54), 2(94)
Non-Executive	Not in daily management; provides oversight	General
Independent	Independent of management/promoters; oversight role	149(6)

Woman	At least one in specified companies	149(1), Rule 3
Nominee	Nominated by institution/Government	General
Additional	Appointed by Board between AGMs	161(1)
Alternate	Deputises for absent director (3+ months abroad)	161(2)
Small Shareholders'	Elected by small shareholders in listed companies	151
Resident	Stayed in India ≥ 182 days in a financial year	149(3)

14.3 Appointment of Directors – Section 152

First Directors

The first directors of a company are the persons named in the articles of association. If the articles do not name the first directors, the subscribers to the memorandum who are individuals shall be deemed to be the first directors of the company and shall hold office until the directors are duly appointed at the first general meeting [Section 152(1)].

Subsequent Directors

After the first directors, subsequent directors are appointed by the members at a general meeting. Section 152(2) provides that every director shall be appointed by the company in a general meeting. No person shall be appointed as a director of a company unless he has been allotted a Director Identification Number (DIN) [Section 152(3)].

The appointment of directors at a general meeting is governed by the following rules:

(a) Individual appointment: Section 162 provides that at a general meeting of a company, a motion for the appointment of two or more persons as directors of the company shall not be moved as a single resolution unless a resolution that it shall be so moved has first been agreed to by the meeting without any vote being cast against it. In simple words, each director must be appointed individually by a separate resolution, unless all members agree unanimously to appoint them collectively. This ensures that the shareholders can exercise their choice in respect of each individual director.

(b) Retirement by rotation: Section 152(6) provides that unless the articles provide for the retirement of all directors at every AGM, not less than two-thirds of the total number of directors of a public company shall be persons whose period of office is liable to determination by retirement of directors by rotation. The remaining one-third may be appointed in any manner provided by the articles. Of the directors who are liable to retire by rotation, one-third shall retire at every AGM. The directors who have been longest in office since their last appointment shall retire first. A retiring director is eligible for reappointment.

Illustration: ABC Ltd. has 9 directors. Two-thirds of 9 = 6 directors are subject to retirement by rotation. One-third of these 6 = 2 directors shall retire at each AGM. The 2 directors who have been longest in office since their last appointment shall retire. They are eligible for reappointment if they offer themselves for reappointment.

(c) Consent to act: Every person proposed as a director must file his consent to act as such with the company [Section 152(5)]. The consent must be filed with the Registrar at the time of appointment in the prescribed form (DIR-2).

Number of Directors – Section 149(1)

Type of Company	Minimum Directors	Maximum Directors
Private Company	2	15 (can be increased by special resolution)

Public Company	3	15 (can be increased by special resolution)
One Person Company	1	15 (can be increased by special resolution)

If a company wants to appoint more than 15 directors, it must pass a special resolution [Section 149(1)(b)]. There is no requirement for Government approval for increasing the number of directors beyond 15 (unlike the 1956 Act which required Central Government approval).

Maximum Directorships – Section 165

Section 165 provides that no person shall hold office as a director, including any alternate directorship, in more than 20 companies at the same time. Out of these 20 companies, the maximum number of public companies in which a person can be a director shall not exceed 10. While counting the limit of 20, private companies which are neither a holding nor a subsidiary company of a public company shall not be included. Section 8 companies are also excluded from the count.

14.4 Qualifications and Disqualifications – Section 164

Qualifications

The Companies Act, 2013 does not prescribe any educational qualifications for becoming a director (except for independent directors who must have relevant expertise). However, the following general requirements must be met:

(a) The person must have been allotted a DIN [Section 152(3)]. (b) He must have given his consent to act as a director [Section 152(5)]. (c) He must not be disqualified under Section 164. (d) In the case of a public company, no person can be appointed as a director unless he is recommended by the Board or unless the requisite notice under Section 160 has been given. (e) For independent directors, the conditions of Section 149(6) must be satisfied.

The articles of the company may prescribe additional qualifications for directors, such as a share qualification (i.e., a requirement to hold a minimum number of shares). However, if the articles do not prescribe a share qualification, none is required by the Act.

Disqualifications – Section 164

Section 164 lists the persons who are disqualified from being appointed as a director. A person shall not be eligible for appointment as a director if:

(1) Unsound mind: He is of unsound mind and stands so declared by a competent court [Section 164(1)(a)].

(2) Insolvent: He is an undischarged insolvent [Section 164(1)(b)].

(3) Application for insolvency pending: He has applied to be adjudicated as an insolvent and his application is pending [Section 164(1)(c)].

(4) Convicted of offence: He has been convicted by a court of any offence, whether involving moral turpitude or otherwise, and sentenced to imprisonment for not less than six months and a period of five years has not elapsed from the date of expiry of the sentence [Section 164(1)(d)]. If the offence involves moral turpitude, he is disqualified even after the five-year period, unless the Central Government grants an exemption.

(5) Court order: An order disqualifying him from being appointed as a director has been passed by a court or Tribunal and the order is in force [Section 164(1)(e)].

(6) Non-payment of calls: He has not paid any calls in respect of any shares of the company held by him, whether alone or jointly with others, and six months have elapsed from the last date fixed for the payment of the call [Section 164(1)(f)].

(7) Convicted under Section 188 (related party transactions): He has been convicted of the offence of related party transactions at any time during the last preceding five years [Section 164(1)(g)].

(8) Non-filing of annual returns/financial statements: Section 164(2) provides that no person who is or has been a director of a company which has not filed financial statements or annual returns for any continuous period of three financial years shall be eligible to be reappointed as a director of that company or appointed in any other company for a period of five years from the date on which the said company fails to do so.

(9) No DIN: He has not been allotted a Director Identification Number [Section 152(3)].

Note: The disqualification under Section 164(2) for non-filing of returns is a very important provision because it motivates the directors to ensure that the company complies with its filing obligations. If a company fails to file its annual returns or financial statements for three consecutive years, all its directors are disqualified for five years not only from that company but from all companies.

14.5 Director Identification Number (DIN)

The Director Identification Number (DIN) is a unique identification number allotted by the Central Government to every person who is a director or intends to be appointed as a director of a company. The concept of DIN was introduced to create a comprehensive database of directors and to track the directorships held by each person.

Section Reference: Section 153 provides that every person who has been appointed as a director of a company, or intends to be appointed as such, shall apply for allotment of a Director Identification Number to the Central Government. Section 154 provides that the Central Government shall allot a Director Identification Number to an applicant.

The DIN is a unique 8-digit number which remains the same throughout the life of the director, regardless of how many companies he is a director of. One person can have only one DIN. If a person already has a DIN, he cannot apply for a second DIN [Section 155].

The application for DIN is made through the SPICe+ form (for new company incorporation) or through Form DIR-3 (for existing directors who do not have a DIN). The applicant must provide his personal details, proof of identity (PAN card, passport, voter ID, etc.), and proof of address. The DIN is allotted online and the applicant receives the DIN number electronically.

Every director must file the KYC (Know Your Customer) details with the MCA on an annual basis through Form DIR-3 KYC. If a director fails to file the KYC, his DIN may be deactivated by the Registrar.

Section 157 provides that every company must file with the Registrar the DIN of every director, along with his name, address, and other particulars, at the time of incorporation or when a new director is appointed. If there is any change in the particulars, the company must file the updated information within 30 days.

14.6 Duties of Directors – Section 166

The duties of directors are codified for the first time in the Companies Act, 2013. Section 166 lays down the duties of directors which are based on common law principles and fiduciary obligations that have been developed by the courts over centuries.

Section Reference: Section 166 provides the following duties:

(1) Duty to act in accordance with the articles – Section 166(1): A director of a company shall act in accordance with the articles of the company. The articles define the powers and limitations of the directors. They must act within the scope of their authority as defined by the articles.

(2) Duty to act in good faith – Section 166(2): A director of a company shall act in good faith in order to promote the objects of the company for the benefit of its members as a whole, and in the best interests of the company, its employees, the shareholders, the community, and for the protection of the environment.

(3) Duty to exercise due care, skill, and diligence – Section 166(3):

A director of a company shall exercise his duties with due and reasonable care, skill, and diligence and shall exercise independent judgment. A director is expected to bring to the performance of his duties the degree of care and skill which a reasonably prudent man would exercise in his own business affairs.

Case: Re City Equitable Fire Insurance Co. Ltd. (1925)

Justice Romer laid down three important propositions regarding the standard of care expected from directors: (a) A director need not exhibit a greater degree of skill than may reasonably be expected from a person of his knowledge and experience. (b) A director is not bound to give continuous attention to the affairs of his company. He is not bound to attend all Board meetings. (c) In respect of all duties that may properly be left to some other official, a director may trust that official to perform such duties honestly in the absence of grounds for suspicion. However, these principles must now be read in the light of Section 166(3) which imposes a higher standard of care.

(4) Duty to avoid conflict of interest – Section 166(4): A director of a company shall not involve in a situation in which he may have a direct or indirect interest that conflicts, or possibly may conflict, with the interest of the company. If a director has a personal interest in any matter which comes before the Board, he must disclose his interest and must not participate in the discussion or vote on such matter.

(5) Duty not to achieve undue gain – Section 166(5): A director of a company shall not achieve or attempt to achieve any undue gain or advantage either to himself or to his relatives, partners, or associates and if such director is found guilty of making any undue gain, he shall be liable to pay an amount equal to that gain to the company.

(6) Duty not to assign office – Section 166(6): A director of a company shall not assign his office and any assignment so made shall be void. This means that a director cannot delegate his office to another person. He must personally perform his duties and responsibilities as a director.

(7) Duty to disclose interest – Section 184: Every director who is in any way, whether directly or indirectly, concerned or interested in a contract or arrangement or proposed contract or arrangement entered into or to be entered into by or on behalf of the company, shall disclose the nature of his concern or interest at the meeting of the Board in which the contract or arrangement is discussed and shall not participate in such meeting.

Section 166(7) provides that if a director of the company contravenes the provisions of Section 166, he shall be punishable with a fine which shall not be less than Rs. 1 lakh but which may extend to Rs. 5 lakhs.

14.7 Powers of Directors – Section 179

The Board of Directors is vested with wide powers to manage the affairs of the company. The directors derive their powers from three sources: (a) the Companies Act, 2013, (b) the Memorandum of Association, and (c) the Articles of Association.

Section Reference: Section 179(1): The Board of Directors of a company shall be entitled to exercise all such powers, and to do all such acts and things, as the company is authorised to exercise and do.

However, Section 179(1) also provides that the Board shall not exercise any power or do any act or thing which is directed or required, whether under this Act or by the memorandum or articles, to be exercised or done by the company in a general meeting. In other words, the Board cannot exercise powers which are reserved for the shareholders at a general meeting.

Powers Exercisable Only by the Board – Section 179(3)

Section 179(3) provides that the Board of Directors of a company shall exercise the following powers only by means of resolutions passed at meetings of the Board:

(a) To make calls on shareholders in respect of money unpaid on their shares. (b) To authorise buy-back of securities under Section 68. (c) To issue securities, including debentures, whether in or outside India. (d) To borrow monies. (e) To invest the funds of the company. (f) To grant loans or give guarantee or provide security in respect of loans. (g) To approve financial statements and the Board's report. (h) To diversify the business of the company. (i) To approve amalgamation, merger, or reconstruction. (j) To take over a company or acquire a controlling or substantial stake in another company. (k) Any other matter which may be prescribed.

Note: The powers listed in Section 179(3) cannot be delegated to any committee of the Board or to the managing director or any other officer of the company. These powers must be exercised by the Board of Directors collectively at a duly convened Board meeting. This ensures that important decisions are taken collectively and not by a single individual.

Powers Exercisable with Shareholders' Approval – Section 180

Section 180 provides that the Board of Directors shall exercise the following powers only with the consent of the company by a special resolution:

(a) To sell, lease, or otherwise dispose of the whole or substantially the whole of the undertaking of the company [Section 180(1)(a)].

(b) To borrow money, where the money to be borrowed, together with the money already borrowed by the company, will exceed the aggregate of its paid-up share capital, free reserves, and securities premium account [Section 180(1)(c)].

(c) To remit, or give time for the repayment of, any debt due from a director [Section 180(1)(b)].

(d) To invest the amount of compensation received by the company in respect of the compulsory acquisition of its undertaking [Section 180(1)(d)].

14.8 Removal of Directors – Section 169

The shareholders of a company have the right to remove a director before the expiry of his term of office. This is a very important right because it ensures that the shareholders retain ultimate control over the management of the company.

Section Reference: Section 169(1): A company may, by ordinary resolution, remove a director, not being a director appointed by the Tribunal under Section 242, before the expiry of the period of his office, notwithstanding anything in this Act or in the articles of the company.

Procedure for Removal

(1) Special notice: A special notice of not less than 14 days must be given to the company of the intention to move a resolution for the removal of a director [Section 169(2)].

(2) Copy to the director: The company must send a copy of the proposed resolution to the director concerned forthwith [Section 169(2)].

(3) Right of representation: The director concerned has the right to be heard on the resolution at the general meeting [Section 169(2)]. He may also make a written representation and request the company to send it to the members.

(4) Ordinary resolution: The resolution for removal requires only an ordinary resolution (i.e., a simple majority of the members present and voting). This is significant because the removal of a director can be effected by a simple majority even if the articles require a special resolution or provide that a director cannot be removed.

(5) Vacancy: A vacancy created by the removal of a director may, if he had been appointed by the company in a general meeting, be filled by the appointment of another director in his place at the same meeting [Section 169(4)]. If the vacancy is not filled at that meeting, it may be filled as a casual vacancy in accordance with the provisions of the Act.

Directors Who Cannot Be Removed Under Section 169

The following directors cannot be removed under Section 169: (a) A director appointed by the Tribunal under Section 242 (in cases of oppression and mismanagement) – he can only be removed by the

Tribunal. (b) A director appointed by proportional representation under Section 163 – during his term of office, he cannot be removed by a resolution under Section 169. (c) Under the 1956 Act, nominee directors could not be removed, but the 2013 Act does not specifically exempt them from removal.

Case: Shuttleworth v. Cox Bros. & Co. (Maidenhead) Ltd. (1927)

The articles of a company provided that a director should vacate office if he was requested to resign by all the other directors. Shuttleworth, a director, refused to give proper accounts and the other directors requested him to resign. He challenged the removal. The Court upheld the removal, holding that the alteration of articles and the subsequent request to resign were made bona fide for the benefit of the company as a whole.

14.9 Resignation of Director – Section 168

A director has the right to resign from his office at any time. Unlike removal (which is done by the shareholders), resignation is a voluntary act of the director himself.

Section Reference: Section 168(1): A director may resign from his office by giving a notice in writing to the company. The Board shall, on receipt of such notice, take note of the same and the company shall intimate the Registrar in such manner, within such time and in such form as may be prescribed, and shall also place the fact of such resignation in the report of directors laid in the immediately following general meeting by the company.

The director must also forward a copy of his resignation along with his reasons for the resignation to the Registrar within 30 days of his resignation in Form DIR-11 [Section 168(1)].

Section 168(2) provides that the resignation of a director shall take effect from the date on which the notice is received by the company or the date, if any, specified by the director in the notice, whichever is later.

Section 168(3) provides that if all the directors of the company resign from their offices, or the Board has no directors, the promoter or, in his absence, the Central Government shall appoint the required number of directors.

Note: A director who has resigned is no longer liable for the acts of the company done after his resignation becomes effective. However, he remains liable for any act done by him or with his knowledge during the period when he was a director. Also, if a director resigns to avoid liability in connection with an ongoing investigation or an offence committed during his tenure, the resignation does not absolve him from such liability.

14.10 Board of Directors – Meetings & Quorum

The directors exercise their powers collectively at meetings of the Board. Individual directors have no power to act on behalf of the company unless the Board has specifically delegated such power to them. Therefore, the rules relating to Board meetings are very important.

Frequency of Board Meetings – Section 173(1)

Section 173(1) provides that every company shall hold a minimum number of four Board meetings every year. Further, the gap between two consecutive Board meetings shall not be more than 120 days. This means that the Board must meet at least once every quarter. For One Person Companies, small companies, and dormant companies, the Board need hold only one meeting in each half of the calendar year and the gap between the two meetings shall not be less than 90 days.

Notice of Board Meeting – Section 173(3)

A meeting of the Board of Directors shall be called by giving not less than 7 days' notice in writing to every director at his address registered with the company. The notice may be sent by hand delivery or by post or by electronic means. A meeting of the Board may be called at shorter notice to transact urgent business, subject to the condition that at least one independent director (if any) shall be present at such meeting. If no independent director is present, the decisions taken at such meeting must be circulated to all the directors and shall be final only on ratification thereof by at least one independent director.

Quorum for Board Meetings – Section 174

Section Reference: Section 174(1): The quorum for a meeting of the Board of Directors of a company shall be one-third of its total strength or two directors, whichever is higher. The participation of the directors by video conferencing or by other audio-visual means shall also be counted for the purposes of quorum.

If the number of interested directors (i.e., directors who have a personal interest in a matter and therefore cannot vote) exceeds or is equal to two-thirds of the total strength, the remaining directors (i.e., the non-interested directors) who are not less than two shall be the quorum [Section 174(3)].

Illustration: If a company has 6 directors, one-third of 6 = 2 directors. Since 2 is not higher than 2, the quorum is 2. If the company has 12 directors, one-third of 12 = 4 directors. Since 4 is higher than 2, the quorum is 4.

Board Meetings Through Video Conferencing – Section 173(2)

Section 173(2) allows directors to participate in Board meetings through video conferencing or other audio-visual means. The Central Government may prescribe the matters which shall not be dealt with in a meeting through video conferencing. Rule 4 of the Companies (Meetings of Board and its Powers) Rules, 2014 lists the matters that cannot be dealt with through video conferencing, including the approval of annual financial statements, the Board's report, the prospectus, and matters relating to amalgamation, merger, etc.

Passing of Resolutions by Circulation – Section 175

Section 175 provides that the Board may also pass resolutions by circulation, without holding a physical meeting. A resolution in writing (including by electronic mode) which has been agreed by a majority of the directors who are entitled to vote on the resolution, but which has not been placed before a meeting, shall be as valid and effectual as if it had been passed at a meeting of the Board duly convened and held. However, if at least one-third of the total number of directors for the time being require that the resolution be decided at a meeting, the chairperson shall put the resolution to be decided at a meeting of the Board.

Minutes of Board Meetings – Section 118

Every company must maintain minutes of all Board meetings. The minutes must contain a fair and correct summary of the proceedings at the meeting. The minutes must be entered in the minutes book within 30 days of the conclusion of the meeting. The minutes must be signed and dated by the chairperson of the meeting or by the chairperson of the next meeting. Each page of the minutes must be initialled or signed by the chairperson. The minutes books must be kept at the registered office of the company and must be open for inspection by the directors.

Chapter 15

Key Managerial Personnel (KMP)

In every company, certain officers occupy the highest managerial positions and are entrusted with the responsibility of managing the affairs of the company on a day-to-day basis. These officers are collectively called 'Key Managerial Personnel' (KMP). The concept of KMP was introduced for the first time by the Companies Act, 2013. Under the earlier Companies Act, 1956, the term 'Key Managerial Personnel' was not used, though the positions of Managing Director, Whole-time Director, Manager, and Secretary were individually defined and regulated. The 2013 Act has brought all these positions under one umbrella term – KMP – and has imposed certain obligations on companies regarding their appointment and conduct.

15.0 Definition of Key Managerial Personnel – Section 2(51) & Section 203

Section Reference: Section 2(51) defines 'Key Managerial Personnel' as: "'Key Managerial Personnel', in relation to a company, means – (i) the Chief Executive Officer or the Managing Director or the Manager; (ii) the Company Secretary; (iii) the Whole-time Director; (iv) the Chief Financial Officer; (v) such other officer, not more than one level below the directors who is in whole-time employment, designated as key managerial personnel by the Board; and (vi) such other officer as may be prescribed."

Section 203(1) provides that every company belonging to such class or classes of companies as may be prescribed shall have the following whole-time key managerial personnel: (i) Managing Director, or Chief Executive Officer, or Manager, and in their absence, a Whole-time Director; (ii) Company Secretary; and (iii) Chief Financial Officer.

Rule 8 of the Companies (Appointment and Remuneration of

Managerial Personnel) Rules, 2014 prescribes that every listed company and every other public company having a paid-up share capital of Rs. 10 crore or more shall have all three whole-time KMPs. Companies not meeting this threshold may have part-time KMPs or may not be required to appoint them.

An important provision of Section 203(2) is that a whole-time KMP shall not hold office in more than one company at the same time, except in its subsidiary company. However, this restriction does not apply to a whole-time KMP of a company that is a subsidiary of another company. Also, Section 203(3) provides that no KMP appointment shall be made without the prior approval of the Board.

Note: The concept of KMP is important because these officers are treated as the top management of the company. They are responsible for compliance with the law, they sign important documents on behalf of the company, they are liable for any defaults committed by the company, and they play a key role in the corporate governance of the company.

15.1 Managing Director – Section 2(54)

Definition

Section Reference: Section 2(54) defines 'Managing Director' as: "'Managing Director' means a director who, by virtue of the articles of a company or an agreement with the company or a resolution passed in its general meeting, or by its Board of Directors, is entrusted with substantial powers of management of the affairs of the company and includes a director occupying the position of managing director, by whatever name called."

The key phrase in this definition is 'substantial powers of management.' A person must be entrusted with substantial powers of management to be called a Managing Director. Merely giving a person the designation of 'Managing Director' is not sufficient – he must actually have substantial powers. Conversely, if a person has substantial powers of management, he is a Managing Director even if he is called by a different name.

The definition also makes it clear that a Managing Director must be a director of the company. A person who is not a director cannot be a Managing Director. He derives his powers from the articles, an agreement, a general meeting resolution, or a Board resolution.

Section Reference: The Explanation to Section 2(54) provides that the power to do administrative acts of a routine nature when authorised by the Board, such as the power to affix the common seal, to draw and endorse negotiable instruments, to effect registration of transfer of shares, shall not be deemed to be 'substantial powers of management.'

Features of a Managing Director

(1) Must be a director: A Managing Director is, first and foremost, a director of the company. He is a member of the Board of Directors and attends Board meetings.

(2) Substantial powers of management: He is entrusted with substantial powers to manage the affairs of the company. This means he has the authority to take important business decisions, control the operations, supervise the employees, and represent the company in its dealings with outsiders.

(3) Full-time officer: A Managing Director is a full-time, whole-time officer of the company. He devotes his entire working time and attention to the affairs of the company.

(4) Powers derived from multiple sources: His powers may be given to him by the articles, by an agreement with the company, by a resolution at a general meeting, or by a resolution of the Board.

(5) Subject to Board's control: Although the Managing Director has substantial powers, he is subject to the superintendence, control, and direction of the Board of Directors. The Board can override the Managing Director's decisions and can revoke or modify his powers at any time.

(6) Cannot hold office in more than one company: Section 203(2) provides that a whole-time KMP (including the Managing Director) cannot hold office in more than one company at the same time, except in its subsidiary company.

Appointment of Managing Director

The appointment of a Managing Director is governed by Section 196 read with Schedule V of the Companies Act, 2013. The following provisions apply:

(a) Board resolution: The appointment must be approved by the Board of Directors at a meeting of the Board. The terms and conditions of appointment, including the remuneration, must be specified in the resolution [Section 196(4)].

(b) Shareholders' approval: The appointment must also be approved by the shareholders at a general meeting by passing an ordinary resolution [Section 196(2)]. In certain cases (e.g., where the remuneration exceeds the limits prescribed by the Act), a special resolution is required.

(c) Central Government approval: Under the earlier regime, Central Government approval was required in many cases. Under the 2013 Act, the requirement of Central Government approval has been largely done away with. However, if the company has no profits or inadequate profits and wants to pay remuneration beyond the limits specified in Schedule V, the approval of the Central Government may be required in certain circumstances.

(d) Term of office: Section 196(3) provides that the term of office of a Managing Director shall not exceed five years at a time. He is eligible for reappointment before the expiry of his term, but not earlier than one year before the expiry of his term. In the case of reappointment, the terms of reappointment must be approved by the Board and the shareholders.

(e) Age limit: No company shall appoint or employ any person as Managing Director who is below the age of 21 years or has attained the age of 70 years [Section 196(3)(a)]. However, the appointment of a person who has attained the age of 70 years may be made by passing a special resolution.

(f) Conditions of Schedule V: The appointment and remuneration of the Managing Director must be in accordance with the conditions specified in Schedule V of the Act, which lays down detailed provisions regarding eligibility, terms of appointment, and maximum permissible remuneration.

Practical Example: In Indian corporate practice, the Managing Director is usually the most senior executive of the company. For example, in many family-run businesses, the promoter himself acts as the Managing Director. In professionally managed companies, the MD is often a professional manager appointed by the Board. Companies like Infosys, Wipro, HUL, and TCS have professional Managing Directors who are appointed based on their qualifications and experience.

15.2 Whole-Time Director – Section 2(94)

Definition

Section Reference: Section 2(94) defines 'Whole-time Director' as: "'Whole-time Director' includes a director in the whole-time employment of the company."

A Whole-time Director (WTD) is a director who is in the whole-time (full-time) employment of the company. The key difference between a Whole-time Director and a Managing Director is that the Managing Director must be entrusted with 'substantial powers of management,' while a Whole-time Director need not have such powers. A Whole-time Director is simply a director who works full-time for the company. He may or may not have substantial management powers.

The distinction is important because in a company, there can be only one Managing Director (or one CEO or one Manager) at a time [Section 203(1)], but there can be more than one Whole-time Director. Many companies have an Executive Chairman, a Managing Director, and one or more Whole-time Directors (sometimes called Executive Directors).

Appointment of Whole-Time Director

The provisions for appointment of a Whole-time Director are similar to those for the Managing Director. The appointment must be approved by the Board of Directors and by the shareholders at a general meeting [Section 196(2)]. The term shall not exceed five years [Section 196(3)]. The age limit of 21 to 70 years applies equally [Section 196(3)(a)]. The conditions of Schedule V regarding remuneration also apply.

Distinction Between Managing Director and Whole-Time Director

Point	Managing Director	Whole-Time Director
Definition	Section 2(54)	Section 2(94)
Powers	Must have substantial powers of management	Need not have substantial powers
Employment	Full-time	Full-time
Number	Only one MD (or CEO or Manager) at a time	More than one WTD possible
Designation	Specifically designated as MD	Called by any designation (Executive Director, etc.)
Control	Subject to Board's superintendence	Subject to Board's control
Section 203	Either MD or CEO or Manager is mandatory	WTD only if MD/CEO/Manager not appointed
Role	Chief executive responsible for management	Assists in management; specific functions assigned

15.3 Manager – Section 2(53)

Definition

Section Reference: Section 2(53) defines 'Manager' as: "'Manager' means an individual who, subject to the superintendence, control, and direction of the Board of Directors, has the management of the whole, or substantially the whole, of the affairs of a company, and includes a director or any other person occupying the position of a manager, by whatever name called, whether under a contract of service or not."

The Manager under the Companies Act is different from the common understanding of the word 'manager.' In common parlance, a manager is any person who manages a department or a function. But under the Companies Act, a Manager is a person who manages the whole or substantially the whole of the affairs of the company. He is essentially the chief operating officer of the company.

Differences Between Manager and Managing Director

(a) A Managing Director must be a director; a Manager need not be a director: A Manager is defined as an 'individual' and may or may not be a director of the company. A Managing Director is, by definition, a director. This is the most fundamental difference between the two.

(b) Management of the whole affairs: Both the Managing Director and the Manager have the management of the affairs of the company, but the Manager is specifically defined as having the management of the 'whole, or substantially the whole, of the affairs' of the company. The Managing Director must have 'substantial powers of management.'

(c) Subject to Board's control: Both the Managing Director and the Manager are subject to the superintendence, control, and direction of the Board of Directors. Neither can act independently of the Board.

(d) Exclusivity: A company can have either a Managing Director or a Manager, but not both at the same time [Section 203(1)]. If a company has a Managing Director, it cannot have a Manager, and vice versa. This is because both positions involve the management of the whole affairs of the company, and having both would create confusion and duplication.

The appointment of a Manager is governed by the same provisions as the Managing Director – Section 196 read with Schedule V. The term shall not exceed five years. The age limit is the same. The remuneration limits of Schedule V apply. The appointment must be approved by the Board and the shareholders.

Note: In practice, the position of 'Manager' as defined under the Companies Act is rarely used in modern Indian companies. Most companies prefer to appoint a Managing Director or a Chief Executive Officer. The term 'Manager' was more common in the earlier era when many Indian companies were managed by 'managing agents' (a system which was abolished in 1969). Today, the position of Manager under the Companies Act is found mainly in certain banking companies, insurance companies, and some older companies.

15.4 Company Secretary – Section 2(24)

Definition

Section Reference: Section 2(24) defines 'Company Secretary' or 'Secretary' as: "'Company Secretary' or 'Secretary' means a company secretary as defined in clause (c) of sub-section (1) of Section 2 of the Company Secretaries Act, 1980 who is appointed by a company to perform the functions of a company secretary under this Act."

Under Section 2(1)(c) of the Company Secretaries Act, 1980, a 'company secretary' means a person who is a member of the Institute of Company Secretaries of India (ICSI). In other words, only a person who has qualified as a company secretary and is a member of ICSI can be appointed as the Company Secretary of a company under the Companies Act, 2013.

Role and Functions of Company Secretary

The Company Secretary is a very important officer of the company. He is the compliance officer, the governance expert, and the principal advisor on company law matters. His role has become increasingly important with the growing emphasis on corporate governance and regulatory compliance. The main functions of the Company Secretary include:

(1) Compliance with laws and regulations: The Company Secretary ensures that the company complies with the provisions of the Companies Act, the rules made thereunder, the SEBI regulations, the listing agreement, and all other applicable laws. He is responsible for filing forms, returns, and documents with the Registrar of Companies and other regulatory authorities within the prescribed time.

(2) Board and General Meetings: The Company Secretary is responsible for organising and conducting the Board meetings and general meetings of the company. He prepares the agenda, circulates the notice, records the minutes, and follows up on the implementation of the decisions taken at the meetings.

(3) Maintenance of statutory records: He is responsible for maintaining all the statutory registers and records of the company, including the register of members, register of directors, register of charges, minutes books, and other records required by the Act.

(4) Advisor to the Board: The Company Secretary advises the Board of Directors on matters of corporate governance, compliance, and legal requirements. He ensures that the Board is aware of the legal and regulatory framework within which it must operate.

(5) Communication and liaison: The Company Secretary is the link between the company and its shareholders, the Registrar of Companies, SEBI, stock exchanges, and other regulatory bodies. He handles the correspondence with these agencies and ensures that the company responds to their queries and requirements in a timely manner.

(6) Share and debenture management: He handles the allotment, transfer, and transmission of shares and debentures. He issues share certificates, maintains the demat records, processes requests for transfer and transmission, and ensures compliance with the procedures prescribed by the Act and the SEBI regulations.

(7) Annual return and compliance certificate: Section 92 requires every company to prepare and file an annual return with the Registrar. The Company Secretary signs the annual return. For listed companies and other specified companies, Section 204 requires a secretarial audit to be conducted by a company secretary in practice, who issues a secretarial audit report.

(8) Representation before various forums: Under Section 432, the Company Secretary is authorised to appear before the NCLT and other regulatory bodies on behalf of the company.

Appointment of Company Secretary

Section 203(1) read with Rule 8 mandates the appointment of a whole-time Company Secretary in every listed company and every public company having a paid-up share capital of Rs. 10 crore or more. The appointment is made by the Board of Directors. The person appointed must be a member of the Institute of Company Secretaries of India (ICSI).

If a company which is required to appoint a whole-time Company Secretary fails to do so, the company and every officer who is in default shall be liable to a penalty of Rs. 5 lakhs and in case of continuing failure, with a further penalty of Rs. 1,000 for each day during which such failure continues, subject to a maximum of Rs. 5 lakhs [Section 203(4)].

Practical Example: In India, the Institute of Company Secretaries of India (ICSI) is the premier professional body that regulates the profession of company secretaries. To become a company secretary, a person must pass the ICSI examinations (Foundation, Executive, and Professional) and complete the practical training requirements. After becoming a member of ICSI, a person can be appointed as the Company Secretary of a company or can practice as a Company Secretary in Practice (CS in Practice) and provide secretarial audit and other services.

15.5 Chief Financial Officer

Definition

Section Reference: Section 2(19) defines 'Chief Financial Officer' as: "'Chief Financial Officer' means a person appointed as the Chief Financial Officer of a company."

This is a very simple definition. Unlike the Company Secretary who must be a member of ICSI, the Act does not prescribe any specific professional qualification for the Chief Financial Officer (CFO). However, in practice, most CFOs are qualified Chartered Accountants (members of the Institute of Chartered Accountants of India – ICAI) or have equivalent financial qualifications and experience.

Role and Functions of the CFO

The Chief Financial Officer is the principal financial officer of the company. He is responsible for all financial matters of the company. His key functions include:

(1) Financial management: The CFO manages the financial resources of the company. He is responsible for financial planning, budgeting, forecasting, and analysis. He ensures that the company has adequate funds to meet its obligations and to finance its growth.

(2) Accounts and financial reporting: He oversees the preparation of the financial statements (balance sheet, profit and loss account, cash flow statement) in compliance with the Companies Act, the Indian Accounting Standards (Ind AS), and other applicable accounting standards. He ensures that the financial statements give a true and fair view of the company's financial position.

(3) Internal controls and audit: The CFO is responsible for establishing and maintaining an adequate system of internal financial controls and ensuring the effectiveness of the internal audit function.

(4) Tax planning and compliance: He ensures that the company complies with all tax laws (income tax, GST, customs, etc.) and files its tax returns within the prescribed time. He also undertakes tax planning to minimise the company's tax liability within the framework of the law.

(5) Treasury management: The CFO manages the company's cash, investments, borrowings, and foreign exchange exposure. He ensures that the company's funds are utilised efficiently and that surplus funds are invested prudently.

(6) Risk management: He identifies, assesses, and manages the financial risks facing the company, including credit risk, liquidity risk, market risk, and operational risk.

(7) Compliance and signing: The CFO, along with the CEO/MD and the Company Secretary, signs the financial statements and other important documents of the company. Under Section 134(1), the financial statements must be signed by the chairperson, the CEO (or MD), the CFO, and the Company Secretary (or a director if there is no CS).

Appointment of CFO

Section 203(1) read with Rule 8 mandates the appointment of a whole-time CFO in every listed company and every public company having a paid-up share capital of Rs. 10 crore or more. The appointment is made by the Board of Directors. The CFO cannot hold office in more than one company at the same time, except in its subsidiary [Section 203(2)]. Though the Act does not prescribe specific qualifications, the Board is expected to appoint a person with appropriate financial qualifications and experience.

Table 15.1: Key Managerial Personnel at a Glance

KMP	Section	Must be Director?	Qualification	Key Role
Managing Director	2(54)	Yes	No specific qualification prescribed	Substantial management powers
Whole-	2(94)	Yes	No specific	Full-time

time Director			qualification prescribed	director; assists in management
Manager	2(53)	Not necessary	No specific qualification prescribed	Manages whole affairs; need not be director
Company Secretary	2(24)	Not necessary	Must be member of ICSI	Compliance, governance, secretary functions
Chief Financial Officer	2(19)	Not necessary	No specific qualification (CA in practice)	Financial management, accounts, reporting

15.6 Managerial Remuneration – Section 197

The Companies Act, 2013 contains detailed provisions regarding the remuneration payable to the directors, including the Managing Director, Whole-time Directors, and Manager. These provisions are designed to ensure that the managerial remuneration is reasonable and is in the best interest of the company and its shareholders. The provisions regarding managerial remuneration are primarily contained in Sections 197 to 200 and Schedule V of the Act.

Overall Maximum Managerial Remuneration – Section 197(1)

Section Reference: Section 197(1): The total managerial remuneration payable by a public company, to its directors, including managing director and whole-time director, and its manager in respect of any financial year shall not exceed eleven per cent of the net profits of that company for that financial year computed in the manner laid down in Section 198, except that the remuneration of the directors shall not be deducted from the gross profits.

This means that the total remuneration of all directors (including MD, WTD, and Manager) combined shall not exceed 11% of the net profits of the company. Within this 11%, there are further sub-limits:

Sub-Limits Within the 11% Ceiling

(a) MD / WTD / Manager: If there is only one MD or WTD or Manager, the remuneration shall not exceed 5% of the net profits. If there is more than one such director, the total remuneration to all of them shall not exceed 10% of the net profits [Section 197(1)(i) and (ii)].

(b) Non-executive Directors: The remuneration payable to directors who are neither the MD nor the WTD nor the Manager shall not exceed (i) 1% of the net profits of the company, if there is a MD or WTD or Manager, or (ii) 3% of the net profits, if there is no MD or WTD or Manager [Section 197(1)(ii)].

(c) Combined ceiling: The total remuneration payable to all directors combined (including MD/WTD/Manager and non-executive directors) shall not exceed 11% of the net profits. In certain cases, the limits specified in Section 197(1) can be exceeded only with the approval of the shareholders by a special resolution.

Illustration: ABC Ltd. has net profits of Rs. 10 crore. The overall limit for managerial remuneration is 11% = Rs. 1.10 crore. If the company has one MD, his remuneration cannot exceed 5% = Rs. 50 lakhs. The non-executive directors' total remuneration cannot exceed 1% = Rs. 10 lakhs (since there is an MD). Together, the total must not exceed Rs. 1.10 crore.

Remuneration When Profits Are Inadequate or Nil – Section 197(3) & Schedule V

A very important practical question arises: What happens if the company has no profits or inadequate profits? Can the company still pay remuneration to its directors and managers? The answer is yes, but subject to the conditions and limits prescribed in Schedule V.

Section 197(3) provides that notwithstanding anything contained in sub-sections (1) and (2), if a company has no profits or its profits are inadequate, the company shall not pay to its directors (including the MD and WTD) any remuneration exclusive of any fees payable to directors under Section 197(5), except in accordance with the provisions of Schedule V.

Schedule V of the Companies Act, 2013 is divided into three Parts:

Part I: Conditions for appointment of managerial personnel (disqualifications, restrictions).

Part II: Maximum remuneration payable by a company having no profits or inadequate profits, without Central Government approval. The limits depend on the effective capital of the company. For example, where the effective capital is negative or less than Rs. 5 crore, the yearly remuneration shall not exceed Rs. 60 lakhs. Where the effective capital is Rs. 5 crore or more but less than Rs. 100 crore, it shall not exceed Rs. 84 lakhs, and so on.

Part III: Provides that a company which has defaulted in payment of dues to any bank or public financial institution or non-convertible debenture holders or any other secured creditor shall not pay managerial remuneration until the default is rectified.

The company may pay remuneration in excess of the limits specified in Schedule V, Part II, only with the approval of the shareholders by a special resolution [Section 197(3)]. The company shall not draw or utilise remuneration from more than one company at a time, unless specifically permitted.

Components of Remuneration – What is Included?

Section 2(78) defines 'remuneration' as any money or its equivalent given or passed to any person for services rendered by him and includes perquisites as defined under the Income Tax Act, 1961. For the purpose of Section 197, 'remuneration' includes the following:

(a) Salary (basic pay). (b) Dearness allowance. (c) Perquisites (such as free accommodation, car, club membership, etc.) valued as per Income

Tax Rules. (d) Commission, whether as a percentage of profits or otherwise. (e) Any contribution to provident fund, superannuation fund, or pension scheme, to the extent it is not part of the employee's statutory obligation. (f) Any other allowances or benefits in kind.

Sitting Fees – Section 197(5)

Section 197(5) provides that a director may receive remuneration by way of a fee for attending meetings of the Board or a committee thereof, or for any other purpose as may be decided by the Board. The sitting fee shall not exceed the amount as may be prescribed. Rule 4 of the Companies (Appointment and Remuneration of Managerial Personnel) Rules, 2014 prescribes that the maximum sitting fee for attending a meeting of the Board or any committee thereof shall be Rs. 1,00,000 per meeting. For independent directors and women directors, the sitting fee shall not be less than the sitting fee payable to other directors.

Sitting fees are not included in the computation of the 11% ceiling of managerial remuneration. This means that directors can receive sitting fees over and above the 11% limit.

Computation of Net Profits – Section 198

Section 198 prescribes the manner in which the net profits of a company shall be computed for the purpose of determining the limits of managerial remuneration. The net profits shall be computed in the following manner:

(a) The net profits shall be calculated in accordance with the provisions of Section 198 and not in accordance with the accounting standards. (b) The following items shall be deducted from the gross profits: all the usual working charges, director's remuneration, bonus or commission to employees, insurance premium, repairs and maintenance, provision for bad and doubtful debts, other usual and necessary provisions, depreciation, interest on loans, and all other outgoings (except those specifically excluded). (c) The following items shall not be deducted: income tax paid or payable, any compensation, damages, or payments by way of penalty under any law, loss of a capital nature, any change in carrying amount of an asset or liability recognised in equity reserves. (d) Credit shall be given for certain items including bounties and subsidies from Government, rent from property, etc.

Penalties for Excess Remuneration – Section 197(9)

If any director draws or receives any remuneration in excess of the limit prescribed by Section 197 or without the approval of the shareholders, he shall refund such sums to the company within two years or such lesser period as may be allowed by the company. If the excess remuneration is not refunded, the company may recover it as a debt [Section 197(9)]. The director shall also hold the remuneration in trust for the company until it is refunded.

Note: The provisions of Section 197 regarding the limit of 11% of net profits apply only to public companies. Private companies are exempt from these limits. However, the remuneration in a private company must still be reasonable and must be approved by the Board of Directors. Also, private companies are exempt from the applicability of Schedule V regarding the payment of managerial remuneration in case of no profits or inadequate profits, unless they are a subsidiary of a public company.

Nomination and Remuneration Committee – Section 178

Section 178 requires certain companies to constitute a Nomination and Remuneration Committee (NRC) of the Board. The NRC must consist of three or more non-executive directors, of whom not less than one-half shall be independent directors. The chairperson of the company may be a member of the NRC but shall not chair such committee.

The functions of the NRC include: (a) To identify persons who are qualified to become directors and who may be appointed in senior management. (b) To recommend to the Board the appointment and removal of directors. (c) To specify the criteria for determining qualifications, positive attributes, and independence of a director. (d) To formulate a policy on Board diversity. (e) To recommend to the Board a policy relating to the remuneration of directors, key managerial personnel, and other employees. (f) To carry out the evaluation of every director's performance.

The requirement of constituting an NRC applies to every listed public company and every public company having a paid-up share capital of Rs. 10 crore or more, or a turnover of Rs. 100 crore or more, or an aggregate outstanding loans, debentures, and deposits exceeding Rs. 50 crore.

Table 15.2: Maximum Managerial Remuneration Limits (Public Companies)

Category	Maximum Remuneration	Section
Overall ceiling (all directors combined)	11% of net profits	197(1)
One MD / WTD / Manager	5% of net profits	197(1)(i)
More than one MD / WTD / Manager	10% of net profits (total)	197(1)(ii)
Non-executive directors (if MD/WTD/Manager exists)	1% of net profits	197(1)(ii)
Non-executive directors (if no MD/WTD/Manager)	3% of net profits	197(1)(ii)
Sitting fee per meeting (maximum)	Rs. 1,00,000 per meeting	197(5), Rule 4
No profit / inadequate profit	As per Schedule V limits	197(3)

Chapter 16

Company Meetings

A company is an artificial person and it makes decisions through its members and directors at meetings. Meetings are the lifeblood of the democratic functioning of a company. It is at the meetings that the shareholders exercise their ultimate control over the management of the company. The directors are accountable to the shareholders and it is at the general meetings that this accountability is enforced. The law of meetings is, therefore, a very important part of company law. The Companies Act, 2013 contains elaborate provisions regarding the convening, conduct, and recording of meetings in Sections 96 to 122.

16.1 Types of General Meetings

Meetings of a company can be broadly classified into three categories:

(A) Meetings of Shareholders (General Meetings): These are meetings of the members (shareholders) of the company. There are two types of general meetings: (i) Annual General Meeting (AGM), and (ii) Extraordinary General Meeting (EGM). The term 'general meeting' means a meeting of the members of the company.

(B) Meetings of the Board of Directors (Board Meetings): These are meetings of the directors of the company. The provisions relating to Board meetings have already been discussed in Section 14.10 of Chapter 14.

(C) Meetings of Creditors and Debenture Holders: These are meetings of the creditors or debenture holders of the company. Such meetings are usually held in connection with schemes of arrangement, compromise, or winding up.

In this chapter, we shall focus primarily on general meetings – AGM and EGM.

Note: Under the Companies Act, 1956, there was a provision for a

'Statutory Meeting' which was the first meeting of the shareholders of a public company held within a specified period after the commencement of business. This provision has been abolished under the Companies Act, 2013. There is no requirement for a statutory meeting under the 2013 Act.

16.2 Annual General Meeting – Section 96

The Annual General Meeting (AGM) is the most important meeting of a company. It is the primary forum where the shareholders exercise their right to oversee the management of the company. It is at the AGM that the shareholders approve the financial statements, declare dividends, appoint auditors, appoint or reappoint directors, and transact other ordinary business.

Mandatory Requirement – Section 96(1)

Section Reference: Section 96(1): Every company other than a One Person Company shall in each year hold, in addition to any other meetings, a general meeting as its annual general meeting and shall specify the meeting as such in the notices calling it.

Thus, every company (other than OPC) must hold an AGM every year. The OPC is exempt from holding an AGM because it has only one member and the decisions can be recorded in the minutes book without a formal meeting.

Time Limit for Holding AGM

(a) First AGM: The first AGM must be held within 9 months from the date of closing of the first financial year of the company [Section 96(1)]. For example, if a company is incorporated on 1st May, 2024, its first financial year will end on 31st March, 2025. The first AGM must be held by 31st December, 2025 (i.e., within 9 months from 31st March, 2025). If the first AGM is held within this period, it is not necessary to hold any AGM in the year of incorporation.

(b) Subsequent AGMs: Subsequent AGMs must be held within 6 months from the date of closing of the financial year [Section 96(1)]. Since the financial year ends on 31st March, the AGM must be held by 30th September of that year.

(c) Gap between two AGMs: The gap between two AGMs must not exceed 15 months [Section 96(1)]. However, this gap can be extended to 18 months for the first AGM.

(d) Extension of time: The Registrar may, for any special reason, extend the time for holding any AGM (other than the first AGM) by a period not exceeding 3 months [Section 96(1), proviso].

Illustration: ABC Ltd.'s financial year ends on 31st March, 2025. Its last AGM was held on 25th September, 2024. The next AGM must be held by: (i) 30th September, 2025 (within 6 months from 31st March, 2025), AND (ii) 25th December, 2025 (within 15 months from the last AGM on 25th September, 2024). The company must hold its AGM by 30th September, 2025 (whichever date is earlier).

Venue of AGM – Section 96(2)

The AGM must be held at the registered office of the company or at some other place within the city, town, or village in which the registered office is situated [Section 96(2)]. The Central Government may exempt any company from this provision, subject to such conditions as it may impose. The AGM cannot be held on a national holiday. It must be held during business hours (between 9 a.m. and 6 p.m.) on any day that is not a national holiday.

Section 96(2) also provides that AGMs of unlisted companies may be held at any place in India if consent is given in writing or by electronic mode by all the members in advance.

Practical Point: The Annual General Meetings of large listed companies like Reliance Industries, TCS, and Infosys are attended by thousands of shareholders. In recent years, many companies have started conducting AGMs through video conferencing and other audio-visual means, especially after the COVID-19 pandemic. The MCA has issued special circulars allowing companies to conduct AGMs through electronic mode.

Business at the AGM – Ordinary and Special Business

The business transacted at an AGM is classified as 'ordinary business' and 'special business.'

Ordinary Business [Section 102(2)]: The following items are considered ordinary business at the AGM: (a) consideration of the financial statements and the reports of the Board of Directors and the auditors, (b) declaration of dividend, (c) appointment of directors in place of those retiring by rotation, and (d) appointment of auditors and fixing their remuneration. All other business transacted at the AGM is special business.

Special Business: Any business other than the four items of ordinary business listed above is special business. For example, alteration of the articles, increase in authorised capital, issue of bonus shares, appointment of a managing director, approval of related party transactions, etc. are all special business. In the case of special business, the explanatory statement under Section 102(1) must be annexed to the notice of the meeting, stating all material facts concerning each item of special business.

Consequences of Not Holding AGM

If a company fails to hold an AGM in accordance with Section 96, the company and every officer of the company who is in default shall be punishable with a fine which may extend to Rs. 1 lakh and in the case of a continuing default, with a further fine which may extend to Rs. 5,000 for every day during which the default continues [Section 99].

If a company fails to hold its AGM, any member of the company may apply to the Tribunal (NCLT), and the Tribunal may call, or direct the calling of, a general meeting of the company and give such ancillary or consequential directions as the Tribunal thinks expedient [Section 97].

16.3 Extraordinary General Meeting – Section 100

An Extraordinary General Meeting (EGM) is any general meeting of the company other than the AGM. It is called to transact urgent or special business which cannot wait until the next AGM. An EGM may be called at any time during the year, as and when the need arises.

Who Can Call an EGM?

(1) Board of Directors: The Board of Directors may, whenever it deems fit, call an EGM of the company [Section 100(1)]. This is the most common method of calling an EGM. The Board passes a resolution to call the EGM and directs the company secretary to issue notices to the members.

(2) Board on Requisition of Members – Section 100(2): The Board of Directors must call an EGM on the requisition of the members. The requisition must be signed by members holding not less than one-tenth of the paid-up share capital of the company carrying the right of voting on the matter (in the case of a company having a share capital) or members having not less than one-tenth of the total voting power (in the case of a company not having a share capital). The requisition must state the matters to be considered at the meeting and must be deposited at the registered office of the company.

On receipt of a valid requisition, the Board must, within 21 days from the date of receipt of the requisition, proceed to call an EGM. The meeting must be held within 45 days from the date of receipt of the requisition [Section 100(3)].

(3) Requisitionists themselves – Section 100(4): If the Board fails to call the EGM within the prescribed time (21 days for calling and 45 days for holding), the requisitionists themselves may call and hold the meeting within 3 months from thc date of the requisition. The meeting so called and held shall be deemed to be a meeting called by the Board. The company must reimburse the requisitionists for any reasonable expenses incurred by them in calling the meeting.

(4) Tribunal – Section 98: If for any reason it is impracticable to call or conduct a meeting in the manner prescribed by the Act, the Tribunal may, either suo motu or on the application of any director or member who would be entitled to vote at the meeting, order a meeting to be called, held, and conducted in such manner as the Tribunal thinks fit.

Case: LIC of India v. Escorts Ltd. (1986)

The Supreme Court held that the right to requisition a general meeting is a statutory right given to the minority shareholders. The Board cannot refuse to call the meeting merely because it disagrees with the purpose for which the meeting is sought. If the requisition is valid in form and content, the Board is bound to call the meeting within the prescribed time.

16.4 Notice of Meeting – Section 101

A valid meeting can be held only if proper notice has been given to all the persons who are entitled to receive it. The purpose of the notice is to inform the members about the time, date, place, and business to be transacted at the meeting, so that they can decide whether to attend the meeting and how to vote on the resolutions.

Requirements of a Valid Notice

(1) Clear 21 days' notice: Section 101(1) provides that a general meeting of a company may be called by giving not less than clear 21 days' notice either in writing or through electronic mode. The word 'clear' means that the day of sending the notice and the day of the meeting are excluded from the count. For example, if the meeting is on 30th September, the notice must be sent on or before 8th September (21 clear days).

(2) Shorter notice: A meeting may be called at shorter notice (i.e., less than 21 days) if consent is given to such shorter notice: (a) in the case of an AGM, by not less than 95% of the members entitled to vote; (b) in the case of an EGM, by members of the company holding not less than 95% of the paid-up share capital or having not less than 95% of the total voting power [Section 101(1), proviso].

(3) Contents of the notice: The notice must specify the place, the date, the day, and the hour of the meeting. It must also contain a statement of the business to be transacted at the meeting [Section 101(1)]. For special business, an explanatory statement must be annexed to the notice under Section 102.

(4) To whom notice must be given: Section 101(3) provides that notice of every meeting shall be given to: (a) every member of the company, legal representative of any deceased member, or assignee of an insolvent member; (b) the auditor or auditors of the company; and (c) every director of the company. If notice is not given to any person who is entitled to receive it, the meeting and the proceedings thereat may be invalid unless the omission is accidental.

(5) Mode of serving notice: The notice may be given to any member by sending it to him by post or by electronic mode or by any other mode as may be prescribed [Section 20]. In the case of a listed company, the notice must also be published on the website of the company and on the website of the stock exchange where the shares are listed.

Explanatory Statement for Special Business – Section 102

Section 102(1) provides that where any items of special business are to be transacted at a general meeting, the notice of the meeting must be accompanied by a statement setting forth all material facts concerning each item of special business. The statement must set out the nature of the concern or interest of every director and manager in the item, and any other information and facts which would enable the members to understand the meaning, scope, and implications of the item and to take a decision thereon.

If the special business involves any contract or arrangement in which any director has a personal interest, the statement must give full particulars of such interest. The statement must also give the memorandum of the contract or arrangement, if any.

The failure to annex the explanatory statement or the inclusion of an inadequate statement may render the resolution passed at the meeting invalid. The members have the right to receive full and complete information about every item of special business to enable them to take an informed decision.

Case: Baillie v. Oriental Telephone and Electric Co. (1915)

The Court held that the notice of a general meeting must be sufficient to enable the members to understand the nature and implications of the business to be transacted. A notice which is vague, misleading, or inadequate may render the proceedings of the meeting invalid. The members must be given fair and clear notice so that they can exercise their rights in an informed manner.

16.5 Quorum – Section 103

A quorum is the minimum number of members who must be present at a meeting to make the proceedings of the meeting valid. If the quorum is not present, the meeting cannot be held and any business transacted at such a meeting would be invalid.

Quorum for General Meetings – Section 103(1)

Section Reference: Section 103(1): Unless the articles of the company provide for a larger number – (a) in case of a public company – (i) five members personally present if the number of members as on the date of meeting is not more than one thousand; (ii) fifteen members personally present if the number of members as on the date of meeting is more than one thousand but up to five thousand; (iii) thirty members personally present if the number of members as on the date of the meeting exceeds five thousand; (b) in the case of a private company, two members personally present, shall be the quorum for a meeting of the company.

Type of Company	Number of Members	Quorum
Public Company	Up to 1,000	5 members
Public Company	1,001 to 5,000	15 members
Public Company	More than 5,000	30 members
Private Company	Any number	2 members

The articles may prescribe a larger quorum, but they cannot prescribe a smaller quorum than the statutory minimum prescribed above.

If Quorum is Not Present – Section 103(2)

Section 103(2) provides that if the quorum is not present within half an hour from the time appointed for holding the meeting:

(a) The meeting shall stand adjourned to the same day in the next week, at the same time and place, or to such other date and such other time and place as the Board may determine.

(b) If at the adjourned meeting also, a quorum is not present within half an hour from the time appointed for holding the meeting, the members present shall be the quorum [Section 103(2)(b)].

However, if the meeting was called on the requisition of members under Section 100, and the quorum is not present, the meeting shall stand cancelled [Section 103(2)(a), proviso].

Note: In the case of a One Person Company (OPC), the sole member present in person or through a proxy (or through video conferencing or other audio-visual means) shall constitute the quorum. Since an OPC has only one member, his presence alone is sufficient.

16.6 Proxies – Section 105

A proxy is a person who is authorised by a member to attend and vote at a general meeting on behalf of the member. Since a member may not always be able to attend the meeting in person, the law allows him to appoint a representative (proxy) to attend and vote on his behalf. The instrument by which a member appoints his proxy is also called a 'proxy.'

Provisions Regarding Proxies

(1) Right to appoint proxy: Section 105(1) provides that any member of a company who is entitled to attend and vote at a meeting of the company shall be entitled to appoint another person as a proxy to attend and vote at the meeting on his behalf. A proxy need not be a member of the company. The right to appoint a proxy cannot be taken away by the articles.

(2) Proxy cannot speak: A proxy cannot speak at the meeting unless the articles otherwise provide [Section 105(1), proviso (b)]. He can only attend and vote. This is an important limitation – a proxy has no right to participate in the discussion unless the articles specifically grant this right.

(3) Proxy must be in writing: The instrument appointing a proxy must be in writing and signed by the member or by his attorney duly authorised in writing [Section 105(4)]. It must be deposited at the registered office of the company not less than 48 hours before the meeting [Section 105(6)].

(4) One proxy for one member: A member can appoint only one proxy for a meeting. However, a person can be appointed as a proxy by more than one member.

(5) Limitation on holding proxies: Section 105(2) provides that no person shall act as a proxy for more than 50 members holding in the aggregate not more than 10% of the total share capital of the company carrying voting rights. However, a member holding more than 10% of the total share capital may appoint a single person as his proxy, and such person shall not act as a proxy for any other person or shareholder.

(6) Voting on poll: A proxy can vote on a poll but cannot vote on a show of hands [Section 107, proviso]. This is because on a show of hands, each member present in person has one vote (irrespective of the number of shares held), and the proxy is not counted as a member present in person.

(7) Notice must mention right to appoint proxy: Every notice calling a meeting must contain a statement that a member entitled to attend and vote is entitled to appoint a proxy and that a proxy need not be a member [Section 105(1)].

(8) Revocation of proxy: A proxy may be revoked by the member at any time before the proxy actually votes at the meeting. If the member himself attends the meeting, the proxy is automatically revoked.

Illustration: Mr. A holds 500 shares in XYZ Ltd. and is unable to attend the AGM. He fills up the proxy form, appoints his friend B as his proxy, signs it, and deposits it with the company 48 hours before the meeting. B attends the AGM on behalf of A. B can vote on the resolutions on behalf of A during a poll, but B cannot speak at the meeting (unless the articles allow it). If A changes his mind and himself attends the meeting, B's proxy is automatically cancelled.

16.7 Resolutions – Ordinary and Special

The decisions of the shareholders at general meetings are expressed in the form of 'resolutions.' A resolution is a formal expression of the will of the members on any matter placed before them. The Companies Act, 2013 recognises two types of resolutions – Ordinary Resolution and Special Resolution.

(1) Ordinary Resolution – Section 114(1)

Section Reference: Section 114(1): A resolution shall be an ordinary resolution if the notice required under this Act has been duly given and the resolution has been passed by the requisite majority. The requisite majority is a majority of the votes cast by the members who, being entitled to vote, vote in person or by proxy or by postal ballot.

In simple words, an ordinary resolution is passed by a simple majority – i.e., more than 50% of the votes cast by the members present and voting (in person or by proxy). For example, if 100 members are present and voting at a meeting, and 51 vote in favour and 49 vote against, the resolution is passed.

Ordinary resolutions are required for most routine matters, including: (a) adoption of financial statements, (b) declaration of dividend, (c) appointment of directors retiring by rotation, (d) appointment of auditors, (e) increase of authorised capital (if authorised by articles), (f) issue of bonus shares, and (g) appointment of Managing Director.

(2) Special Resolution – Section 114(2)

Section Reference: Section 114(2): A resolution shall be a special resolution when – (a) the intention to propose the resolution as a special resolution has been duly specified in the notice calling the general meeting or other intimation given to the members of the resolution; (b) the notice required under this Act has been duly given; and (c) the votes cast in favour of the resolution, whether on a show of hands, or electronically or on a poll, as the case may be, by members who, being entitled so to do, vote in person or by proxy or by postal ballot, are required to be not less than three times the number of the votes, if any, cast against the resolution by members so entitled and voting.

In simple words, a special resolution requires: (a) the notice must specify that the resolution is to be proposed as a special resolution, (b) proper notice must be given, and (c) the resolution must be passed by a majority of not less than three-fourths (75%) of the votes cast. For example, if 100 votes are cast, at least 75 must be in favour and not more than 25 against.

Special resolutions are required for important and fundamental matters, including: (a) alteration of the memorandum (objects, name, registered office), (b) alteration of the articles, (c) change of name, (d) shifting of registered office from one State to another, (e) reduction of share capital, (f) buy-back of shares (above 10%), (g) issue of sweat equity shares, (h) conversion of public company into private, (i) voluntary winding up, and many other matters specified in the Act.

Table 16.1: Ordinary Resolution vs. Special Resolution

Point	Ordinary Resolution	Special Resolution
Majority Required	Simple majority (> 50% of votes cast)	Three-fourths majority (≥ 75% of votes cast)
Notice	Ordinary notice (21 days)	Must specify it is a special resolution in the notice
Section	Section 114(1)	Section 114(2)
Used for	Routine matters (accounts, dividend, auditors)	Fundamental matters (alter MOA/AOA, name change, etc.)
Filing with ROC	Some need filing; not all	Must be filed with ROC within 30 days (Section 117)
Examples	Adoption of accounts, dividend, director reappointment	Alter articles, buy-back, sweat equity, change name

(3) Resolution Requiring Special Notice – Section 115

Certain resolutions require 'special notice' from the member who proposes them. Special notice must be given not less than 14 days before the meeting to the company. On receipt of such notice, the company must give its members notice of the resolution at the same time and in the same manner as it gives notice of the meeting [Section 115(2)]. The matters for which special notice is required include: (a) removal of a director under Section 169, (b) removal of an auditor under Section 140(4)(i), and (c) appointment of an auditor other than the retiring auditor.

Voting Methods

Voting at a general meeting can be done in the following ways:

(a) Show of hands: This is the default method of voting. Each member present in person has one vote, irrespective of the number of shares held. The chairperson counts the number of members raising their hands in favour and against. Proxies cannot vote on a show of hands.

(b) Poll: A poll may be demanded by any member or members holding at least one-tenth of the total voting power or holding shares on which Rs. 5 lakh or more has been paid up [Section 109]. On a poll, voting rights are proportionate to the shareholding – each member has one vote for each share held. Proxies can vote on a poll. A poll gives a more accurate result than a show of hands because it reflects the actual shareholding.

(c) Electronic voting (e-voting): Section 108 provides that the Central Government may prescribe the class or classes of companies and the resolutions in respect of which voting may be done through electronic means. Every listed company and every company having 1,000 or more shareholders must provide the facility of e-voting for every resolution. E-voting allows shareholders to vote remotely through a secure electronic platform without attending the meeting in person.

16.8 Postal Ballot – Section 110

Postal ballot is a mechanism by which the shareholders can vote on certain resolutions without attending the meeting in person. Instead of voting at the meeting, the members vote by sending their votes in a prescribed form to the company by post or through electronic means. This is particularly useful for widely-held companies where it is impractical for all shareholders to attend a single meeting.

Provisions of Section 110

(1) Mandatory postal ballot: Section 110(1) provides that a company shall transact certain prescribed items of business only by means of postal ballot instead of transacting such business at a general meeting. Rule 22 of the Companies (Management and Administration) Rules, 2014 prescribes the items which must be passed through postal ballot, including: (a) alteration of the objects clause of the memorandum, (b) alteration of the articles relating to the appointment of directors, (c) issue of shares with differential voting rights, (d) change of registered office from one State to another, (e) sale of the whole or substantially the whole of the company's undertaking, (f) variation in the rights attached to a class of shares or debentures, (g) buy-back of company's own shares, and (h) appointment of a person other than a retiring auditor.

(2) Optional postal ballot: Any item of business, other than ordinary business and any business in respect of which directors or auditors have a right to be heard at the meeting, may be transacted by postal ballot [Section 110(1)].

(3) Procedure: The company shall send a notice to all the shareholders, along with a draft resolution and the reasons thereof, by registered post or speed post or through electronic means. The notice must provide a postal ballot form and a self-addressed business reply envelope. The members shall send their assent or dissent in writing on the postal ballot form within 30 days from the date of issue of the notice. Alternatively, members may send their vote through electronic means (e-voting).

(4) Scrutiniser: The Board shall appoint one scrutiniser, who is not in the employment of the company and who is a Chartered Accountant, Cost Accountant, or Company Secretary in practice, or an advocate, to scrutinise the postal ballot forms in a fair and transparent manner. The scrutiniser shall submit his report to the chairperson within 30 days from the last date of receipt of postal ballot.

(5) Result: The result of the postal ballot shall be declared by the chairperson or any person authorised by him. The date of declaration of the result shall be deemed to be the date of passing of the resolution. The resolution shall be deemed to have been passed at a general meeting.

(6) No postal ballot for OPC and private company: A company having up to 200 members is not required to transact any business through postal ballot. However, it may voluntarily opt for postal ballot if it so desires.

Note: The postal ballot mechanism has become increasingly important in the era of e-voting. Most listed companies now conduct postal ballots through electronic means (e-voting) rather than physical postal ballots. SEBI has also mandated e-voting for all listed companies for all resolutions. The e-voting platform is usually provided by agencies like NSDL (National Securities Depository Limited) or CDSL (Central Depository Services India Limited).

16.9 Minutes of Meetings – Section 118

Minutes are the official record of the proceedings of the meetings. They serve as documentary evidence of what was discussed and decided at the meeting. The maintenance of proper minutes is a statutory obligation imposed on every company.

Obligation to Maintain Minutes – Section 118(1)

Section Reference: Section 118(1): Every company shall cause minutes of the proceedings of every general meeting, of every meeting of its Board of Directors, and of every meeting of every committee of the Board, to be prepared and signed in such manner as may be prescribed, and kept within 30 days of the conclusion of every such meeting.

Rules Regarding Minutes

(1) Contents: The minutes must contain a fair and correct summary of the proceedings at the meeting. They must record: (a) the appointment of the chairperson of the meeting, (b) the number of members present (quorum), (c) the business transacted at the meeting, (d) the resolutions passed with the voting results, (e) the names of directors dissenting from any resolution (if any), and (f) any other material facts. The minutes must also note the time at which the meeting commenced and concluded.

(2) Signing: The minutes of each meeting must be signed and dated by the chairperson of the meeting or the chairperson of the next succeeding meeting [Section 118(2)]. Each page of the minutes must be initialled or signed by the chairperson.

(3) Time limit: The minutes must be entered in the minutes book within 30 days of the conclusion of the meeting [Section 118(1)].

(4) Minutes book: The minutes must be kept in a separate minutes book maintained for the purpose. The pages of the minutes book must be consecutively numbered. The minutes book must be kept at the registered office of the company.

(5) Evidentiary value: Section 118(8) provides that minutes of the proceedings of every general meeting kept in accordance with the provisions of this section shall be evidence of the proceedings recorded therein. Section 118(9) provides that where minutes have been kept in accordance with the provisions of this section, until the contrary is proved, the meeting shall be deemed to have been duly called, held, and conducted, and all proceedings thereat shall be deemed to have been duly taken.

(6) Inspection of minutes of general meeting: Section 119 provides that the minutes of general meetings must be open for inspection by any member of the company during business hours, without charge. Any member is entitled to be furnished with a copy of any minutes, within 7 working days of the request, on payment of the prescribed fee. However, the minutes of Board meetings are not available for inspection by the members – only by the directors.

(7) Preservation: The minutes books must be preserved permanently. They cannot be destroyed. The Secretary of the company is usually responsible for maintaining the minutes books.

(8) Penalty: If a company fails to maintain minutes as required, the company and every officer who is in default shall be punishable with a fine of up to Rs. 1 lakh and in the case of continuing default, with a further fine of up to Rs. 5,000 for every day during which the default continues.

Case: Kerr v. John Motram Ltd. (1940)

The Court held that the minutes, when properly signed, are prima facie evidence of the proceedings of the meeting. However, they are not conclusive evidence. If it can be proved that the minutes do not correctly record the proceedings, the court may go behind the minutes and determine the true facts. But until the contrary is proved, the minutes are accepted as a true record of what happened at the meeting.

Table 16.2: Summary of Key Provisions on Company Meetings

Provision	AGM	EGM
Section	96	100
Frequency	Once every year	As and when needed
Notice Period	21 clear days	21 clear days
Who Calls?	Board of Directors	Board / Requisitionists / Tribunal
Shorter Notice	95% members' consent	95% voting power consent
Venue	City/town of registered office	Any place as decided
Business	Ordinary + Special	Only Special
Quorum (Public)	5 / 15 / 30 based on members	5 / 15 / 30 based on members
Quorum (Private)	2 members	2 members
Adjourned meeting quorum	Members present = quorum	Requisition meeting: stands cancelled

Penalty for default	Up to Rs. 1 lakh + Rs. 5,000/day	No specific penalty; members can approach Tribunal

Chapter 17

Accounts, Audit & Auditors

The keeping of proper books of accounts, the preparation of financial statements, and the independent audit of those statements are the cornerstones of corporate financial discipline. The shareholders, creditors, employees, Government, and the general public all depend on the financial statements of the company to understand its financial health and performance. If the accounts are not properly maintained or if the financial statements are misleading, the very foundation of trust in the corporate system is shaken. It is for this reason that the Companies Act, 2013 contains very detailed and stringent provisions regarding the maintenance of books of accounts, the preparation and presentation of financial statements, and the appointment, powers, and duties of auditors. These provisions are primarily contained in Sections 128 to 148 of the Act.

17.1 Books of Accounts – Section 128

Section Reference: Section 128(1): Every company shall prepare and keep at its registered office books of account and other relevant books and papers and financial statement for every financial year which give a true and fair view of the state of the affairs of the company, including that of its branch office or offices, if any, and explain the transactions effected both at the registered office and its branches.

The term 'books of account' includes records maintained in respect of: (a) all sums of money received and expended by the company and the matters in respect of which the receipt and expenditure takes place; (b) all sales and purchases of goods and services by the company; (c) the assets and liabilities of the company; and (d) the items of cost as may be prescribed under Section 148 in the case of a company which belongs to any class of companies specified by the Central Government under that section.

Where Must Books Be Kept?

The books of account must be kept at the registered office of the company or at such other place in India as the Board of Directors may decide [Section 128(1)]. If the Board decides to keep the books at a place other than the registered office, it must file a notice of the full address of that place with the Registrar within 7 days [Section 128(1)]. If the company has a branch office, whether in India or outside India, the proper books of account relating to the transactions effected at the branch must be kept at the branch. Proper summarised returns must be sent by the branch to the company at its registered office or other place at intervals of not more than three months [Section 128(2)].

Electronic Form – Section 128(3)

Section 128(3) provides that the books of account and other books and papers maintained by the company may be kept in electronic mode in such manner as may be prescribed. This is a very practical provision because most companies today maintain their accounts on computers using accounting software like Tally, SAP, Oracle, etc. Rule 3 of the Companies (Accounts) Rules, 2014 prescribes the conditions for maintenance of books of accounts in electronic mode, including requirements for backup, accessibility, and security.

Preservation of Books – Section 128(5)

The books of account, together with the vouchers relevant to any entry in such books, must be preserved for a period of not less than 8 financial years immediately preceding a financial year. If the company has been in existence for a period less than 8 years, the books must be kept for the entire period. In the case of an investigation by the Serious Fraud Investigation Office (SFIO), the Central Government may order the company to preserve the books for a longer period.

Penalty for Non-Compliance – Section 128(6)

If the Managing Director, the Whole-time Director in charge of finance, the Chief Financial Officer, or any other person charged by the Board with the duty of complying with the provisions of Section 128, fails to take all reasonable steps to secure compliance, such person shall, in respect of each offence, be punishable with imprisonment for a term which may extend to one year or with a fine which shall not be less than Rs. 50,000 but which may extend to Rs. 5 lakhs, or with both. If it is proved that the books of account were kept with intent to defraud the creditors of the company or any other person, or for any other fraudulent purpose, the persons responsible shall be punishable with imprisonment for a term which shall not be less than one year but which may extend to six years or with a fine which shall not be less than one lakh rupees but which may extend to ten lakh rupees, or with both.

17.2 Financial Statements – Section 129

The preparation and presentation of financial statements is the most important aspect of corporate financial reporting. The financial statements are the primary means through which the shareholders and the public come to know about the financial position and performance of the company.

What Are Financial Statements? – Section 2(40)

Section Reference: Section 2(40) defines 'financial statement' as: "'Financial statement' in relation to a company, includes – (i) a balance sheet as at the end of the financial year; (ii) a profit and loss account, or in the case of a company carrying on any activity not for profit, an income and expenditure account for the financial year; (iii) cash flow statement for the financial year; (iv) a statement of changes in equity, if applicable; and (v) any explanatory note annexed to, or forming part of, any document referred to in sub-clause (i) to (iv)."

However, the financial statement of a One Person Company, small company, and dormant company may not include the cash flow statement [Section 2(40), proviso].

Preparation of Financial Statements – Section 129(1)

Section 129(1) provides that the financial statements shall give a true and fair view of the state of affairs of the company or companies, comply with the accounting standards notified under Section 133, and shall be in the form or forms as may be provided for different class or classes of companies in Schedule III of the Act.

The phrase 'true and fair view' is of utmost importance. It means that the financial statements must present the financial position, financial performance, and cash flows of the company in a manner that faithfully represents the underlying transactions and events. The accounts must not be misleading or deceptive. They must be prepared in accordance with the applicable accounting standards and must contain adequate disclosures.

Schedule III: Schedule III of the Companies Act, 2013 prescribes the form of the balance sheet and the statement of profit and loss. It is divided into two parts – Part I deals with the form of balance sheet and Part II deals with the form of statement of profit and loss. Schedule III requires a vertical format for the balance sheet (unlike the horizontal format used under the 1956 Act) and classifies assets and liabilities into current and non-current categories.

Accounting Standards – Section 133

Section 133 provides that the Central Government may prescribe the standards of accounting or any addendum thereto, as recommended by the Institute of Chartered Accountants of India (ICAI), constituted under the Chartered Accountants Act, 1949, in consultation with and after examination of the recommendations made by the National Financial Reporting Authority (NFRA). These are called the Indian Accounting Standards (Ind AS).

The Ind AS are converged with the International Financial Reporting Standards (IFRS) and are applicable to specified classes of companies based on their net worth, turnover, and listing status. Companies not covered by Ind AS continue to follow the existing Accounting Standards

(AS) notified under the Companies (Accounting Standards) Rules, 2006.

Consolidated Financial Statements – Section 129(3)

Section 129(3) provides that where a company has one or more subsidiaries or associate companies, it shall, in addition to its own financial statements (called 'standalone financial statements'), prepare a consolidated financial statement of the company and of all the subsidiaries and associate companies in the same form and manner as that of its own. The consolidated financial statements shall be laid before the AGM along with the laying of its financial statement. The consolidated financial statements shall also be prepared in compliance with the applicable accounting standards.

The purpose of consolidated financial statements is to present the financial position and performance of the entire group (holding company and all its subsidiaries and associates) as if it were a single economic entity. This gives the shareholders and the public a complete picture of the group's financial health, rather than the financial position of only the holding company in isolation.

Laying Before AGM and Filing with ROC

Section 129(2) read with Section 137(1) requires that the financial statements, together with the Board's report and the auditor's report, must be laid before every AGM. Section 137(1) provides that the company must file with the Registrar a copy of the financial statements (including consolidated statements, if applicable), along with the auditor's report and all other documents required to be attached thereto, within 30 days of the date of the AGM. If the financial statements have been revised or a revised Board's report has been prepared, the revised statements must be filed within 30 days of revision [Section 130 & 131].

Note: The financial year of every company, irrespective of its date of incorporation, shall end on the 31st day of March every year [Section 2(41)]. However, a company incorporated outside India and having a principal place of business in India may have a different financial year.

Also, a company or body corporate which is a holding company or a subsidiary of a company incorporated outside India may, with the approval of the Tribunal, have a financial year ending on a date other than 31st March.

17.3 Directors' Report – Section 134

The Board of Directors is required to prepare and present a report on the affairs of the company to the shareholders at every AGM. This report is called the 'Board's Report' or the 'Directors' Report.' It is attached to the financial statements and is an important document because it provides the directors' perspective on the company's performance, operations, and future outlook.

Contents of the Board's Report – Section 134(3)

Section 134(3) prescribes the matters which must be included in the Board's Report. The report must contain the following:

(a) Extract of annual return: An extract of the annual return as provided under Section 92(3), or a web-link to the annual return on the company's website.

(b) Number of Board meetings: The number of meetings of the Board held during the financial year.

(c) Directors' Responsibility Statement: A statement by the directors that (i) the applicable accounting standards have been followed in preparation of the annual accounts with proper explanations for material departures; (ii) the directors have selected appropriate accounting policies and applied them consistently and made judgments and estimates that are reasonable and prudent; (iii) the directors have taken proper and sufficient care for the maintenance of adequate accounting records for safeguarding the assets of the company and for preventing and detecting fraud and other irregularities; (iv) the directors have prepared the annual accounts on a going concern basis; (v) the directors have laid down internal financial controls to be followed by the company and that such controls are adequate and operating effectively;

(vi) the directors have devised proper systems to ensure compliance with the provisions of all applicable laws and that such systems are adequate and operating effectively.

(d) Declaration by independent directors: A statement that the company has received declarations from all independent directors under Section 149(7) that they meet the criteria of independence.

(e) Company's policy on directors' appointment and remuneration: The policy developed and implemented on the appointment and remuneration of directors and other employees, including criteria for determining qualifications, positive attributes, independence, and the policy on remuneration of directors, KMP, and other employees.

(f) Explanations for audit qualifications: If the auditors have made any qualifications, reservations, adverse remarks, or disclaimers in their report, the Board must provide an explanation or comment on every such qualification, etc.

(g) Particulars of loans, guarantees, and investments: Under Section 186.

(h) Particulars of related party transactions: Under Section 188.

(i) State of company's affairs: A general description of the state of the company's affairs and the results of its operations during the year, including the amount proposed to carry to any reserves and the recommended dividend.

(j) Material changes: Material changes and commitments, if any, affecting the financial position of the company which have occurred between the end of the financial year and the date of the report.

(k) Conservation of energy, technology absorption, foreign exchange: Particulars regarding conservation of energy, technology absorption, and foreign exchange earnings and outgo.

(l) Risk management policy: A statement indicating development and implementation of a risk management policy for the company, including identification of elements of risk which may threaten the existence of the company.

(m) CSR policy: Details about the policy developed and implemented by the company on Corporate Social Responsibility initiatives taken during the year (if applicable under Section 135).

(n) Other prescribed matters: Such other matters as may be prescribed.

Signing of the Board's Report – Section 134(6)

The Board's Report and any annexures thereto must be signed by the chairperson of the company if he is authorised by the Board, and by at least two directors, one of whom must be the Managing Director [Section 134(6)]. In the case of a One Person Company, the Board's report must be signed by only one director.

Signing of Financial Statements – Section 134(1)

The financial statements, including consolidated financial statements, must be approved by the Board of Directors before they are signed on behalf of the Board by the chairperson of the company where he is authorised by the Board, or by two directors out of which one shall be the Managing Director and the Chief Executive Officer, if he is a director in the company, and the Chief Financial Officer, and the Company Secretary of the company, wherever they are appointed [Section 134(1)].

17.4 Corporate Social Responsibility – Section 135

Corporate Social Responsibility (CSR) is one of the landmark provisions of the Companies Act, 2013. India became one of the first countries in the world to mandate CSR spending by companies. The objective of CSR is to make companies contribute to the social and economic development of the country, especially in the areas of education, health, environment, poverty alleviation, and gender equality.

Applicability – Section 135(1)

Section Reference: Section 135(1): Every company having net worth of rupees five hundred crore or more, or turnover of rupees one thousand crore or more or a net profit of rupees five crore or more during the immediately preceding financial year shall constitute a Corporate Social Responsibility Committee of the Board consisting of three or more directors, out of which at least one director shall be an independent director.

Thus, the CSR provisions apply to every company (whether public or private) which meets any one of the following criteria in the immediately preceding financial year: (a) Net worth of Rs. 500 crore or more, OR (b) Turnover of Rs. 1,000 crore or more, OR (c) Net profit of Rs. 5 crore or more.

A private company which does not have an independent director on its Board (because it is not required to have one) need not include an independent director on the CSR Committee. The CSR Committee must have at least two members.

CSR Committee – Functions – Section 135(3)

The CSR Committee shall: (a) formulate and recommend to the Board a Corporate Social Responsibility Policy which shall indicate the activities to be undertaken by the company as specified in Schedule VII; (b) recommend the amount of expenditure to be incurred on the activities; and (c) monitor the Corporate Social Responsibility Policy of the company from time to time.

CSR Spending – Section 135(5)

Section Reference: Section 135(5): The Board of every company referred to in sub-section (1) shall ensure that the company spends, in every financial year, at least two per cent of the average net profits of the company made during the three immediately preceding financial years, or where the company has not completed the period of three financial years since its incorporation, during such immediately preceding financial years, in pursuance of its Corporate Social Responsibility Policy.

If the company fails to spend the required 2% amount, the Board must specify the reasons for not spending the amount in its report under Section 134(3)(o). Under the Companies (Amendment) Act, 2020, if the company fails to spend the CSR amount, the unspent amount relating to any ongoing project must be transferred to a special account called the 'Unspent Corporate Social Responsibility Account' within 30 days from the end of the financial year and shall be spent within a period of three financial years. If the unspent amount does not relate to any ongoing project, it shall be transferred to a Fund specified in Schedule VII (such as the Prime Minister's National Relief Fund, PM CARES Fund, etc.) within six months of the expiry of the financial year.

Activities Covered Under CSR – Schedule VII

Schedule VII of the Companies Act, 2013 lists the activities which may be included by companies in their CSR policies. These include:

(a) Eradicating hunger, poverty, and malnutrition, promoting health care including preventive health care and sanitation, including contribution to the Swachh Bharat Kosh. (b) Promoting education, including special education and employment enhancing vocation skills especially among children, women, elderly, and the differently abled, and livelihood enhancement projects. (c) Promoting gender equality, empowering women, setting up homes and hostels for women and orphans. (d) Ensuring environmental sustainability, ecological balance, protection of flora and fauna, animal welfare, agroforestry, conservation of natural resources. (e) Protection of national heritage, art, and culture including restoration of buildings and sites of historical importance. (f) Measures for the benefit of armed forces veterans, war widows, and their dependents. (g) Training to promote rural sports, nationally recognised sports, Paralympic sports, and Olympic sports. (h) Contribution to the Prime Minister's National Relief Fund or any other fund set up by the Central Government. (i) Contributions to incubators or research and development projects in the field of science, technology, engineering, and medicine, funded by the Central or State Government. (j) Rural development projects. (k) Slum area development. (l) Disaster management, including relief, rehabilitation, and reconstruction activities.

Illustration: Reliance Industries spends over Rs. 900 crore annually on CSR activities in areas like education (Jio Institute, Dhirubhai Ambani International School), healthcare (Sir H.N. Reliance Foundation Hospital), rural transformation, and disaster relief. Tata Group companies collectively spend thousands of crores on CSR through the Tata Trusts and various group company CSR initiatives.

Note: CSR expenditure shall not include any activity undertaken in the normal course of business of the company. Activities undertaken by the company on a commercial basis shall not qualify as CSR. Also, only activities in India qualify for CSR – activities outside India do not count towards the 2% spending requirement (with certain exceptions for training Indian sports personnel and promoting internationally recognised sports).

17.5 Appointment of Auditors – Section 139

The audit of the financial statements of a company is one of the most important safeguards for the protection of shareholders and creditors. The auditor is an independent professional who examines the books of accounts and the financial statements of the company and gives his opinion on whether the financial statements give a 'true and fair view' of the company's financial position and performance.

First Auditor – Section 139(6)

The first auditor of a company (other than a Government company) must be appointed by the Board of Directors within 30 days from the date of registration of the company [Section 139(6)]. If the Board fails to appoint within 30 days, it shall inform the members of the company who shall, within 90 days at an EGM, appoint such auditor. The first auditor shall hold office until the conclusion of the first AGM.

In the case of a Government company, the first auditor shall be appointed by the Comptroller and Auditor General (CAG) of India within 60 days from the date of registration. If the CAG does not appoint within 60 days, the Board shall appoint the first auditor within the next 30 days [Section 139(7)].

Subsequent Auditors – Section 139(1)

Section Reference: Section 139(1): Subject to the provisions of this Chapter, every company shall, at the first annual general meeting, appoint an individual or a firm as an auditor who shall hold office from the conclusion of that meeting till the conclusion of its sixth annual general meeting and thereafter till the conclusion of every sixth meeting.

In simple words, the auditor is appointed at the AGM for a term of 5 years (from the conclusion of one AGM to the conclusion of the sixth AGM). The appointment must be approved by the members at the AGM by an ordinary resolution. Before the appointment, the written consent of the auditor and a certificate from him confirming his eligibility must be obtained [Section 139(1)].

The company must inform the Registrar within 15 days of the appointment about the name and address of the auditor appointed [Section 139(1)].

Rotation of Auditors – Section 139(2)

Section 139(2) is one of the most significant provisions introduced by the 2013 Act. It provides for the mandatory rotation of auditors for certain classes of companies. The provisions apply to:

(a) All listed companies. (b) All unlisted public companies having a paid-up share capital of Rs. 10 crore or more. (c) All private limited companies having a paid-up share capital of Rs. 50 crore or more. (d) All companies having public borrowings from financial institutions, banks, or public deposits of Rs. 50 crore or more.

For these companies, the following rotation rules apply:

(i) Individual auditor: An individual auditor cannot be appointed for more than one term of five consecutive years [Section 139(2)]. After completing one term of five years, there must be a cooling-off period of five years before the same individual can be reappointed as auditor of the same company.

(ii) Audit firm: An audit firm cannot be appointed for more than two terms of five consecutive years each [Section 139(2)]. After completing two terms (i.e., ten years), there must be a cooling-off period of five years before the same firm can be reappointed. However, if the audit firm has common partners with other audit firms, the incoming firm shall not be eligible if any partner of the outgoing firm is also a partner of the incoming firm for the same period.

Type of Auditor	Maximum Consecutive Term	Cooling-off Period
Individual Auditor	One term of 5 years	5 years
Audit Firm	Two terms of 5 years each (total 10 years)	5 years

Ratification of Appointment – Section 139(1)

Every appointment of an auditor must be ratified by the members at every subsequent AGM during the term. However, the Companies (Amendment) Act, 2017 has done away with the requirement of ratification at every AGM. Now, once the auditor is appointed at the AGM for a term of 5 years, no annual ratification is required. The auditor continues in office till the conclusion of the sixth AGM.

Who Can Be Appointed as Auditor?

Only a Chartered Accountant (a member of the Institute of Chartered Accountants of India) can be appointed as the auditor of a company [Section 141(1)]. A firm can be appointed if a majority of its partners practicing in India are qualified for appointment as auditors. An LLP of CAs can also be appointed. A body corporate (i.e., a company) cannot be appointed as an auditor.

Who Cannot Be Appointed as Auditor? – Section 141(3)

Section 141(3) lists the persons who are disqualified from being appointed as auditors:

(a) A body corporate other than an LLP. (b) An officer or employee of the company. (c) A person who is a partner of, or who is in the employment of, an officer or employee of the company. (d) A person, or his relative, or partner, who holds any security of or interest in the company or its subsidiary, or holding, or associate company. However, a relative may hold securities or interest having face value not exceeding Rs. 1 lakh. (e) A person who is indebted to the company, or its subsidiary, or holding, or associate company, or subsidiary of such holding company, for an amount exceeding Rs. 5 lakhs. (f) A person who has given any guarantee or provided any security in connection with the indebtedness of any third person to the company for an amount exceeding Rs. 1 lakh. (g) A person or a firm who, whether directly or indirectly, has a business relationship with the company, or its subsidiary, or holding, or associate company or subsidiary of such holding company. (h) A person whose relative is a director or is in the employment of the company as a director or KMP. (i) A person who is in full-time employment elsewhere, or a person or a partner of a firm holding appointment as its auditor if such person or partner is at the date of such appointment or reappointment holding appointment as auditor of more than 20 companies, other than OPCs, dormant companies, and small companies. (j) A person who has been convicted by a court of an offence involving fraud and a period of 10 years has not elapsed from the date of such conviction.

Note: The disqualifications in Section 141(3) are very stringent and are designed to ensure the complete independence of the auditor from the company and its management. The idea is that the auditor must have no financial interest, personal relationship, or business relationship with the company which could compromise his independence and objectivity.

17.6 Powers and Duties of Auditors – Section 143

The auditor occupies a unique position in the corporate structure. He is appointed by the shareholders but he reports on the accounts which are prepared by the management. His primary duty is to report to the shareholders whether the financial statements give a true and fair view of the company's financial position and performance. To perform this duty effectively, the Act gives him wide powers of access and investigation.

Rights (Powers) of the Auditor

(1) Right of access to books of accounts – Section 143(1): The auditor shall have a right of access at all times to the books of account and vouchers of the company kept at the registered office or at any other place. He can require information and explanations from the officers of the company as he may consider necessary for the performance of his duties as auditor.

(2) Right to attend general meetings – Section 146: All notices of, and other communications relating to, any general meeting shall be forwarded to the auditor. The auditor has the right to attend any general meeting and to be heard at such meeting on any part of the business which concerns him as auditor. He may also make representations regarding his removal.

(3) Right to visit branch offices – Section 143(8): Where the company has branch offices, the auditor has the right to visit any branch office and access the books and records maintained there.

(4) Right to receive remuneration – Section 142: The remuneration of the auditor shall be fixed by the company in its general meeting or in such manner as the members may determine.

(5) Right to seek legal and professional advice: The auditor may seek legal and professional advice at the expense of the company when necessary for the proper discharge of his duties.

Duties of the Auditor

(1) Duty to report – Section 143(2) & (3): The auditor must make a report to the members of the company on the accounts examined by him and on every financial statement which is required to be laid before the AGM. The auditor's report shall state: (a) whether he has sought and obtained all the information and explanations which to the best of his knowledge and belief were necessary for the purposes of his audit; (b) whether, in his opinion, proper books of account have been kept by the company as required by law; (c) whether the company's balance sheet and profit and loss account dealt with in the report are in agreement with the books of account; (d) whether, in his opinion, the financial statements comply with the Accounting Standards; (e) observations or comments of the auditors on financial transactions or matters which have any adverse effect on the functioning of the company; (f) whether any director is disqualified from being appointed as a director under Section 164(2); (g) any qualification, reservation, or adverse remark relating to the maintenance of accounts and other matters connected therewith; and (h) whether the company has adequate internal financial controls with reference to financial statements in place and the operating effectiveness of such controls [Section 143(3)].

(2) Duty to report fraud – Section 143(12): If an auditor of a company, in the course of the performance of his duties as auditor, has reason to believe that an offence involving fraud is being or has been committed against the company by officers or employees of the company, he shall immediately report the matter to the Central Government within 60 days. If the fraud involves an amount of Rs. 1 crore or more, the auditor must report to the Central Government. If the fraud involves less than Rs. 1 crore, the auditor must report to the Audit Committee or the Board within 2 days. The auditor must also report the fraud in his audit report.

(3) Duty of confidentiality: The auditor has a duty to maintain confidentiality regarding the company's affairs. He must not disclose any information obtained in the course of his audit to any unauthorised person. However, this duty does not apply when disclosure is required by law (e.g., reporting fraud under Section 143(12)).

(4) Duty of care and skill: The auditor must exercise reasonable care and skill in the performance of his duties. He is not an insurer or a guarantor of the accuracy of the accounts. But he must be reasonably vigilant and must not turn a blind eye to suspicious transactions.

Case: London and General Bank (No. 2) (1895)

Lord Justice Lindley described the duty of an auditor: 'An auditor is not bound to be a detective, or to approach his work with suspicion, or with a foregone conclusion that there is something wrong. He is a watchdog, but not a bloodhound. He is justified in believing tried servants of the company in whom confidence is placed by the company. He is entitled to assume that they are honest, and to rely upon their representations, provided he takes reasonable care. If there is anything calculated to excite suspicion, he should probe it to the bottom.' This statement has become the classic description of the auditor's duty in company law.

Case: Kingston Cotton Mill Co. (No. 2) (1896)

Lord Justice Lopes made the famous statement: 'It is the duty of an auditor to bring to bear on the work he has to perform that skill, care, and caution which a reasonably competent, careful, and cautious auditor would use. He is not an insurer; he does not guarantee that the books do correctly show the true position of the company's affairs. What he does guarantee is that he has taken reasonable care and skill before believing what appears in the books of the company.'

Auditor's Report – Section 143(2)

The auditor's report is addressed to the members of the company. It must be attached to every financial statement laid before the AGM. The report must clearly state the auditor's opinion on whether the financial statements give a true and fair view. The report may contain one of the following opinions:

(a) Unqualified opinion (clean report): The financial statements give a true and fair view. (b) Qualified opinion: The financial statements give a true and fair view except for certain specific matters mentioned in the report. (c) Adverse opinion: The financial statements do not give a true and fair view. (d) Disclaimer of opinion: The auditor is unable to form an opinion because of certain limitations on the scope of the audit.

17.7 Removal and Resignation of Auditors

Removal of Auditor – Section 140(1)

Section 140(1) provides that the auditor appointed under Section 139 may be removed from his office before the expiry of his term only by a special resolution of the company, after obtaining the prior approval of the Central Government in that behalf. The company must file an application with the Central Government within 30 days of the resolution passed by the Board. The Central Government may issue an order within 30 days of receipt of the application.

The requirement of Central Government approval is a safeguard against the arbitrary removal of the auditor by the management. Since the auditor is expected to be independent of the management, the law ensures that the management cannot remove the auditor simply because the auditor has given an unfavourable report.

Resignation of Auditor – Section 140(2)

The auditor may resign from his office by filing a notice in writing with the company. In addition, he must file a statement in the prescribed form with the Registrar within 30 days of the date of resignation. The statement must indicate the reasons and other facts as may be relevant with regard to his resignation [Section 140(2)].

In the case of a Government company, the auditor must also file the statement with the Comptroller and Auditor General (CAG). In the case of companies other than Government companies, the auditor must file the statement with the company and the Registrar. If the auditor does not comply with this requirement, he shall be punishable with a fine of Rs. 50,000 or an amount equal to the remuneration of the auditor, whichever is less, and in case of continuing failure, with a further fine of Rs. 500 for each day during which the default continues, subject to a maximum of Rs. 5 lakhs [Section 140(3)].

Auditor Not to Be Reappointed – Section 140(4)

The Tribunal may, on an application made by the Central Government, if it is satisfied that the auditor has acted in a manner which amounts to fraud, direct the company to change its auditor [Section 140(5)]. If the Tribunal is satisfied, it shall, within 15 days of receipt of such application, direct the company to change the auditor. The auditor against whom the order is made shall not be eligible to be appointed as an auditor of any company for a period of 5 years from the date of passing of the order and shall be liable to action under Section 447 (fraud).

17.8 Cost Audit and Secretarial Audit

Cost Audit – Section 148

Section 148 provides that the Central Government may, by order, require the audit of cost records of certain classes of companies. The audit of cost records is called 'cost audit.' The cost audit is conducted by a Cost Accountant who is a member of the Institute of Cost Accountants of India (ICMAI, formerly ICWAI).

The Central Government may direct that the cost records of such class of companies as may be prescribed shall be audited by a Cost Accountant. The cost auditor is appointed by the Board of Directors on the recommendation of the Audit Committee. The remuneration of the cost auditor is fixed by the Board and ratified by the members at the AGM.

The cost auditor must submit his report to the Board within 180 days from the closure of the financial year. The company must file the cost audit report with the Central Government within 30 days from the date of receipt of the report. The cost audit is applicable mainly to companies engaged in the manufacture of goods or engaged in production, processing, mining, or generation activities.

Secretarial Audit – Section 204

Section Reference: Section 204(1): Every listed company and a company belonging to such other class of companies as may be prescribed shall annex with its Board's report a secretarial audit report, given by a company secretary in practice, in such form as may be prescribed.

The secretarial audit is conducted by a Company Secretary in Practice (CSP) who is a member of the Institute of Company Secretaries of India (ICSI). The secretarial audit checks whether the company has complied with the provisions of the Companies Act, the rules made thereunder, the SEBI regulations, the listing agreement, and other applicable laws.

The secretarial audit is mandatory for: (a) every listed company, (b) every public company having a paid-up share capital of Rs. 50 crore or more, and (c) every public company having a turnover of Rs. 250 crore or more.

The secretarial auditor must issue a secretarial audit report in Form MR-3 which must be annexed to the Board's Report. If the secretarial auditor makes any qualification, reservation, or adverse remark in his report, the Board must explain the same in the Board's Report.

Table 17.1: Statutory Audit vs. Cost Audit vs. Secretarial Audit

Point	Statutory Audit	Cost Audit	Secretarial Audit
Section	139–147	148	204
Conducted by	Chartered Accountant (ICAI)	Cost Accountant (ICMAI)	Company Secretary in Practice (ICSI)
Scope	Financial statements and	Cost records and cost statements	Compliance with laws and

	books of accounts		regulations
Applicability	All companies	Prescribed classes of companies	Listed companies and specified public companies
Appointment by	Members at AGM	Board on Audit Committee recommendation	Board of Directors
Report filed with	Members + ROC	Central Government	Annexed to Board's Report

PART – V : CORPORATE GOVERNANCE & COMPLIANCE

Chapter 18

Corporate Governance

In the last two decades, corporate governance has become one of the most widely discussed topics in the field of company law and business management. The collapse of major corporations like Enron, WorldCom, and Lehman Brothers in the United States, and the Satyam Computer Services scandal in India, exposed the severe consequences of poor corporate governance. These corporate failures resulted in huge losses for shareholders, employees, creditors, and the economy at large. The lesson learnt was clear – good corporate governance is not merely a matter of compliance; it is essential for the survival and growth of the corporate sector. The Companies Act, 2013 has incorporated many provisions aimed at strengthening corporate governance in Indian companies.

18.1 Meaning and Importance of Corporate Governance

Meaning of Corporate Governance

Corporate governance is a broad and multi-dimensional concept. There is no single universally accepted definition of corporate governance. Different experts, committees, and organisations have defined it in different ways. Let us look at some of the important definitions:

According to the Cadbury Committee (UK, 1992): "Corporate governance is the system by which companies are directed and controlled." This is the most widely cited definition. It emphasises that corporate governance is about the way companies are run – the processes, structures, and mechanisms through which the company is managed and its affairs are conducted.

According to the OECD (Organisation for Economic Co-operation and Development): "Corporate governance involves a set of relationships between a company's management, its board, its shareholders, and other stakeholders. Corporate governance also provides the structure through which the objectives of the company are set, and the means of attaining those objectives and monitoring performance are determined."

According to the Kumar Mangalam Birla Committee (India, 1999): "Corporate governance is about commitment to values, about ethical business conduct, and about making a distinction between personal and corporate funds in the management of a company."

According to N.R. Narayana Murthy Committee (India, 2003): "Corporate governance is the acceptance by management of the inalienable rights of shareholders as the true owners of the corporation and of their own role as trustees on behalf of the shareholders."

In simple words, corporate governance can be understood as the set of rules, practices, and processes by which a company is directed and controlled. It involves balancing the interests of a company's many stakeholders – shareholders, management, customers, suppliers, creditors, Government, and the community. Good corporate governance ensures that the company is run in a transparent, fair, and accountable manner, and that the interests of all stakeholders are protected.

Importance of Corporate Governance

Corporate governance is important for the following reasons:

(1) Protection of shareholders' interests: Good corporate governance ensures that the shareholders, who are the owners of the company, are treated fairly and equitably. It protects the rights of minority shareholders and prevents the misuse of power by the controlling shareholders and the management.

(2) Accountability and transparency: Corporate governance makes the management accountable to the Board and the Board accountable to the shareholders. It ensures transparency in the company's operations, financial reporting, and decision-making.

(3) Attracts investment: Companies with good corporate governance practices attract more investment from domestic and foreign investors. Investors are more willing to invest in companies where they feel their money is safe and the management is trustworthy.

(4) Improves performance: Good governance leads to better decision-making, efficient use of resources, and improved financial performance. Well-governed companies tend to be more profitable and more sustainable in the long run.

(5) Prevents fraud and mismanagement: Strong corporate governance mechanisms, such as independent directors, audit committees, and internal controls, act as checks against fraud, corruption, and mismanagement.

(6) Protects stakeholder interests: Corporate governance is not only about shareholders. It also protects the interests of employees, creditors, customers, suppliers, and the community. A well-governed company treats all its stakeholders fairly and ethically.

(7) Builds public confidence: Good corporate governance builds public trust and confidence in the corporate sector. When companies are well-governed, the public has faith in the capital markets, the banking system, and the economy as a whole.

(8) Legal compliance: Good corporate governance ensures that the company complies with all applicable laws and regulations. It reduces the risk of legal penalties, regulatory action, and reputational damage.

Indian Context: The Satyam Computer Services fraud (2009) is the most notorious example of corporate governance failure in India. The chairman, Mr. Ramalinga Raju, admitted to inflating the company's cash balances by over Rs. 7,000 crore. The fraud wiped out the savings of thousands of investors and employees. This incident led to major reforms in corporate governance in India and was one of the driving forces behind the enactment of the Companies Act, 2013 with its stronger governance provisions.

18.2 Principles and Theories of Corporate Governance

Principles of Corporate Governance

The OECD Principles of Corporate Governance (first adopted in 1999 and revised in 2004 and 2015) are considered the international benchmark for corporate governance. The key principles are:

(1) Rights and equitable treatment of shareholders: The corporate governance framework should protect and facilitate the exercise of shareholders' rights and ensure the equitable treatment of all shareholders, including minority and foreign shareholders.

(2) Role of stakeholders: The framework should recognise the rights of stakeholders established by law or through mutual agreements and encourage active co-operation between the company and its stakeholders in creating wealth, jobs, and the sustainability of financially sound enterprises.

(3) Disclosure and transparency: The framework should ensure that timely and accurate disclosure is made on all material matters regarding the company, including the financial situation, performance, ownership, and governance of the company.

(4) Responsibilities of the Board: The framework should ensure the strategic guidance of the company, the effective monitoring of management by the Board, and the Board's accountability to the company and the shareholders.

(5) Ensuring a sound basis for corporate governance: The framework should promote transparent and fair markets, and the efficient allocation of resources.

(6) Institutional investors, stock markets, and intermediaries: The framework should provide sound incentives throughout the investment chain and provide for stock markets to function in a way that contributes to good corporate governance.

Theories of Corporate Governance

(1) Agency Theory

The Agency Theory is the most influential theory of corporate governance. It was developed by Jensen and Meckling (1976). The theory is based on the principal-agent relationship. In a company, the shareholders (principals) delegate the management of the company to the directors and managers (agents). The problem arises because the interests of the agents may not always align with the interests of the principals. The directors may pursue their own interests (such as higher salaries, perquisites, and empire building) at the expense of the shareholders' interests (such as maximising shareholder wealth). This conflict of interest is called the 'agency problem.' Corporate governance mechanisms (such as independent directors, audit committees, executive compensation policies, and disclosure requirements) are designed to reduce the agency problem and align the interests of the agents with those of the principals.

(2) Stewardship Theory

The Stewardship Theory takes a more optimistic view of the managers. It argues that the managers are not always self-interested agents. They may act as responsible stewards of the company's resources and may be motivated by factors other than financial self-interest, such as professional pride, job satisfaction, and a sense of duty. According to this theory, the managers are trustworthy and will act in the best interests of the company without the need for extensive monitoring and control mechanisms. The theory suggests that corporate governance should be based on trust, empowerment, and collaboration rather than on suspicion and control.

(3) Stakeholder Theory

The Stakeholder Theory, propounded by R. Edward Freeman (1984), argues that the company has a responsibility not only to its shareholders but to all its stakeholders – employees, customers, suppliers, creditors, the Government, and the community. According to this theory, the purpose of corporate governance is to balance the interests of all stakeholders and to ensure that the company creates value for all of them, not just for the shareholders. The Companies Act, 2013 reflects this theory in its provisions on CSR (Section 135), the duty of directors to promote the objects of the company for the benefit of members, employees, shareholders, the community, and the environment (Section 166(2)).

(4) Resource Dependency Theory

This theory focuses on the role of the Board of Directors as a link between the company and the external resources it needs to survive and grow. According to this theory, directors are appointed not only for their monitoring function but also for the resources and connections they bring to the company. Independent directors, in particular, can provide access to external expertise, networks, and legitimacy. The composition of the Board should reflect the company's need for different types of resources.

18.3 Corporate Governance under Companies Act, 2013

The Companies Act, 2013 has significantly strengthened the corporate governance framework in India compared to the earlier Companies Act, 1956. The key governance provisions of the 2013 Act are spread across various sections. The following are the major corporate governance provisions:

(1) Mandatory independent directors (Section 149): Every listed public company must have at least one-third of the total number of directors as independent directors. This ensures that the Board has an adequate number of directors who are independent of the management and can provide unbiased oversight.

(2) Woman director (Section 149(1)): Certain classes of companies must have at least one woman director. This promotes gender diversity on the Board.

(3) Duties of directors codified (Section 166): For the first time, the duties of directors have been codified, including the duty to act in good faith, avoid conflict of interest, and exercise due care and diligence.

(4) Mandatory Board committees: The Act requires certain companies to constitute the Audit Committee (Section 177), the Nomination and Remuneration Committee (Section 178), the Stakeholders Relationship Committee (Section 178(5)), and the CSR Committee (Section 135).

(5) Related party transactions (Section 188): The Act requires the approval of the Board and, in certain cases, the approval of the shareholders for transactions between the company and its related parties. This prevents self-dealing by directors and promoters.

(6) Rotation of auditors (Section 139): Mandatory rotation of auditors ensures that the auditor does not develop a cosy relationship with the management over time.

(7) Class action suits (Section 245): Members and depositors can file class action suits before the NCLT to hold the management accountable for oppressive or prejudicial conduct.

(8) Corporate Social Responsibility (Section 135): Mandatory CSR spending ensures that companies contribute to the social and economic development of the country.

(9) Vigil mechanism / Whistle blower policy (Section 177(9) & (10)): Every listed company and every company which accepts deposits from the public or has borrowed money from banks or public financial institutions in excess of Rs. 50 crore must establish a vigil mechanism (whistle blower policy) for directors and employees to report genuine concerns about unethical behaviour, actual or suspected fraud, or violation of the company's code of conduct.

(10) Secretarial audit (Section 204): Mandatory secretarial audit for listed and specified public companies ensures compliance with laws and regulations.

(11) Internal financial controls (Section 134(5)(e)): The directors must ensure that the company has adequate internal financial controls and that these controls are operating effectively.

(12) Fraud reporting by auditors (Section 143(12)): Auditors are mandated to report fraud to the Central Government, strengthening the detection and prevention of fraud.

18.4 Role of Independent Directors

Independent directors are the cornerstone of modern corporate governance. They bring an independent, objective, and unbiased perspective to the Board's deliberations. They act as a check on the management and the promoters and protect the interests of minority shareholders and other stakeholders.

Definition and Qualifications – Section 149(6)

The definition and qualifications of independent directors have been discussed in detail in Chapter 14 (Section 14.2). To briefly recapitulate, an independent director must be a person of integrity with relevant expertise, must not be a promoter or related to promoters/directors, must have no pecuniary relationship with the company, and must meet all the other criteria specified in Section 149(6).

Code for Independent Directors – Schedule IV

Schedule IV of the Companies Act, 2013 contains a Code for Independent Directors. The Code lays down the following guidelines:

(a) Professional conduct: Independent directors shall uphold ethical standards of integrity and probity, act objectively and constructively, exercise their responsibilities in a bona fide manner, devote sufficient time and attention to their professional obligations, and not allow any extraneous considerations that will vitiate their exercise of objective independent judgment.

(b) Role and functions: Independent directors shall help in bringing an independent judgment to bear on the Board's deliberations, especially on issues of strategy, performance, risk management, resources, key appointments, and standards of conduct. They shall satisfy themselves on the integrity of financial information and that the financial controls and risk management systems are robust. They shall safeguard the interests of all stakeholders, particularly the minority shareholders. They shall balance the conflicting interests of the stakeholders. They shall determine appropriate levels of remuneration of executive directors, KMP, and senior management.

(c) Duties: Independent directors shall undertake appropriate induction and regularly update and refresh their skills, knowledge, and familiarity with the company. They shall seek appropriate clarification or amplification of information and, where necessary, take appropriate professional advice and opinion of outside experts at the expense of the company. They shall strive to attend all meetings of the Board and its committees. They shall participate constructively and actively in the meetings. They shall keep themselves well-informed about the company and the external environment in which it operates.

(d) Evaluation: The performance of independent directors shall be evaluated by the entire Board of Directors, excluding the director being evaluated. On the basis of this evaluation, the Board shall determine whether to extend or continue the term of appointment of the independent director.

(e) Separate meetings: The independent directors shall hold at least one meeting in a year, without the attendance of non-independent directors and members of the management. At this meeting, they shall review the performance of non-independent directors and the Board as a whole, assess the quality, quantity, and timeliness of the flow of information between the company management and the Board, and discuss any other matter they deem fit.

Indian Context: In the Satyam scandal, the independent directors on the Board failed to detect or prevent the massive fraud committed by the chairman. This exposed the weakness of the independent director system – independent directors may not be truly independent if they owe their appointment to the promoters or if they do not have access to adequate information. The Companies Act, 2013 has tried to address these issues by prescribing stricter eligibility criteria, limiting the tenure, and providing for separate meetings of independent directors.

18.5 Audit Committee and Other Committees

(A) Audit Committee – Section 177

The Audit Committee is the most important Board committee from the perspective of corporate governance. It plays a crucial role in ensuring the integrity of financial reporting, the effectiveness of internal controls, and the independence of the audit process.

Section Reference: Section 177(1): The Board of Directors of every listed public company and such other class or classes of companies, as may be prescribed, shall constitute an Audit Committee.

Rule 6 of the Companies (Meetings of Board and its Powers) Rules, 2014 prescribes that the following companies must also constitute an Audit Committee: (a) all public companies having a paid-up share capital of Rs. 10 crore or more, (b) all public companies having a turnover of Rs. 100 crore or more, (c) all public companies having outstanding loans or borrowings or debentures or deposits exceeding Rs. 50 crore or more.

Composition – Section 177(2)

The Audit Committee must consist of a minimum of 3 directors with independent directors forming a majority. The majority of members of the Audit Committee, including its chairperson, shall be persons with ability to read and understand the financial statement. At least one member must have accounting or related financial management expertise.

Functions – Section 177(4)

Section 177(4) specifies the following functions of the Audit Committee:

(a) Recommendation for appointment, remuneration, and terms of appointment of auditors of the company. (b) Review and monitoring of the auditor's independence and performance, and effectiveness of audit process. (c) Examination of the financial statement and the auditors' report thereon. (d) Approval or any subsequent modification of transactions of the company with related parties. (e) Scrutiny of inter-corporate loans and investments. (f) Valuation of undertakings or assets of the company, wherever it is necessary. (g) Evaluation of internal financial controls and risk management systems. (h) Monitoring the end use of funds raised through public offers and related matters.

Vigil Mechanism – Section 177(9) & (10)

Section 177(9) requires every listed company or a company which accepts deposits from the public or has borrowed money from banks and public financial institutions in excess of Rs. 50 crore to establish a vigil mechanism for directors and employees to report genuine concerns. Section 177(10) provides that the vigil mechanism shall provide for adequate safeguards against victimisation of persons who use such mechanism and also provide for direct access to the chairperson of the Audit Committee in appropriate or exceptional cases. The whistle blower policy must be disclosed on the company's website and in the Board's Report.

(B) Nomination and Remuneration Committee – Section 178

The Nomination and Remuneration Committee (NRC) has been discussed in Chapter 15 (Section 15.6). It must consist of 3 or more non-executive directors, of whom at least half must be independent directors. Its functions include identifying qualified persons for directorship, recommending appointments, formulating criteria for independence, and recommending remuneration policies.

(C) Stakeholders Relationship Committee – Section 178(5)

Section Reference: Section 178(5): The Board of Directors of a company which consists of more than one thousand shareholders, debenture-holders, deposit-holders, and any other security holders at any time during a financial year shall constitute a Stakeholders Relationship Committee consisting of a chairperson who shall be a non-executive director and such other members as may be decided by the Board.

The Stakeholders Relationship Committee considers and resolves the grievances of shareholders, debenture holders, and other security holders. It deals with matters such as non-receipt of share certificates, non-receipt of dividends, non-receipt of annual reports, complaints regarding transfer and transmission of shares, and other matters of investor grievance. The committee ensures that investor complaints are resolved promptly and effectively.

(D) CSR Committee – Section 135

The CSR Committee has been discussed in detail in Chapter 17 (Section 17.4). It must consist of 3 or more directors, of whom at least one must be an independent director (except for private companies exempt from appointing independent directors). Its functions include formulating the CSR policy, recommending CSR expenditure, and monitoring implementation.

Table 18.1: Mandatory Board Committees at a Glance

Committee	Section	Composition	Applicability
Audit Committee	177	Min 3 directors; majority independent; chairperson independent; one with financial expertise	Listed companies; public companies with Rs. 10 cr+ capital or Rs. 100 cr+ turnover or Rs. 50 cr+ borrowings
Nomination & Remuneration Committee	178	3+ non-executive directors; at least half independent	Listed companies; public companies with Rs. 10 cr+ capital or Rs. 100 cr+ turnover or Rs. 50 cr+ borrowings

Stakeholders Relationship Committee	178(5)	Chairperson must be non-executive; other members as per Board	Companies with 1,000+ shareholders/debenture-holders/deposit-holders/security holders
CSR Committee	135	3+ directors; at least 1 independent (except private cos.)	Companies with Rs. 500 cr+ net worth or Rs. 1,000 cr+ turnover or Rs. 5 cr+ net profit

18.6 Related Party Transactions – Section 188

Related party transactions are transactions between the company and its directors, key managerial personnel, their relatives, or any firm or body corporate in which a director or KMP has a significant interest. Such transactions carry the risk of self-dealing and conflict of interest because the director or KMP may benefit at the expense of the company. The Companies Act, 2013 contains strict provisions to regulate related party transactions.

Who is a Related Party? – Section 2(76)

Section 2(76) defines 'related party' with reference to a company. A related party includes: (a) a director or his relative, (b) a key managerial personnel or his relative, (c) a firm in which a director, manager, or his relative is a partner, (d) a private company in which a director or manager or his relative is a member or director, (e) a public company in which a director or manager is a director and holds along with his relatives more than 2% of its paid-up share capital, (f) a body corporate whose Board of Directors, managing director, or manager is accustomed to act in accordance with the advice, directions, or instructions of a director or manager, (g) any person on whose advice, directions, or instructions a director or manager is accustomed to act, (h) any body corporate which is a holding, subsidiary, or associate company of such company, or a subsidiary of a holding company to which it is also a subsidiary, (i) a director (other than an independent director) or KMP of the holding company or his relative.

Transactions Requiring Approval – Section 188(1)

Section 188(1) provides that no company shall enter into any of the following contracts or arrangements with a related party except with the consent of the Board of Directors given by a resolution at a meeting of the Board, and subject to such conditions as may be prescribed:

(a) Sale, purchase, or supply of any goods or materials. (b) Selling or otherwise disposing of, or buying, property of any kind. (c) Leasing of property of any kind. (d) Availing or rendering of any services. (e) Appointment of any agent for purchase or sale of goods, materials, services, or property. (f) Such related party's appointment to any office or place of profit in the company, its subsidiary company, or associate company. (g) Underwriting the subscription of any securities or derivatives thereof, of the company.

When is Shareholders' Approval Required?

Rule 15 of the Companies (Meetings of Board and its Powers) Rules, 2014 prescribes the monetary thresholds above which shareholders' approval is required. The thresholds depend on the type of transaction and the paid-up capital of the company. For example, in the case of sale/purchase/supply of goods, shareholders' approval is required if the transaction exceeds 10% of the annual turnover or Rs. 100 crore, whichever is lower. For listed companies, SEBI LODR Regulations prescribe additional requirements, including the approval of shareholders by ordinary resolution with the related party abstaining from voting.

Section 188(1) also requires that the contract or arrangement must be referred to in the Board's Report along with a justification for entering into such contract or arrangement. In the case of a listed company, the related party transactions must also be disclosed in the annual report as per the SEBI LODR Regulations.

Consequences of Non-Compliance – Section 188(3) & (4)

Where a contract or arrangement is entered into without the approval of the Board or the shareholders (as the case may be), the contract shall be voidable at the option of the Board or the shareholders, as the case may be [Section 188(3)]. If the contract or arrangement is found to be detrimental to the interest of the company, the director or member who had voted in favour of the resolution shall indemnify the company against any loss incurred by the company [Section 188(3)]. Any director or other employee of a company who had entered into or authorised the contract or arrangement in violation of Section 188 shall be punishable with imprisonment for a term which may extend to one year or with a fine of Rs. 25,000 to Rs. 5 lakhs, or with both [Section 188(5)].

Case / Report: Satyam Computer Services Scandal (2009)

In the Satyam scandal, the chairman proposed to use the company's funds to acquire two companies owned by his family members – Maytas Properties and Maytas Infra. This was a classic case of related party transaction aimed at benefiting the promoter family at the expense of the company's shareholders. The proposal was withdrawn after strong opposition from institutional investors and the market. This incident highlighted the importance of strict regulation of related party transactions and the need for shareholder approval for such transactions.

18.7 SEBI's LODR Regulations (Overview)

For listed companies, corporate governance requirements are primarily governed by the SEBI (Listing Obligations and Disclosure Requirements) Regulations, 2015 (commonly called SEBI LODR Regulations). These regulations replaced the earlier Listing Agreement (Clause 49 of which dealt with corporate governance). The SEBI LODR Regulations apply to all companies whose securities are listed on any recognised stock exchange in India.

Key Corporate Governance Requirements Under SEBI LODR

(1) Board composition: The Board of a listed company must have an optimum combination of executive and non-executive directors with at least one woman director. At least one-third of the Board must consist of independent directors. If the chairperson is a non-executive director, at least one-third must be independent; if the chairperson is an executive director or is related to a promoter, at least half the Board must be independent [Regulation 17].

(2) Board meetings: The Board must meet at least four times a year with a maximum gap of 120 days between two meetings. The quorum must include at least one independent director [Regulation 17].

(3) Mandatory committees: Listed companies must constitute the Audit Committee, the Nomination and Remuneration Committee, the Stakeholders Relationship Committee, and the Risk Management Committee (for top listed companies based on market capitalisation) [Regulations 18-21].

(4) Related party transactions: All related party transactions must be approved by the Audit Committee. Material related party transactions require the approval of the shareholders by ordinary resolution, and the related parties must abstain from voting. The threshold for 'material' related party transaction has been prescribed by SEBI from time to time [Regulation 23].

(5) Disclosures: Listed companies must make extensive disclosures to the stock exchanges and shareholders, including quarterly and annual financial results, shareholding patterns, corporate governance reports, and disclosures of material events [Regulations 30-36].

(6) Independent directors: Independent directors of listed companies are subject to additional requirements regarding their qualification, appointment, and evaluation. Listed companies must conduct a formal annual evaluation of the Board, its committees, and individual directors [Regulation 17(10) and Schedule II Part D].

(7) Code of conduct: The Board must lay down a code of conduct for all Board members and senior management. All Board members and senior management must affirm compliance with the code on an annual basis. The Annual Report must contain a declaration signed by the CEO that all Board members and senior management personnel have affirmed compliance [Regulation 17(5)].

(8) CEO/CFO certification: The CEO and CFO must certify to the Board that the financial statements are true and fair, the internal controls are adequate, and that they have reported any fraud or significant changes in internal controls to the auditors and the Audit Committee [Regulation 17(8) and Schedule II Part B].

(9) Corporate governance report: Every listed company must submit a quarterly compliance report on corporate governance to the stock exchanges. It must also include a separate section on corporate governance in its annual report, together with a certificate from a practicing company secretary or statutory auditors regarding compliance with the conditions of corporate governance [Regulation 27 and Schedule V Part C].

(10) Whistle blower mechanism: Listed companies must establish a whistle blower mechanism and disclose its details on the company's website. No employee shall be denied access to the Audit Committee [Regulation 22].

Note: The SEBI LODR Regulations are more detailed and prescriptive than the Companies Act, 2013 when it comes to corporate governance for listed companies. Listed companies must comply with both the Companies Act and the SEBI LODR Regulations. Where the SEBI regulation prescribes a higher standard, the company must comply with the higher standard. Non-compliance with SEBI LODR can result in penalties imposed by SEBI, suspension of trading of securities, and delisting from the stock exchange.

Table 18.2: Major Indian Committees on Corporate Governance

Committee	Year	Key Recommendation
Kumar Mangalam Birla Committee	1999	First formal code; Clause 49 introduced in Listing Agreement
Naresh Chandra Committee	2002	Auditor-company relationship; independent directors
N.R. Narayana Murthy Committee	2003	Strengthened Clause 49; whistle blower policy; audit committee role
Uday Kotak Committee	2017	Separation of chairperson and MD/CEO; enhanced role of independent directors; reduced board size
Companies Act, 2013	2013	Codified governance norms into statute; CSR; rotation of auditors; class action suits

Chapter 19

Oppression and Mismanagement

In every company, there is always a risk that the persons in control – the majority shareholders, the promoters, or the management – may conduct the affairs of the company in a manner which is oppressive to the minority shareholders or prejudicial to the interests of the company. The minority shareholders, by definition, do not have the voting power to protect themselves through the democratic process of passing resolutions. They are at the mercy of the majority. If the majority misuses its power, the minority has no remedy through the normal corporate machinery. It is for this reason that the Companies Act provides special remedies for the prevention of oppression and mismanagement. These remedies are contained in Sections 241 to 246 of the Companies Act, 2013.

The provisions for prevention of oppression and mismanagement are one of the most important safeguards for the protection of minority shareholders. They represent the law's recognition that the democratic principle of majority rule must be tempered with the principle of fairness and justice. The majority has the right to rule, but it does not have the right to oppress or be unjust to the minority.

19.1 Prevention of Oppression – Section 241

Meaning of Oppression

The term 'oppression' has not been defined in the Companies Act, 2013. However, the courts have interpreted the term in several landmark cases. Oppression, in the context of company law, means conduct which is harsh, burdensome, and wrongful, and which is lacking in fair dealing. It refers to a situation where the persons in control of the company conduct the affairs of the company in a manner which is unfair, unjust, and prejudicial to the interests of some members.

Case: Scottish Co-operative Wholesale Society Ltd. v. Meyer (1959)

Lord Cooper defined oppression as: 'Oppression involves, at the lowest, a visible departure from the standards of fair dealing and a violation of the conditions of fair play on which every shareholder who entrusts his money to a company is entitled to rely.' Viscount Simonds said the word 'oppressive' means 'burdensome, harsh, and wrongful.' This case is one of the most important cases on the meaning of oppression.

Case: Needle Industries (India) Ltd. v. Needle Industries Newey (India) Holding Ltd. (1981)

The Supreme Court of India held that oppression involves an element of lack of probity and fair dealing in the affairs of the company to the prejudice of some portion of its members. It said that the conduct must be oppressive to some part of the members and not merely to an individual member. The conduct must be oppressive in the sense that it is burdensome, harsh, and wrongful. Mere lack of confidence between the majority shareholders and the minority shareholders does not amount to oppression.

It is important to understand that not every act of the majority which the minority dislikes can be termed as 'oppression.' The Act protects the minority from genuine oppression, not from the legitimate exercise of majority power. Mere dissatisfaction or disagreement is not oppression. The conduct must be such that it can be described as unfair, unjust, burdensome, and harsh, and it must amount to a visible departure from the standards of fair dealing.

Grounds for Filing an Application – Section 241(1)

Section Reference: Section 241(1): Any member of a company who complains that – (a) the affairs of the company have been or are being conducted in a manner prejudicial to public interest or in a manner prejudicial or oppressive to him or any other member or members or in a manner prejudicial to the interests of the company; or (b) the material change, not being a change brought about by, or in the interests of, any creditors, including debenture holders or any class of shareholders of the company, has taken place in the management or control of the company, whether by an alteration in the Board of Directors, or manager, or in the ownership of the company's shares, or if it has no share capital, in its membership, or in any other manner whatsoever, and that by reason of such change, it is likely that the affairs of the company will be conducted in a manner prejudicial to its interests or its members or any class of members – may apply to the Tribunal, provided such member has a right to apply under Section 244.

From Section 241(1), the following grounds can be identified for filing an application:

(a) Affairs conducted in a manner prejudicial to public interest: If the company's affairs are being conducted in a way that is harmful to the public interest, any eligible member can file an application. For example, if a company is polluting the environment or engaging in activities harmful to public health.

(b) Affairs conducted in a manner oppressive to any member: If the affairs of the company are being conducted in a manner that is oppressive to any member or group of members, such as denial of dividends, exclusion from management, unfair allotment of shares to dilute minority holdings, removal of directors representing the minority, siphoning off company funds, and similar acts.

(c) Affairs conducted in a manner prejudicial to the interests of the company: If the conduct is harmful to the company itself, even if it is not directly oppressive to any particular member. For example, if the directors are entering into fraudulent transactions or wasting the company's assets.

(d) Material change in management or control: If there has been a material change in the management or control of the company (such as a change in the Board of Directors, change in ownership of shares, etc.)

and as a result of such change, it is likely that the affairs of the company will be conducted in a manner prejudicial to the interests of the company or its members.

Who Can File an Application? – Section 244

Section Reference: Section 244(1): The following members of a company shall have the right to apply under Section 241: (a) in the case of a company having a share capital, not less than one hundred members of the company or not less than one-tenth of the total number of its members, whichever is less, or any member or members holding not less than one-tenth of the issued share capital of the company, subject to the condition that the applicant or applicants has or have paid all calls and other sums due on his or their shares; (b) in the case of a company not having a share capital, not less than one-fifth of the total number of its members.

In simple words, the following persons can apply:

(a) In a company with share capital: at least 100 members, or at least one-tenth of total members (whichever is less), or member(s) holding at least one-tenth of the issued share capital (provided all calls are paid up).
(b) In a company without share capital: at least one-fifth of total members.

Section 244(2) provides that the Central Government may, if in its opinion the circumstances so warrant, authorise any member or members of the company to apply to the Tribunal under Section 241 notwithstanding the fact that the requirements of Section 244(1) are not met. This gives the Central Government the power to enable even a single shareholder to file an application if the circumstances justify it.

Note: The right to apply under Section 241 is a right given to the minority shareholders for their protection. However, the application can only be filed with the Tribunal (NCLT). The ordinary civil courts do not have jurisdiction to entertain applications under Section 241. This is because company matters are specialised matters which require specialised knowledge and expertise.

Examples of Oppressive Conduct

The courts have recognised the following types of conduct as oppressive:

(a) Persistent non-payment of dividends when the company has adequate profits. (b) Issue of shares to the majority at an artificially low price to dilute the minority's shareholding. (c) Exclusion of minority directors from the Board or from the management. (d) Misappropriation of company funds by the directors or majority shareholders. (e) Sale of company's assets at undervalue to a related party. (f) Diversion of company's business to a competing company owned by the majority. (g) Manipulation of accounts to show lower profits or losses. (h) Refusal to register transfer of shares to prevent change of control. (i) Payment of excessive remuneration to directors who are majority shareholders. (j) Unfair allotment of shares without giving pre-emptive rights to existing shareholders.

Case: Shanti Prasad Jain v. Kalinga Tubes Ltd. (1965)

The Supreme Court held that the oppression must involve an element of lack of probity and fair dealing in the affairs of the company to the prejudice of some part of its members. The Court said that the jurisdiction to grant relief is not intended to be exercised simply because the person in control of the company is being high-handed or is acting in a way which the minority finds disagreeable. There must be a continuous course of oppressive conduct. A single isolated act of the majority may not constitute oppression unless it is of such severity as to justify the relief.

19.2 Prevention of Mismanagement – Section 242

Meaning of Mismanagement

Mismanagement, like oppression, has not been defined in the Act. In general terms, mismanagement refers to the conduct of the company's affairs in a manner which is not in the best interests of the company. It may include incompetence, negligence, waste of the company's resources, fraudulent dealing, and any other conduct which causes or is likely to cause harm to the company and its stakeholders.

While oppression relates to conduct which is harmful to some members of the company, mismanagement relates to conduct which is harmful to the company itself or to the public interest. However, in practice, the two concepts often overlap. An act which is oppressive to the minority may also be an act of mismanagement, and vice versa. The Companies Act, 2013 deals with both oppression and mismanagement together in Sections 241 and 242.

Powers of the Tribunal – Section 242

Section 242 gives the Tribunal (NCLT) very wide powers to grant relief in cases of oppression and mismanagement. The Tribunal may, with a view to bringing to an end the matters complained of, make such order as it thinks fit. Section 242(1) provides that the Tribunal may make any of the following orders:

(a) Regulation of the company's affairs: The Tribunal may pass an order regulating the conduct of the company's affairs in the future. This may include directions regarding the management, the financial policies, the appointment and removal of directors, and any other matter relating to the conduct of the company's affairs [Section 242(1)(a)].

(b) Purchase of shares by majority from minority or vice versa: The Tribunal may order the purchase of the shares or interests of any members of the company by other members thereof or by the company itself. If the company purchases its own shares, it must reduce its share capital accordingly [Section 242(1)(b)]. This is a very important power because it provides an exit route for the oppressed minority shareholders. The Tribunal can order the majority to buy out the minority at a fair price, or in some cases, order the minority to buy out the majority.

(c) Restriction on transfer or allotment of shares: The Tribunal may place restrictions on the transfer of shares or on the allotment of shares [Section 242(1)(c)]. This can prevent the majority from further diluting the minority's holding.

(d) Removal of Managing Director, Manager, or Director: The Tribunal may terminate, set aside, or modify any agreement between the company and its managing director, or any director or manager, and may direct that the managing director, director, or manager who was a party to such agreement shall not be the managing director, director, or manager of the company or any other company for a period of up to 5 years [Section 242(1)(d)].

(e) Recovery of undue gains: The Tribunal may direct that the director or manager who has been guilty of mismanagement shall not receive any remuneration from the company. The Tribunal can also order the recovery of any undue gains made by any director, manager, or other person [Section 242(1)(e)].

(f) Setting aside fraudulent transactions: The Tribunal may set aside any transfer, delivery of goods, payment, execution, or other act relating to property made or done by or against the company within 3 months before the date of the application under Section 241, which would have been regarded as a fraudulent preference if made within 3 months before the making of a winding-up order [Section 242(1)(f)].

(g) Appointment of directors: The Tribunal may provide for the appointment of such number of persons as directors of the company as the Tribunal may consider necessary [Section 242(1)(g)]. The director appointed by the Tribunal cannot be removed by the company without the leave of the Tribunal.

(h) Alteration of MOA or AOA: The Tribunal may direct the alteration of the memorandum or the articles of the company if it considers it necessary to protect the interests of the members or the public [Section 242(2)(a)]. If the Tribunal orders such alteration, the company cannot make any further alteration in the memorandum or articles which is inconsistent with the Tribunal's order without the leave of the Tribunal [Section 242(3)].

(i) Any other order: The Tribunal may make any other order as it thinks just and equitable in the circumstances of the case. This is a residuary power which gives the Tribunal the flexibility to craft appropriate remedies for different situations.

Illustration: In a private company, the two promoter-brothers (holding 60% shares) systematically excluded the sister (holding 40% shares) from all management decisions, paid themselves excessive salaries, refused to declare dividends, and attempted to dilute her shareholding by issuing shares to their own nominees. The sister filed an application under Section 241. The Tribunal found oppression and ordered the brothers to buy the sister's shares at a fair value determined by a registered valuer. The Tribunal also restrained the brothers from issuing any further shares without Tribunal's approval.

Section 243 – Consequences of Removal of Director by Tribunal

Section 243(1) provides that if an order under Section 242 terminates or sets aside any agreement and directs that a managing director or director or manager shall not hold the office of managing director or director or manager in any company for a period of up to 5 years, then such person shall not directly or indirectly act as managing director, director, or manager of that or any other company during that period without the leave of the Tribunal.

Section 243(2) provides that any person who contravenes the above provision shall be punishable with imprisonment for a term which may extend to 6 months or with a fine which may extend to Rs. 5 lakhs, or with both.

Note: The powers of the Tribunal under Section 242 are very wide and discretionary. The Tribunal exercises these powers keeping in mind the principles of equity, justice, and good conscience. The objective is to bring the matters complained of to an end and to protect the interests of the aggrieved members and the company as a whole. The Tribunal is not bound to grant any specific relief – it may grant such relief as it considers just and equitable in the circumstances of each case.

19.3 Class Action Suit – Section 245

The concept of class action suit is a new and significant introduction in the Companies Act, 2013. Before the 2013 Act, there was no provision in Indian company law for class action suits. A class action suit enables a group of persons who have suffered a common grievance to jointly sue the company or its management for relief.

Definition and Purpose

Section Reference: Section 245(1): Such number of member or members, depositor or depositors or any class of them, as the case may be, as are indicated in sub-section (3), may, if they are of the opinion that the management or conduct of the affairs of the company are being conducted in a manner prejudicial to the interests of the company or its members or depositors, file an application before the Tribunal on behalf of the members or depositors for seeking all or any of the following orders, namely:—

The orders which may be sought in a class action suit include:

(a) To restrain the company from committing an act which is ultra vires the articles or memorandum of the company [Section 245(1)(a)].

(b) To restrain the company from committing breach of any provision of the company's memorandum or articles [Section 245(1)(b)].

(c) To declare a resolution altering the memorandum or articles of the company as void if the resolution was passed by suppression of material facts or obtained by misstatement to the members or depositors [Section 245(1)(c)].

(d) To restrain the company and its directors from acting on such resolution [Section 245(1)(d)].

(e) To restrain the company from doing an act which is contrary to the provisions of the Act or any other law for the time being in force [Section 245(1)(e)].

(f) To restrain the company from taking action contrary to any resolution passed by the members [Section 245(1)(f)].

(g) To claim damages or compensation or demand any other suitable action from or against the company or its directors for any fraudulent, unlawful, or wrongful act or omission, or the conduct of the company or its directors [Section 245(1)(g)].

(h) To claim damages or compensation or demand any other suitable action from the auditor including audit firm of the company for any improper or misleading statement of particulars made in his audit report or for any fraudulent, unlawful, or wrongful act or conduct [Section 245(1)(h)].

(i) To claim damages or compensation or demand any other suitable action from the expert or consultant or any other person for any incorrect or misleading statement made to the company or its members or for any fraudulent, unlawful, or wrongful act or conduct [Section 245(1)(i)].

Who Can File a Class Action Suit? – Section 245(3)

The following persons are eligible to file a class action suit:

Category	Company with Share Capital	Company without Share Capital
Members	Not less than 100 members or not less than such percentage of total members as prescribed (whichever is less); or member(s) holding not less than such percentage of issued share capital as prescribed (subject to all dues being paid up)	Not less than one-fifth of the total number of its members
Depositors	Not less than 100 depositors or not less than	Same thresholds

	such percentage of total depositors as prescribed (whichever is less); or depositor(s) to whom the company owes not less than such percentage of total deposits as prescribed	

Important Provisions of Section 245

(1) Admissibility: Section 245(4) provides that the Tribunal shall consider the application under Section 245 only if it is satisfied that the application is in good faith, that there is prime facie case in favour of the members or depositors, and that the application is in the interest of the company.

(2) Binding effect: Section 245(5) provides that any order passed by the Tribunal shall be binding on the company and all its members, depositors, and auditors, including the auditing firm or audit firm of the company. This means that the order benefits all the members/depositors of the class and not just those who filed the application.

(3) No withdrawal without Tribunal's permission: The application admitted under Section 245 shall not be withdrawn without the leave of the Tribunal [Section 245(7)].

(4) Costs: Section 245(9) provides that the company shall bear the costs of the class action suit if the application is successful. If the suit is frivolous, the Tribunal may impose costs on the applicants.

(5) Protection from similar suits: Section 245(6) provides that a similar application by any member or depositor is not maintainable in any court or Tribunal once an application under Section 245 is admitted.

(6) Not applicable to banking companies: Section 245(8) provides that the class action suit provisions do not apply to a banking company.

Note: The class action suit is a powerful tool for the protection of minority shareholders and depositors. It enables them to collectively fight against oppression, fraud, and mismanagement by the majority or the management. The advantage of a class action suit is that the costs of litigation are shared among the members of the class, and the order benefits all the members of the class. This is particularly useful when individual claims are too small to justify individual litigation.

Indian Context: In 2020, some minority shareholders of a well-known Indian company attempted to use Section 245 to challenge certain related party transactions which they alleged were detrimental to the company's interests. Although class action suits are still relatively rare in India compared to the United States, the provision provides a powerful tool that is increasingly being explored by shareholder activists and institutional investors

Table 19.1: Oppression (Section 241) vs. Class Action (Section 245)

Point	Oppression & Mismanagement (Sec 241)	Class Action Suit (Sec 245)
Purpose	Relief from oppressive/prejudicial conduct	Relief from fraudulent, wrongful, or unlawful acts
Filed by	Members (100 or one-tenth threshold)	Members or depositors (100 or prescribed percentage)
Filed against	The company / its management	Company, directors, auditors, experts, consultants
Tribunal's power	Wide – can regulate affairs, order buy-out, alter MOA/AOA	Wide – can restrain acts, award damages, declare resolutions void

Binding effect	On the parties to the application	On the company and ALL members/depositors of the class
Banking companies	Applicable	Not applicable (Section 245(8))
Section	241–244	245

19.4 National Company Law Tribunal (NCLT)

The National Company Law Tribunal (NCLT) is a quasi-judicial body established under the Companies Act, 2013 to adjudicate matters relating to companies. The NCLT was constituted on 1st June, 2016. It has replaced the Company Law Board (CLB) and has taken over the jurisdiction of the High Courts in several company law matters.

Constitution – Section 408

Section Reference: Section 408(1): The Central Government shall, by notification, constitute, with effect from such date as may be specified therein, a Tribunal to be known as the National Company Law Tribunal consisting of such number of judicial and technical members, not exceeding the prescribed number, as the Central Government may deem necessary, to be appointed by it by notification, to exercise and discharge such powers and functions as are, or may be, conferred on it by or under this Act or any other law for the time being in force.

The NCLT consists of a President and such number of judicial and technical members as the Central Government may deem necessary. The President must be a person who is or has been a Judge of a High Court for at least 5 years. A judicial member must be a person who is or has been a judge of a High Court or is or has been a District Judge for at least 5 years. A technical member must be a person who has been a member of the Indian Corporate Law Service or the Indian Legal Service for at least 15 years, or who has practiced as a Chartered Accountant, Cost Accountant, or Company Secretary for at least 15 years.

Benches and Jurisdiction

The NCLT has its principal bench in New Delhi. In addition, various benches have been constituted across India in cities like Mumbai, Chennai, Kolkata, Ahmedabad, Hyderabad, Bengaluru, Chandigarh, Jaipur, Kochi, Allahabad, Guwahati, Cuttack, Amaravati, and Indore. Each bench exercises jurisdiction over the companies registered within its territorial jurisdiction.

Each bench consists of a judicial member and a technical member. The President may constitute benches with a single member (judicial or technical) for certain categories of cases. Matters relating to rehabilitation, restructuring, and winding up are heard by benches comprising both a judicial member and a technical member.

Powers and Jurisdiction of the NCLT

The NCLT has jurisdiction over a wide range of company law matters, including:

(a) Applications for oppression and mismanagement under Sections 241–246. (b) Applications for class action suits under Section 245. (c) Applications relating to compromise, arrangement, amalgamation, and merger under Sections 230–234. (d) Applications for winding up of companies under Sections 271–365. (e) Applications relating to corporate insolvency resolution process under the Insolvency and Bankruptcy Code, 2016. (f) Applications for reduction of share capital under Section 66. (g) Applications for conversion of public company into private company under Section 14. (h) Applications for rectification of register of members under Section 59. (i) Applications relating to deposits and depositors. (j) Applications for compounding of offences under Section 441. (k) Any other matter which the Central Government may prescribe.

The NCLT has the same powers as a civil court in respect of: (a) summoning and enforcing attendance of witnesses, (b) requiring the discovery and production of documents, (c) receiving evidence on affidavit, (d) issuing commissions for examination of witnesses, (e) any other matter as may be prescribed [Section 424].

Procedure Before the NCLT

The NCLT follows its own rules of procedure as prescribed by the Central Government – the National Company Law Tribunal Rules, 2016. The proceedings before the NCLT are less formal than the proceedings in civil courts. The Tribunal may follow the principles of natural justice but is not bound by the strict rules of evidence under the Indian Evidence Act, 1872. The Tribunal must decide every application within 3 months from the date of presentation, unless extended for reasons to be recorded in writing [Section 422].

Appeals Against NCLT Orders – Section 421

Any person aggrieved by an order of the NCLT may file an appeal to the National Company Law Appellate Tribunal (NCLAT) within 45 days from the date of the order. The appeal must be accompanied by a certified copy of the order and the prescribed fee. The NCLAT may extend the time for filing the appeal by a further period not exceeding 45 days if it is satisfied that the appellant was prevented by sufficient cause from filing the appeal within the prescribed period.

Note: The establishment of the NCLT has been a landmark reform in Indian company law. Before the NCLT, company law matters were scattered across multiple forums – the Company Law Board, the High Courts, the Board for Industrial and Financial Reconstruction (BIFR), and the Appellate Authority for Industrial and Financial Reconstruction (AAIFR). The NCLT has consolidated all these jurisdictions into a single specialised tribunal, resulting in faster disposal of cases and greater consistency in decision-making.

19.5 National Company Law Appellate Tribunal (NCLAT)

The National Company Law Appellate Tribunal (NCLAT) is the appellate body established under the Companies Act, 2013 to hear appeals against the orders of the NCLT. The NCLAT was also constituted on 1st June, 2016.

Constitution – Section 410

Section Reference: Section 410: The Central Government shall, by notification, constitute, with effect from such date as may be specified therein, an Appellate Tribunal to be known as the National Company Law Appellate Tribunal consisting of a Chairperson and such number of Judicial and Technical Members, not exceeding eleven, as the Central Government may deem fit, to be appointed by it by notification, for hearing appeals against the orders of the Tribunal.

The NCLAT consists of a Chairperson and such number of judicial and technical members (not exceeding eleven) as the Central Government may deem fit. The Chairperson must be a person who is or has been a Judge of the Supreme Court or the Chief Justice of a High Court. The qualifications for the judicial and technical members are similar to those prescribed for the NCLT.

The NCLAT has its principal office in New Delhi. It may also sit at such other places as the Central Government may prescribe.

Jurisdiction of the NCLAT

The NCLAT has jurisdiction to hear and dispose of:

(a) Appeals against the orders of the NCLT: Any person aggrieved by any order of the NCLT may prefer an appeal to the NCLAT [Section 421].

(b) Appeals under the Insolvency and Bankruptcy Code, 2016: The NCLAT also acts as the appellate tribunal under the Insolvency and Bankruptcy Code (IBC), 2016. It hears appeals against the orders of the NCLT passed under the IBC.

(c) Appeals under the Competition Act, 2002: With effect from 2017, the NCLAT has also been designated as the appellate tribunal for appeals against the orders of the Competition Commission of India (CCI) under the Competition Act, 2002. This jurisdiction was earlier with the Competition Appellate Tribunal (COMPAT) which has since been merged with the NCLAT.

Appeals Against NCLAT Orders

Any person aggrieved by any order of the NCLAT may file an appeal to the Supreme Court of India within 60 days from the date of receipt of the order [Section 423]. The appeal to the Supreme Court is limited to questions of law only. The Supreme Court may extend the time for filing the appeal by a further period not exceeding 60 days if it is satisfied that the appellant was prevented by sufficient cause from filing the appeal within the prescribed period.

Table 19.2: NCLT and NCLAT at a Glance

Feature	NCLT	NCLAT
Section	408	410
Nature	Tribunal (First instance)	Appellate Tribunal (Appeals)
Head	President (HC Judge with 5 years' experience)	Chairperson (SC Judge or HC Chief Justice)
Members	Judicial + Technical members	Judicial + Technical members (max 11)
Constituted on	1st June, 2016	1st June, 2016
Benches	Multiple benches across India (15+ cities)	Principal office in New Delhi
Jurisdiction	All company law matters, winding up, IBC	Appeals from NCLT, IBC, Competition Act
Appeal against orders	To NCLAT within 45 days	To Supreme Court within 60 days (on law only)
Replaced	Company Law Board,	COMPAT (for

	BIFR, AAIFR, HC jurisdiction	Competition Act appeals)
Decision timeline	3 months from date of application	As per NCLAT Rules

Indian Context: The NCLT has become one of the busiest tribunals in India, particularly after the enactment of the Insolvency and Bankruptcy Code, 2016. Major corporate insolvency cases like Essar Steel, Bhushan Steel, Alok Industries, Amtek Auto, and Jaypee Infratech have been resolved through the NCLT/NCLAT process. The NCLT bench at Indore handles company law matters and IBC cases for companies registered in Madhya Pradesh and Chhattisgarh.

PART – VI : WINDING UP & OTHER PROVISIONS

Chapter 20

Winding Up of Companies

Just as a company is born through the process of incorporation, a company dies through the process of winding up. Winding up is the process by which the life of a company is brought to an end. It is the process of collecting the assets of the company, paying off its debts and liabilities, and distributing the surplus, if any, among the members in proportion to their shareholding. After the winding up is completed, the company is dissolved and ceases to exist as a legal entity. Winding up does not mean the immediate death of the company. The company continues to exist as a legal entity until it is formally dissolved. During the period of winding up, the company cannot carry on any business except to the extent necessary for the beneficial winding up of its affairs.

20.1 Meaning and Modes of Winding Up

Meaning of Winding Up

Winding up is the process by which the management of a company's affairs is taken out of the hands of the directors and entrusted to a person called the 'liquidator,' who collects the assets, pays the debts, and distributes the surplus among the contributories (members) in accordance with their rights. It is a legal proceeding under the supervision of the Tribunal (NCLT) or, in the case of voluntary winding up, under the supervision of the members and creditors.

It is very important to distinguish between 'winding up' and 'dissolution.' Winding up is the process; dissolution is the end result. During the winding up process, the company continues to exist as a legal entity and can sue and be sued in its own name. The company is dissolved only after the winding up process is completed and the

Tribunal passes an order of dissolution. On dissolution, the company ceases to exist.

Modes of Winding Up

Under the Companies Act, 2013, winding up of a company may be done in two ways:

(1) Winding Up by the Tribunal (Compulsory Winding Up): This is winding up ordered by the National Company Law Tribunal (NCLT) on an application (petition) made by the company, its creditors, contributories, the Registrar, or any person authorised by the Central Government. This is governed by Sections 271 to 365 of the Companies Act, 2013 read with the Insolvency and Bankruptcy Code, 2016.

(2) Voluntary Winding Up: Under the original Companies Act, 2013, voluntary winding up was provided for in Sections 304 to 323. However, after the enactment of the Insolvency and Bankruptcy Code (IBC), 2016, the provisions relating to voluntary winding up under the Companies Act, 2013 have been substantially replaced by Section 59 of the IBC, 2016. Now, voluntary liquidation of a corporate person is governed by the IBC and not by the Companies Act.

Note: Under the Companies Act, 1956, there were three modes of winding up: (a) Compulsory winding up by the Court, (b) Voluntary winding up (further divided into Members' Voluntary Winding Up and Creditors' Voluntary Winding Up), and (c) Winding up subject to the supervision of the Court. The Companies Act, 2013 originally retained only two modes – winding up by Tribunal and voluntary winding up. After the IBC came into effect, the voluntary winding up provisions of the 2013 Act were omitted and replaced by the voluntary liquidation process under the IBC.

Mode	Authority	Governing Law
Winding Up by the Tribunal	National Company Law Tribunal (NCLT)	Companies Act, 2013 (Sections 271–365)
Voluntary Liquidation	Members / Creditors + Insolvency Professional	Insolvency and Bankruptcy Code, 2016 (Section 59)

20.2 Winding Up by Tribunal – Section 271

Winding up by the Tribunal is also called compulsory winding up because it is ordered by the Tribunal even if the company or its management does not want it. The Tribunal orders winding up on the basis of a petition filed by a qualified person on one or more of the grounds specified in the Act.

Grounds for Winding Up by the Tribunal – Section 271

Section Reference: Section 271(1): A company may, on a petition under Section 272, be wound up by the Tribunal – (a) if the company has, by special resolution, resolved that the company be wound up by the Tribunal; (b) if the company has acted against the interests of the sovereignty and integrity of India, the security of the State, friendly relations with foreign States, public order, decency, or morality; (c) if on an application made by the Registrar or any other person authorised by the Central Government by notification under this Act, the Tribunal is of the opinion that the affairs of the company have been conducted in a fraudulent manner or the company was formed for fraudulent and unlawful purpose or the persons concerned in the formation or management of its affairs have been guilty of fraud, misfeasance, or misconduct in connection therewith and that it is proper that the company be wound up; (d) if the company has made a default in filing with the Registrar its financial statements or annual returns for immediately preceding five consecutive financial years; or (e) if the Tribunal is of the opinion that it is just and equitable that the company should be wound up.

Let us examine each of these grounds in detail:

(a) Special Resolution: The company itself may resolve that it should be wound up by the Tribunal. This resolution must be a special resolution (i.e., passed by a three-fourths majority). This ground is used when the members themselves want to close down the company and prefer the Tribunal's supervision for the winding up process.

(b) Against sovereignty, security, public order, decency, or morality: If the company has acted in a manner which is against the sovereignty and integrity of India, the security of the State, friendly relations with foreign States, public order, decency, or morality, the Tribunal may order its winding up. This is a very serious ground and is invoked in cases where the company's activities are harmful to the nation or to public interest.

(c) Fraudulent conduct: If the affairs of the company have been conducted in a fraudulent manner, or the company was formed for a fraudulent or unlawful purpose, or the persons concerned in its management have been guilty of fraud, misfeasance, or misconduct, the Tribunal may order winding up. This ground can be invoked by the Registrar or any person authorised by the Central Government. This is an important ground because it targets companies which are involved in fraudulent activities.

(d) Non-filing of financial statements or annual returns: If the company has not filed its financial statements or annual returns with the Registrar for five consecutive financial years, the Tribunal may order winding up. This is a relatively new ground introduced by the 2013 Act. It is aimed at companies which are dormant or defunct and have not complied with their statutory filing obligations.

(e) Just and equitable: The Tribunal may order winding up if it is of the opinion that it is just and equitable to do so. This is the widest ground and gives the Tribunal a very broad discretion. The Tribunal can order winding up on this ground even if none of the other grounds exist, if it is satisfied that the circumstances are such that it is just and equitable to wind up the company.

Just and Equitable Ground – Detailed Analysis

The 'just and equitable' ground is the most flexible and frequently invoked ground for winding up. The courts and tribunals have ordered winding up on this ground in the following types of situations:

(i) Deadlock in management: Where there is a complete deadlock in the management of the company and the directors cannot agree on anything, making it impossible for the company to function. This is particularly common in private companies with equal shareholding where the two groups of shareholders are unable to work together.

Case: Yenidje Tobacco Co. Ltd. (1916)

Two persons, Y and R, formed a company with equal shareholding. Each was a director. They quarrelled and could not agree on anything. They stopped speaking to each other and communicated only through the company secretary. The business came to a standstill. The Court ordered winding up on the just and equitable ground, holding that the relationship between the two director-shareholders was analogous to a partnership and since the partnership between them had broken down irretrievably, it was just and equitable to wind up the company.

(ii) Loss of substratum (main object): Where the main object or purpose for which the company was formed has failed or become impossible, and the company has lost its substratum (i.e., there is no business left for the company to carry on), winding up may be ordered.

Case: Re German Date Coffee Co. (1882)

A company was formed with the object of manufacturing coffee from dates under a German patent. The patent was never obtained. The Court held that the main object of the company had failed and there was no business left for the company to carry on. The substratum of the company was gone. It was just and equitable to wind up the company.

(iii) Fraud or illegal purpose: Where the company was formed for a fraudulent or illegal purpose, or where the business is carried on by means of fraud.

(iv) Oppression of minority: Where the majority shareholders are oppressing the minority to such an extent that winding up is the only remedy available. However, the Tribunal will first consider whether a less drastic remedy (such as an order under Section 242) would be appropriate before ordering winding up.

(v) Financial difficulties: Where the company is so heavily indebted that it cannot pay its debts and there is no reasonable prospect of it becoming solvent. However, after the IBC, 2016, insolvency-related winding up is now primarily dealt with under the IBC rather than under Section 271.

(vi) Bubble companies: Where the company was formed merely to issue shares and never had any genuine business. Such companies are sometimes called 'bubble companies' because they are formed like bubbles and burst soon after.

Note: The 'just and equitable' ground is not to be used lightly. The Tribunal must be satisfied that there are no alternative remedies available and that winding up is the only just and proper course of action. The Tribunal will consider all the circumstances of the case and will not order winding up merely because the petitioner is unhappy or dissatisfied with the management. The petitioner must show that there are genuine grounds which make it just and equitable to wind up the company.

Who Can File a Petition? – Section 272

Section Reference: Section 272(1): A petition to the Tribunal for the winding up of a company shall be presented by – (a) the company; (b) any contributory or contributories; (c) all or any of the persons specified in clauses (a) and (b); (d) the Registrar; (e) any person authorised by the Central Government in that behalf; or (f) in a case falling under clause (b) of Section 271, by the Central Government or a State Government.

A 'contributory' means every person liable to contribute to the assets of a company in the event of its being wound up [Section 2(26)]. It includes present and past members of the company. However, a past member is not liable to contribute if he ceased to be a member more than one year before the commencement of the winding up.

The Registrar can file a winding up petition only with the previous sanction of the Central Government and on the following grounds: (a) fraudulent conduct under Section 271(1)(c); (b) non-filing of returns for five consecutive years under Section 271(1)(d); (c) just and equitable ground under Section 271(1)(e); and (d) if the company has acted against the sovereignty, security, etc. under Section 271(1)(b).

Procedure for Winding Up by Tribunal

The following is the general procedure for winding up by the Tribunal:

(1) Filing of petition: A petition is filed with the NCLT by any of the persons mentioned in Section 272, along with the prescribed fee and supporting documents. The petition must state the grounds for winding up and the relief sought.

(2) Admission of petition: The Tribunal examines the petition and, if it is satisfied that a prima facie case is made out, admits the petition and issues notice to the company and other interested persons.

(3) Advertisement: The admitted petition is advertised in a newspaper having circulation in the district where the registered office of the company is situated. This enables creditors, contributories, and other interested persons to participate in the proceedings.

(4) Hearing: The Tribunal hears the petitioner, the company, the creditors, and the contributories. The Tribunal may appoint a provisional liquidator at this stage if it considers it necessary to protect the assets of the company [Section 273].

(5) Winding up order: After hearing all parties, the Tribunal may make one of the following orders: (a) dismiss the petition, (b) make any interim order as it thinks fit, (c) appoint a provisional liquidator, (d) make an order for winding up of the company, or (e) make any other order as it thinks fit [Section 273(1)]. The winding up is deemed to commence on the date of the filing of the petition [Section 357].

(6) Appointment of liquidator: On the making of the winding up order, the Tribunal appoints an Official Liquidator or a Company Liquidator to conduct the winding up proceedings [Section 275]. The liquidator takes over the management of the company from the directors.

(7) Realisation of assets and payment of debts: The liquidator collects the assets of the company, realises them (sells them), and uses the proceeds to pay the debts of the company in the order of priority prescribed by the Act.

(8) Distribution of surplus: After paying all the debts and the costs of winding up, if there is any surplus, it is distributed among the contributories (members) in proportion to their shareholding.

(9) Dissolution: After the winding up is completed, the liquidator files a report with the Tribunal. The Tribunal, on being satisfied that the affairs of the company have been completely wound up, passes an order of dissolution. The company ceases to exist as a legal entity from the date of the dissolution order [Section 302].

20.3 Voluntary Winding Up (Under IBC, 2016)

As mentioned earlier, voluntary winding up (now called 'voluntary liquidation') is now governed by Section 59 of the Insolvency and Bankruptcy Code, 2016 and the IBBI (Voluntary Liquidation Process) Regulations, 2017. The original provisions for voluntary winding up under the Companies Act, 2013 (Sections 304 to 323) have been omitted.

When Can a Company Opt for Voluntary Liquidation?

Section 59(1) of the IBC provides that a corporate person who intends to liquidate itself voluntarily and has not committed any default (i.e., has paid all its debts or made adequate provision for payment of its debts) may initiate voluntary liquidation proceedings.

The voluntary liquidation can be initiated in two ways: (a) By a declaration of the majority of the directors, verified by an affidavit, that the company has no debt or that it will be able to pay its debts in full from the proceeds of assets to be sold in the voluntary liquidation, and that the company is not being liquidated to defraud any person. (b) By a special resolution of the members in case of a members' voluntary liquidation, or by a resolution of the members where the company owes debts and the creditors representing two-thirds in value of the debt of the company approve the resolution within seven days.

Procedure for Voluntary Liquidation Under IBC

(1) Declaration of solvency: The majority of the directors must make a declaration (verified by affidavit) that the company has no debts or that it will be able to pay its debts in full. This declaration must be accompanied by the audited financial statements and a report of the valuation of the assets of the company.

(2) Special resolution: The company must pass a special resolution in a general meeting appointing an insolvency professional as the liquidator to conduct the voluntary liquidation process. The resolution must also fix the remuneration of the liquidator.

(3) Creditors' approval (if debts exist): If the company has any debts, the creditors representing two-thirds in value of the debts must approve the resolution within seven days of the special resolution.

(4) Public announcement: Within five days of the special resolution, the liquidator must make a public announcement calling upon the stakeholders to submit their claims within 30 days. He must also inform the Registrar and the IBBI (Insolvency and Bankruptcy Board of India) about the commencement of voluntary liquidation.

(5) Verification of claims: The liquidator verifies the claims of the creditors and prepares a list of stakeholders.

(6) Realisation and distribution: The liquidator realises the assets of the company, pays the debts in the order of priority specified in the IBC, and distributes the surplus (if any) to the members.

(7) Final report and dissolution: The liquidator prepares a final report and submits it to the members, creditors, and the NCLT. The

NCLT, on being satisfied that the voluntary liquidation process has been completed, passes an order of dissolution. The company is dissolved from the date of the NCLT's order.

The entire voluntary liquidation process must be completed within a period of 12 months from the date of commencement. The NCLT may, on an application made by the liquidator, extend the period for a maximum period of up to two years.

Table 20.1: Winding Up by Tribunal vs. Voluntary Liquidation

Point	Winding Up by Tribunal	Voluntary Liquidation (IBC)
Nature	Compulsory – ordered by NCLT	Voluntary – initiated by company itself
Governing Law	Companies Act, 2013 (Sec 271–365)	IBC, 2016 (Sec 59) + IBBI Regulations
Initiated by	Company, creditors, contributories, Registrar, Central Govt	Company (members + creditors)
Precondition	Grounds under Section 271	Company must have no default or must be solvent
Resolution	Special resolution (ground (a)) or petition	Special resolution + creditors' approval (if debts exist)
Liquidator	Official Liquidator / Company Liquidator (appointed by Tribunal)	Insolvency Professional (appointed by members)
Supervision	Under Tribunal's supervision throughout	Under Insolvency Professional; NCLT at

		dissolution stage
Time frame	No fixed time limit	Must be completed within 12 months (extendable to 2 years)
Dissolution	Order by NCLT after completion	Order by NCLT on liquidator's application
Main use	Fraudulent companies, insolvent companies, deadlocked companies	Solvent companies wanting orderly closure

20.4 Liquidator – Powers and Duties

The liquidator is the central figure in the winding up process. He takes over the management of the company from the directors and is responsible for collecting the assets, paying the debts, and distributing the surplus. His role is similar to that of an executor of a will who carries out the last wishes of the deceased.

Appointment of Liquidator

In winding up by the Tribunal, the Tribunal appoints the liquidator. Section 275 provides that the Tribunal shall, at the time of passing the order of winding up, appoint an Official Liquidator or a liquidator from a panel maintained by the Central Government. The liquidator must be a professional – a Chartered Accountant, a Company Secretary, a Cost Accountant, or an Advocate of at least 10 years' standing who has experience of winding up affairs. In voluntary liquidation under the IBC, the liquidator is an insolvency professional registered with the IBBI who is appointed by the members.

Powers of the Liquidator – Section 290

Section 290 gives the Company Liquidator very wide powers to enable him to carry out the winding up effectively. These powers are divided into two categories:

(A) Powers Exercisable with the Sanction of the Tribunal –

Section 290(1)(a)

The following powers can be exercised by the liquidator only with the prior approval (sanction) of the Tribunal:

(i) To institute or defend any suit, prosecution, or other legal proceeding, civil or criminal, in the name and on behalf of the company.

(ii) To carry on the business of the company so far as may be necessary for the beneficial winding up of the company.

(iii) To sell the immovable and movable property of the company by public auction or private contract, with power to transfer the whole thereof to any person or to sell the same in parcels.

(iv) To raise any money required on the security of the assets of the company.

(v) To do all such other things as may be necessary for winding up the affairs of the company and distributing its assets.

(B) Powers Exercisable Without the Sanction of the Tribunal – Section 290(1)(b)

The following powers can be exercised by the liquidator without the Tribunal's sanction:

(i) To execute, in the name and on behalf of the company, all deeds, receipts, and other documents.

(ii) To prove, rank, and claim in the insolvency of any contributory for any balance against his estate.

(iii) To draw, accept, make, and endorse any negotiable instrument in the name and on behalf of the company.

(iv) To take out, in his official name, letters of administration to any deceased contributory and to do any other act necessary for obtaining payment of any money due from a contributory or his estate.

Duties of the Liquidator

The main duties of the liquidator include:

(1) To take into his custody or under his control all the property, effects, and actionable claims to which the company is or appears to be

entitled [Section 281].

(2) To settle the list of contributories and make calls on them for any money due [Section 285].

(3) To collect all debts due to the company.

(4) To investigate the affairs of the company, including the conduct of its promoters, directors, and officers, and to report any fraud, misfeasance, or misconduct to the Tribunal.

(5) To pay the debts of the company in the order of priority prescribed by the Act.

(6) To distribute the surplus, if any, among the contributories.

(7) To file periodic reports with the Tribunal on the progress of the winding up.

(8) To apply to the Tribunal for the dissolution of the company after the winding up is completed.

20.5 Consequences of Winding Up

The making of a winding up order has several important legal consequences:

(1) Directors' powers cease: On the making of the winding up order, all the powers of the directors cease. The directors cannot exercise any power on behalf of the company, except with the sanction of the liquidator or the Tribunal [Section 278(a)]. The management of the company is transferred from the directors to the liquidator.

(2) Employees terminated: The winding up order operates as a notice of discharge to the officers, employees, and workmen of the company, except when the business of the company is continued by the liquidator [Section 278(b)]. However, the employees are entitled to their wages and dues in priority over other creditors.

(3) Stay of suits: When a winding up order has been made, no suit or other legal proceeding shall be commenced or continued against the company except with the leave of the Tribunal [Section 279]. This is to protect the assets of the company and to ensure that all claims are dealt with in the winding up proceedings itself.

(4) Effect on share transfers: Any transfer of shares made after the commencement of winding up is void unless the Tribunal orders otherwise [Section 281(2)]. Similarly, any alteration in the status of the members made after the commencement of winding up is void.

(5) Disposition of property void: Any disposition of the property (including actionable claims) of the company, and any transfer of shares in the company, or alteration in the status of members, made after the commencement of the winding up shall be void, unless the Tribunal otherwise orders [Section 334]. This prevents the directors or the majority shareholders from dissipating the assets of the company after the winding up process has begun.

(6) Fraudulent preference void: Any transfer or charge on the company's property made within a specified period before the commencement of winding up, with the intent to give a preference to certain creditors over others, shall be deemed a fraudulent preference and shall be void [Section 328].

(7) Floating charge invalid: A floating charge on the company's property created within 12 months (or 2 years if in favour of a related party) before the commencement of winding up shall be invalid, unless it is proved that the company, immediately after the creation of the charge, was solvent [Section 332].

Order of Priority for Payment of Debts – Section 326 & 327

The debts of the company are paid in the following order of priority:

(a) First: The costs of winding up, including the remuneration of the liquidator. (b) Second: Workmen's dues for the preceding 24 months and secured creditors' debts (pari passu – equally). Section 326 provides that workmen's dues and debts due to secured creditors shall be paid in priority over all other debts. The workmen's dues and the secured creditors' debts rank equally and shall be paid proportionately if the assets are insufficient. (c) Third: Wages and salaries of employees (other than workmen) for the preceding 24 months. (d) Fourth: All revenues, taxes, cesses, and other dues of the Central and State Governments and local authorities. (e) Fifth: All other unsecured debts. (f) Sixth: Any surplus remaining after payment of all debts is distributed among the contributories (members) – first to preference shareholders (up to the amount of their capital), and the remaining surplus to equity shareholders in proportion to their shareholding.

Note: The order of priority for payment of debts is very important in the winding up process. In most cases, the assets of the company are insufficient to pay all the debts, and the creditors receive only a fraction of their dues. The employees and the Government have priority over unsecured creditors, and the shareholders are the last to receive any payment. In many winding up cases, the shareholders receive nothing because the assets are not sufficient even to pay the creditors in full.

20.6 Striking Off of Company Name – Section 248

Striking off is a relatively simpler and faster process of removing a company from the register of companies. It is not the same as winding up. Winding up involves a detailed process of collecting assets, paying debts, and distributing surplus. Striking off is an administrative process by which the Registrar removes the name of a defunct or inactive company from the register.

When Can the Registrar Strike Off? – Section 248(1)

Section 248(1) provides that the Registrar may strike off the name of a company from the register if he has reasonable cause to believe that – (a) the company is not carrying on any business or operation for a period of two immediately preceding financial years and has not made any application within such period for obtaining the status of a dormant company under Section 455; (b) the subscribers to the memorandum have not paid the subscription which they had undertaken to pay at the time of incorporation of a company and a declaration under Section 10A(1)(a) has not been filed within 180 days of its incorporation; and (c) the company is not carrying on any business or operations, as revealed after the physical verification carried out under Section 12(9).

Before striking off, the Registrar must send a notice to the company and all its directors giving them at least 30 days to send their representations. The Registrar must also cause a notice to be placed on the MCA website for at least 30 days. If no representation is received or the representation is not satisfactory, the Registrar may strike off the name of the company.

Application by Company for Striking Off – Section 248(2)

Section 248(2) provides that a company may also apply to the Registrar for striking off its name from the register if it has not commenced business within one year of its incorporation, or if it is not carrying on any business or operation for a period of two immediately preceding financial years and has no intention of doing so. The application must be made by the company after obtaining the consent of 75% of the members (in terms of paid-up share capital), and the company must have no assets and no liabilities at the time of the application.

The company must file an application in Form STK-2 along with the prescribed fee and a statement of accounts (not older than 30 days from the date of application). The Registrar, on being satisfied, will publish a notice in the Official Gazette and on the website of the MCA. If no objection is received within 30 days, the Registrar may strike off the name of the company.

Effect of Striking Off

Section 248(6) provides that the striking off shall not affect the liability (if any) of every officer and member of the company. The liability continues and may be enforced as if the company had not been struck off. This means that even though the company's name has been removed from the register, the directors, officers, and members remain liable for any obligations that existed before the striking off.

Section 248(7) provides that any aggrieved person may file an appeal to the Tribunal (NCLT) against the order of the Registrar striking off the name of the company. The Tribunal may, if it is satisfied that the company was carrying on business or that it is otherwise just to restore, order the restoration of the name of the company to the register. The Tribunal must dispose of the application within 3 years.

Point	Winding Up	Striking Off
Nature	Full legal process of liquidation	Administrative removal from register
Authority	NCLT (Tribunal)	Registrar of Companies
Process	Collection of assets, payment of debts, distribution of surplus	Simple removal of name; no liquidation process
Suitable for	Companies with assets, debts, and operations	Defunct / inactive companies with no assets and no liabilities
Liability after	Liability discharged through liquidation	Liability continues even after striking off (Sec 248(6))
Restoration possible?	Not applicable (dissolution is final)	Yes – appeal to NCLT within 3 years (Sec 248(7))
Section	271–365	248

Indian Context: The MCA has been conducting periodic 'clean-up drives' to strike off defunct and inactive companies from the register. In 2017-18, the MCA struck off over 2 lakh companies which had not filed their annual returns for three or more years. This exercise was aimed at removing shell companies and reducing the number of inactive companies on the register. Many of these struck-off companies were suspected of being used for money laundering and other fraudulent purposes.

Chapter 21

Compromises, Arrangements & Amalgamations

In the modern business world, companies do not always remain as separate, independent entities throughout their lifetime. Business strategies often require companies to come together, combine their resources, or restructure their operations. Sometimes, a company may need to settle disputes with its creditors by offering them a compromise. Sometimes, two companies may decide to join together to form a stronger entity. Sometimes, a large company may absorb a smaller one. All these transactions – compromises, arrangements, mergers, and amalgamations – are governed by Sections 230 to 240 of the Companies Act, 2013. These provisions are of great practical importance in the corporate world today, as mergers and acquisitions (M&A) have become a routine feature of business strategy.

21.1 Compromise and Arrangement – Section 230

Meaning of Compromise and Arrangement

The terms 'compromise' and 'arrangement' have not been precisely defined in the Companies Act, 2013. However, they have been given a wide meaning by the courts.

Compromise: A compromise is a settlement of a dispute between the company and its creditors or members by mutual concession. It presupposes the existence of a dispute or a claim. Both parties give up something and agree to meet halfway. For example, if a company owes Rs. 10 crore to its creditors and offers to pay Rs. 6 crore in full and final settlement, and the creditors agree, it is a compromise.

Arrangement: An arrangement is a wider term than a compromise. It includes any scheme of reorganisation of the share capital, any alteration of rights, any scheme for the amalgamation of two or more companies, and any other arrangement between the company and its creditors or members. An arrangement does not necessarily presuppose a dispute. It is simply a plan or scheme agreed upon between the company and its creditors or members for the reorganisation of the company's affairs.

The Supreme Court of India has given a very wide interpretation to the term 'arrangement.' In several cases, the Court has held that the word 'arrangement' is of very wide import and includes any scheme that rearranges the rights and obligations of the members or creditors of the company.

Case: Re T.B. & S. Motor Service (Mysore) Pvt. Ltd. (1959)

The Karnataka High Court observed that the word 'arrangement' is a word of very wide meaning. It is wider than a compromise. Every compromise is an arrangement but every arrangement is not a compromise. An arrangement may include the reconstruction of a company, the merger of two companies, a scheme of demerger, and any other reorganisation of the company's capital structure or business.

Who Can Propose a Scheme? – Section 230(1)

Section Reference: Section 230(1): Where a compromise or arrangement is proposed – (a) between a company and its creditors or any class of them; or (b) between a company and its members or any class of them – the Tribunal may, on the application of the company or of any creditor or member of the company, or in the case of a company which is being wound up, of the liquidator, order a meeting of the creditors or class of creditors, or of the members or class of members, as the case may be, to be called, held, and conducted in such manner as the Tribunal directs.

Thus, a scheme of compromise or arrangement can be proposed between the company and: (a) its creditors or any class of creditors, or (b) its members or any class of members. The application to the Tribunal can be made by the company itself, or by any creditor, or by any member, or by the liquidator (if the company is being wound up).

Procedure for Compromise and Arrangement

(1) Application to the Tribunal: The company (or any creditor or member or the liquidator) makes an application to the NCLT proposing the scheme of compromise or arrangement. The application must be accompanied by the scheme itself, a disclosure statement containing all material facts, a copy of the auditor's report, and such other documents as may be prescribed.

(2) Notice of objection from regulators – Section 230(5): A notice of the application must be sent to the Central Government, the income tax authorities, the Reserve Bank of India, SEBI, the Registrar, the stock exchanges, the Official Liquidator, the Competition Commission of India, and such other sectoral regulators or authorities as may be relevant. These authorities may file their objections or representations before the Tribunal within 30 days. This provision ensures that the scheme does not adversely affect the public interest, tax revenue, or competition.

(3) Order for meeting: If the Tribunal is satisfied that the scheme is workable and not against public interest, it orders a meeting of the creditors or members (or classes thereof) to consider the scheme. The Tribunal gives directions regarding the manner in which the meeting is to be called, held, and conducted.

(4) Disclosure in the notice of meeting – Section 230(3): With every notice calling the meeting, there must be sent a statement disclosing: (a) the terms of the compromise or arrangement, (b) the material interests of the directors, KMP, and debenture trustees, (c) the effect of the scheme on the above persons, (d) a report adopted by the directors and the auditors' opinion on the scheme.

(5) Approval at the meeting: The scheme must be approved by a majority in number representing three-fourths in value of the creditors or members (or class thereof) present and voting either in person or by proxy at the meeting [Section 230(6)]. This is called the 'dual majority' test – both majority in number and three-fourths in value must be satisfied.

Illustration: If 100 creditors are present at the meeting holding claims worth Rs. 50 crore, the scheme must be approved by more than 50 creditors (majority in number) AND the approving creditors must represent at least Rs. 37.5 crore (three-fourths in value) of the total claims of the creditors present. Both conditions must be met simultaneously.

(6) Sanction by the Tribunal – Section 230(7): After the scheme is approved at the meeting, the company must file a petition with the Tribunal for its sanction. The Tribunal, after hearing the company and the objectors (if any), may sanction the scheme with or without modifications. The Tribunal shall not sanction the scheme unless it is satisfied that the scheme is fair and reasonable and is not against public interest.

(7) Filing with the Registrar: A certified copy of the Tribunal's order must be filed with the Registrar within 30 days [Section 230(7)].

(8) Binding effect: Once the Tribunal sanctions the scheme, it is binding on the company, all the creditors (or class of creditors), all the members (or class of members), and, in the case of a company being wound up, on the liquidator and the contributories of the company [Section 230(7)]. Even those creditors or members who voted against the scheme are bound by it, provided the requisite majority approved it.

Power of the Tribunal to Enforce Compromise – Section 230(12)

Section 230(12) provides that the Tribunal may enforce the compromise or arrangement by making such orders as it deems fit, including orders for the transfer of property and for the carrying on of any business. If the Tribunal is satisfied that the compromise or arrangement cannot be implemented satisfactorily with or without modifications, it may order the winding up of the company.

Minority Shareholders' Protection – Section 230(11)

Section 230(11) provides that where, at a meeting held under Section

230, a scheme is approved by a majority in number representing three-fourths in value, the Tribunal may, if it is satisfied that the scheme is fair and reasonable, sanction the same. However, the minority shareholders who did not consent to the scheme have the right to represent to the Tribunal that the scheme is not fair or is prejudicial to their interests. The Tribunal will consider their objections before sanctioning the scheme. This is an important safeguard for the protection of minority shareholders.

Note: The scheme of compromise or arrangement under Section 230 is a very powerful tool in corporate restructuring. It can be used for a wide variety of purposes, including settlement with creditors, reduction of capital, conversion of debentures into shares, reorganisation of share capital, demerger of business divisions, and any other arrangement that the company may need. The key requirement is that it must be approved by the requisite majority and sanctioned by the Tribunal.

21.2 Merger and Amalgamation – Section 232

Meaning of Merger and Amalgamation

The terms 'merger' and 'amalgamation' are often used interchangeably, but there are subtle differences between them.

Merger (or Absorption): A merger takes place when one company is absorbed by another company. The absorbed company (called the 'transferor company') ceases to exist, and its assets, liabilities, and business are taken over by the absorbing company (called the 'transferee company'). The transferee company continues to exist with its own identity. The shareholders of the transferor company receive shares or other consideration from the transferee company.

Illustration: Company A merges with Company B. After the merger, Company A ceases to exist. All the assets, liabilities, and business of A are transferred to B. The shareholders of A receive shares in B. B continues to exist with its original identity but now has the combined assets and business of both A and B. This is a merger or absorption.

Amalgamation (or Consolidation): An amalgamation takes place when two or more companies combine to form a new company. The old companies (transferor companies) cease to exist, and a new company (transferee company) is formed which takes over the assets, liabilities, and business of all the old companies. The shareholders of the old companies receive shares in the new company.

Illustration: Company A and Company B amalgamate to form a new Company C. After the amalgamation, both A and B cease to exist. All the assets, liabilities, and business of A and B are transferred to C. The shareholders of A and B receive shares in C. C is a new company with the combined assets and business of A and B. This is an amalgamation or consolidation.

Demerger (or Splitting): A demerger is the reverse of a merger. It is the process by which one or more divisions or businesses of a company are transferred to a newly formed company or an existing company. The original company continues to exist with its remaining business. The shareholders of the original company receive shares in the new company in addition to their shares in the original company. Although the term 'demerger' is not specifically defined in the Companies Act, 2013, it is recognised under the Income Tax Act, 1961 [Section 2(19AA)] and is commonly used in corporate restructuring.

Indian Example: Some of the biggest mergers and acquisitions in Indian corporate history include: Vodafone India – Idea Cellular merger (2018, now Vi – Vodafone Idea Ltd.), Tata Steel's acquisition of Corus Group (2007), Flipkart's acquisition by Walmart (2018), Zee Entertainment – Sony Pictures Networks merger (2023-24), HDFC Ltd. – HDFC Bank merger (2023, one of the largest in Indian financial sector), and Reliance's merger of Jio Financial Services demerger (2023).

Provisions of Section 232

Section Reference: Section 232(1): Where an application is made to the Tribunal under Section 230 for the sanctioning of a compromise or arrangement proposed between a company (the transferor company) and any other company (the transferee company) and it involves the merger or amalgamation of the two companies, the Tribunal may order a meeting of the creditors and/or members.

Section 232 read with Section 230 lays down the procedure for merger and amalgamation. The procedure is essentially the same as for a compromise or arrangement under Section 230, with some additional requirements specific to mergers and amalgamations.

Procedure for Merger and Amalgamation

(1) Application to the Tribunal: Both the transferor company (company being absorbed or dissolved) and the transferee company (absorbing company or new company) must file an application with the NCLT. The application must be accompanied by the scheme of merger/amalgamation, the draft valuation report, the swap ratio (the ratio at which shares of the transferor company will be exchanged for shares of the transferee company), and other prescribed documents.

(2) Notice to regulators – Section 230(5): Notice must be given to the Central Government, income tax authorities, RBI, SEBI, Registrar, stock exchanges, CCI, and other relevant authorities. These bodies have 30 days to file objections.

(3) Meetings of creditors and members: The Tribunal orders meetings of the creditors and members (or classes thereof) of both the transferor and the transferee companies. The scheme must be approved at each meeting by the dual majority test (majority in number representing three-fourths in value).

(4) Sanction by the Tribunal: After the scheme is approved at the meetings, both companies file petitions with the Tribunal for sanction. The Tribunal, after hearing all parties and considering any objections, may sanction the scheme.

(5) Transfer of assets and liabilities – Section 232(3): The Tribunal's order shall provide for the transfer of the whole or any part of the undertaking, property, and liabilities of the transferor company to the transferee company. The order may also provide for the allotment of shares, debentures, or other securities of the transferee company to the members of the transferor company.

(6) Dissolution of the transferor company: In a merger, the Tribunal's order provides for the dissolution of the transferor company without the process of winding up. This is a significant advantage because the company is dissolved simply by the Tribunal's order, without going through the lengthy and expensive winding up process.

(7) Filing with the Registrar: The order must be filed with the Registrar of both companies within 30 days. The Registrar of the transferor company shall strike off the name of the company from the register.

What the Tribunal's Order May Contain – Section 232(3)

The Tribunal's order sanctioning the merger/amalgamation may provide for all or any of the following matters:

(a) The transfer to the transferee company of the whole or any part of the undertaking, property, or liabilities of the transferor company. (b) The allotment or appropriation by the transferee company of any shares, debentures, policies, or other instruments. (c) The continuation by or against the transferee company of any legal proceedings pending by or against the transferor company. (d) The dissolution, without winding up, of the transferor company. (e) The provision to be made for any persons who dissent from the compromise or arrangement. (f) Such incidental, consequential, and supplemental matters as are necessary to ensure that the merger/amalgamation is fully and effectively carried out.

Accounting Treatment – Section 232(2)(d)

Section 232(2)(d) requires that the Tribunal shall fix a fair and reasonable consideration for the shares or other securities of the transferor company. The accounting treatment of the merger must be in compliance with the Indian Accounting Standards (Ind AS) prescribed under Section 133. Under Ind AS 103 (Business Combinations), the purchase method (now called the 'acquisition method') is used for accounting for mergers and amalgamations.

Protection of Dissenting Shareholders – Section 235

Section 235 provides special protection to dissenting shareholders in cases of merger or amalgamation. If a scheme or contract involving the transfer of shares of one company to another (the 'transferee company') has been approved by holders of not less than nine-tenths in value of the shares whose transfer is involved, the transferee company may, within two months after the expiry of four months from the date of the offer, give notice to the dissenting shareholders that it desires to acquire their shares. The dissenting shareholders are then bound to transfer their shares to the transferee company at the same price and on the same terms as the other shareholders.

However, the dissenting shareholders may, within one month from the date of the notice, apply to the Tribunal expressing their dissent. The Tribunal may, if it thinks fit, order that the shares shall not be acquired, or it may modify the terms of acquisition. This provision protects the minority from being forced out at an unfair price, while also allowing the majority to complete the acquisition.

Case: Hindustan Lever Ltd. v. SEBI (1998)

The Supreme Court considered the scheme of amalgamation of Tata Oil Mills Co. Ltd. (TOMCO) with Hindustan Lever Ltd. (HLL). The Court upheld the scheme after being satisfied that it was fair and reasonable, that the swap ratio was determined by independent valuers, and that the interests of the shareholders and creditors were adequately protected. This case established several important principles regarding the Tribunal's role in scrutinising merger schemes.

21.3 Cross-Border Mergers – Section 234

With the globalisation of business, companies often need to merge with or acquire companies in other countries. Cross-border mergers are mergers between an Indian company and a foreign company. The Companies Act, 2013 has, for the first time, specifically provided for cross-border mergers.

Provisions of Section 234

Section Reference: Section 234(1): The provisions of this Chapter shall apply to mergers and amalgamations between companies registered under this Act and companies incorporated in the jurisdictions of such countries as may be notified from time to time by the Central Government. However, the merger or amalgamation of a company registered under this Act shall be in accordance with the provisions of Sections 230 to 232 of this Act.

Section 234 allows two types of cross-border mergers:

(a) Inbound merger: Where a foreign company merges into an Indian company (i.e., the Indian company is the transferee company and the foreign company is the transferor company). After the merger, the Indian company survives and the foreign company ceases to exist.

(b) Outbound merger: Where an Indian company merges into a foreign company (i.e., the foreign company is the transferee company and the Indian company is the transferor company). After the merger, the foreign company survives and the Indian company ceases to exist.

Conditions for Cross-Border Mergers

The following conditions must be complied with for cross-border mergers:

(1) Prior RBI approval: The merger must be approved by the Reserve Bank of India. Since cross-border mergers involve the transfer of assets and liabilities across national boundaries, the RBI's approval is necessary to ensure compliance with the foreign exchange laws (FEMA, 1999). The RBI has issued the Foreign Exchange Management (Cross Border Merger) Regulations, 2018 which prescribe the detailed procedure and conditions for cross-border mergers.

(2) Compliance with the laws of the foreign jurisdiction: The merger must also be in compliance with the laws of the country in which the foreign company is incorporated. The Central Government has notified certain countries (jurisdictions) whose companies can participate in cross-border mergers with Indian companies.

(3) NCLT approval: The scheme of cross-border merger must be approved by the NCLT in the same manner as a domestic merger under Sections 230 to 232.

(4) Valuation by registered valuer: The assets and liabilities of both the Indian and the foreign company must be valued by a registered valuer.

(5) Transferee company must comply with Indian laws: In the case of an inbound merger (where the transferee is an Indian company), the resulting Indian company must comply with all provisions of the Companies Act, SEBI regulations, and other Indian laws. In the case of an outbound merger (where the transferee is a foreign company), the Indian shareholders must receive consideration in accordance with the FEMA regulations.

21.4 Fast Track Merger – Section 233

The Companies Act, 2013 has introduced a simplified and faster procedure for the merger and amalgamation of certain classes of companies. This is called the 'Fast Track Merger' process. The purpose of this provision is to reduce the time and cost involved in the merger process for smaller companies and for mergers between holding and subsidiary companies.

Which Companies Can Use the Fast Track Merger Process?

Section Reference: Section 233(1): Notwithstanding the provisions of Sections 230 to 232, a scheme of merger or amalgamation may be entered into between – (a) two or more small companies; or (b) between a holding company and its wholly-owned subsidiary company; or (c) such other class or classes of companies as may be prescribed – by filing an application with the Central Government, Registrar, and Official

Liquidator, and obtaining the approval in the manner laid down in this section.

Thus, the fast track merger process is available for: (a) mergers between two or more small companies (as defined in Section 2(85)); (b) mergers between a holding company and its wholly-owned subsidiary company; and (c) such other classes of companies as the Central Government may prescribe.

Rule 25 of the Companies (Compromises, Arrangements and Amalgamations) Rules, 2016 prescribes the additional class of companies as 'a start-up company merging with a small company.'

Procedure for Fast Track Merger

(1) Filing of scheme: The companies must file the scheme of merger with the Central Government, the Registrar of Companies, and the Official Liquidator (in case of companies being wound up).

(2) Notice to members and creditors: A notice must be given to the members and creditors of the companies proposing the merger. The notice must be accompanied by the scheme and the valuation report. The members and creditors are given 30 days to raise their objections.

(3) Approval by members and creditors: The scheme must be approved by the members holding at least 90% of the total number of shares in each company and by the majority of creditors representing 9/10th in value of the creditors or class of creditors of the respective companies. The approval may be obtained at a meeting or by postal ballot or by electronic voting.

(4) Approval by the Central Government (Regional Director): Instead of the NCLT, the scheme in a fast track merger is approved by the Central Government (through the Regional Director). The Regional Director must confirm the scheme within 30 days of receipt of the application. If the Regional Director has any objection, he may file an application before the NCLT. If no objection is raised within 30 days, the scheme is deemed to have been confirmed [Section 233(6)].

(5) Registrar's report: The Registrar may also submit his observations to the Central Government within 30 days. Similarly, the Official Liquidator may also give his report within 30 days.

(6) Effective date: The scheme takes effect from the date specified therein or from the date of filing with the Registrar, whichever is later.

(7) Filing with the Registrar: The scheme must be filed with the Registrar of both companies within 30 days. The Registrar of the transferor company strikes off its name from the register.

Advantages of Fast Track Merger

(a) Faster process – the entire process can be completed in about 2 to 3 months, compared to 6 to 12 months or more for a regular merger under Section 232. (b) Lower cost – the filing fees and professional costs are lower because the process is simpler and does not involve lengthy Tribunal hearings. (c) No NCLT involvement (unless there are objections) – the scheme is approved by the Regional Director, which is a simpler administrative process. (d) Suitable for small companies and holding-subsidiary mergers where the interests of minority shareholders and creditors are adequately protected.

Table 21.1: Regular Merger vs. Fast Track Merger

Point	Regular Merger (Sec 232)	Fast Track Merger (Sec 233)
Applicable to	All companies	Small companies, holding-wholly owned subsidiary, start-ups
Approval Authority	NCLT (Tribunal)	Central Government (Regional Director)
Member approval	Majority in number + 3/4th in value	Members holding 90% + shares
Creditor	Majority in number +	Creditors representing

approval	3/4th in value	9/10th in value
Notice to regulators	Central Govt, RBI, SEBI, IT, CCI, etc.	Central Govt, ROC, Official Liquidator
Time taken	6–12 months or more	2–3 months approximately
Cost	Higher (Tribunal fees, legal costs)	Lower (simpler process)
NCLT involvement	Mandatory	Only if Regional Director objects
Section	230–232	233

Table 21.2: Merger vs. Amalgamation vs. Demerger

Point	Merger (Absorption)	Amalgamation (Consolidation)	Demerger (Splitting)
Meaning	One company absorbed by another	Two+ companies combine into new company	One company splits its business into separate entities
Transferor	Absorbed company (ceases to exist)	Both old companies (cease to exist)	Original company (continues with remaining business)
Transferee	Absorbing company (survives)	New company (newly formed)	New/existing company (receives transferred business)
Identity	Transferee	Entirely new	Both entities

	retains its identity	identity	continue separately
Example	Company A merges into Company B; A dissolves	A + B form new Company C; A and B dissolve	A transfers its IT division to new Company B; A continues
Also called	Absorption	Consolidation, Fusion	Splitting, Hive-off

Indian Example: The HDFC Ltd.–HDFC Bank merger (effective 1st July 2023) was one of the largest mergers in Indian corporate history. HDFC Ltd. (the mortgage lender) was the transferor company which merged into HDFC Bank (the transferee company). After the merger, HDFC Ltd. ceased to exist and HDFC Bank continued with the combined business. The shareholders of HDFC Ltd. received 42 shares of HDFC Bank for every 25 shares held in HDFC Ltd. The scheme was approved by the NCLT after extensive regulatory approvals from the RBI, SEBI, CCI, and other authorities.

Chapter 22

E-Governance and Miscellaneous Provisions

The Companies Act, 2013 is not merely a law about how companies are formed, managed, and wound up. It also contains several important provisions relating to the use of technology in corporate administration (e-governance), the investigation of corporate fraud, the punishment for offences, the compounding of offences, and the powers of the Central Government. In addition, the enactment of the Insolvency and Bankruptcy Code, 2016 has fundamentally changed the way corporate insolvency and bankruptcy are handled in India. This chapter covers these miscellaneous but very important provisions which a student of company law must know.

22.1 E-Governance under Companies Act – Section 120

The use of electronic means in the administration of companies is one of the most significant modern developments in company law. The Companies Act, 2013 has given statutory recognition to e-governance in company affairs, making India one of the countries which have formally incorporated technology into their corporate legal framework.

Provisions of Section 120

Section Reference: Section 120(1): The Central Government may prescribe the maintenance and inspection of documents in electronic form, the filing of documents through electronic form, the issue of any certificate or other document by the Registrar in electronic form, and the payment of fees or any other charges under the Act through electronic mode.

Section Reference: Section 120(2): Notwithstanding anything contained in this Act or in any other law for the time being in force, any document, record, register, minutes, books of account, or any such other document required to be kept by a company or allowed to be inspected or copies to be given to any person, may be kept or inspected or copies given, as the case may be, in electronic form in such manner as may be prescribed.

The above provisions empower the Central Government to mandate that all company records, documents, and filings may be maintained, filed, and inspected in electronic form. This has transformed the way companies and the Registrar of Companies interact.

Key Areas of E-Governance in Company Administration

(1) MCA Portal (www.mca.gov.in): The Ministry of Corporate Affairs (MCA) has developed a comprehensive online portal through which all filings, registrations, and communications between companies and the Government are done electronically. The portal is called MCA21 (now upgraded to MCA21 Version 3.0). All forms – annual returns, financial statements, incorporation forms, change of directors, charge registration, etc. – are filed electronically through this portal.

(2) SPICe+ (Simplified Proforma for Incorporating Company Electronically Plus): As discussed in Chapter 7, the SPICe+ form is an integrated web form which allows the incorporation of a company along with the allotment of DIN, PAN, TAN, GST registration, EPFO registration, ESIC registration, and opening of bank account – all through a single online application.

(3) Electronic filing of annual returns and financial statements: Every company must file its annual return (Form MGT-7 or MGT-7A) and financial statements (Form AOC-4 or AOC-4 XBRL) electronically through the MCA portal. XBRL (eXtensible Business Reporting Language) filing is mandatory for specified classes of companies.

(4) E-voting: Section 108 provides for voting through electronic means. Every listed company and every company having 1,000 or more shareholders must provide the facility of e-voting for every resolution. E-voting is conducted through platforms provided by NSDL and CDSL.

(5) Electronic maintenance of registers and records: Section 120(2) allows companies to maintain their statutory registers (register of members, register of directors, register of charges, etc.) in electronic form. The books of account can also be maintained in electronic form under Section 128(3).

(6) Board meetings through video conferencing: Section 173(2) allows directors to participate in Board meetings through video conferencing or other audio-visual means. Similarly, AGMs and EGMs can also be conducted through video conferencing in certain circumstances, as permitted by the MCA from time to time.

(7) Digital signatures: All documents filed with the Registrar must be digitally signed by the authorised person (director, company secretary, or other authorised signatory). The digital signature certificate (DSC) is issued by certifying authorities licensed by the Controller of Certifying Authorities under the Information Technology Act, 2000.

(8) Electronic communication: Section 20 allows the service of documents, notices, and other communications through electronic mode. Companies can send notices of meetings, annual reports, and other documents to shareholders through email, provided the shareholders have given their consent and registered their email addresses with the company.

Indian Context: The MCA21 portal has revolutionised the interaction between companies and the Registrar. Before the introduction of MCA21 in 2006, all filings were done physically – companies had to prepare documents on paper, get them stamped, and physically submit them at the ROC office. Today, all filings are done online from anywhere in India, 24 hours a day. The latest version, MCA21 V3.0, includes features like integrated web forms, a new company search function, the XBRL filing system for financial statements, and a compliance management system. This has significantly improved the ease of doing business in India.

Note: The COVID-19 pandemic (2020-21) accelerated the adoption of e-governance in company affairs. The MCA issued several circulars allowing companies to conduct AGMs and EGMs entirely through video conferencing or other audio-visual means. Board meetings were also allowed through video conferencing without any restriction on agenda items. Although some of these relaxations were temporary, the trend towards digital governance has become permanent and irreversible.

22.2 Inspection, Inquiry and Investigation

The Companies Act, 2013 gives the Central Government, the Registrar, and certain other authorities the power to inspect the books and papers of a company, to conduct inquiries into the affairs of a company, and to investigate the management of a company. These powers are essential for enforcing the law and detecting fraud and mismanagement. The provisions relating to inspection, inquiry, and investigation are contained in Sections 206 to 229 of the Act.

(A) Inspection – Section 206

Section 206 empowers the Registrar to call for information, returns, or documents from a company. The Registrar may also conduct an inspection of the books and papers of a company. The purpose of inspection is to verify whether the company is complying with the provisions of the Act and the rules made thereunder.

Section 206(1) provides that where the Registrar has reasonable cause to believe that a company has failed to comply with the provisions of the Act, or that there are circumstances suggesting that the company's affairs are being conducted in a manner prejudicial to public interest, he may call upon the company to furnish such information or explanation within such time as may be specified.

Section 206(4) provides that the Registrar may, after considering the information or explanation furnished, order an investigation into the affairs of the company if he is of the opinion that there are circumstances suggesting fraud or mismanagement.

(B) Inquiry – Section 210

Section 210 provides that the Central Government may order an inquiry into the affairs of a company in the following circumstances:

(a) On receipt of a report from the Registrar under Section 208,

(b) On intimation of a special resolution passed by a company that its affairs ought to be investigated,

(c) In the public interest,

(d) On request from any State Government,

The inquiry is conducted by an inspector appointed by the Central Government. The inspector has the power to examine on oath any person who is or has been an officer, employee, or agent of the company. The inspector must submit his report to the Central Government within the prescribed time.

(C) Investigation – Sections 210 to 227

Investigation is a more detailed and thorough process than inquiry. It involves a comprehensive examination of the affairs of the company, including its management, finances, and operations. Investigation is ordered in cases of suspected fraud, serious mismanagement, or oppression.

(1) Investigation by the Central Government – Section 210: The Central Government may appoint one or more competent persons as inspectors to investigate the affairs of a company if it is of the opinion that it is necessary in the public interest or in the interest of the company or its members or creditors. The inspectors must submit a report to the Central Government.

(2) Investigation by the SFIO – Section 211: The Serious Fraud Investigation Office (SFIO) is a specialised investigation agency established under Section 211 of the Companies Act, 2013. The SFIO investigates serious cases of fraud and mismanagement relating to companies. The Central Government may assign the investigation of a case to the SFIO if it believes that the case involves complex transactions, interlinking of companies, international ramifications, or substantial public interest. The SFIO has wide powers of investigation, including the power to arrest persons involved in the fraud.

(3) Investigation of ownership – Section 216: The Central Government may appoint inspectors to investigate the ownership of shares and debentures of a company, to determine the true persons who are financially interested in the company and who control or materially influence the company's policy.

Powers of Inspectors – Sections 217 to 219

The inspectors have very wide powers:

(a) To require the production of books, accounts, and documents [Section 217]. (b) To examine on oath any person who is or has been an officer or employee of the company [Section 217(3)]. (c) To investigate the affairs of any related body corporate [Section 219]. (d) To seize books and documents if there is a risk that they may be destroyed, mutilated, or falsified [Section 209]. (e) To require any person to appear before the inspector and give evidence [Section 217].

Consequences of Investigation – Section 224 & 225

After the investigation is completed and the inspector submits his report, the Central Government may take the following actions: (a) direct the company to take such action as it thinks fit [Section 224(1)]; (b) file a petition before the NCLT for the winding up of the company [Section 224(2)]; (c) file a petition before the NCLT for relief under Sections 241 and 242 (oppression and mismanagement) [Section 224(3)]; (d) institute a prosecution against any person who is found guilty of fraud or any other offence [Section 224(4)]; (e) recover the cost of investigation from the company or any person who is responsible for the fraud [Section 225].

Feature	Inspection	Inquiry	Investigation
Section	206–209	210	210–227
Authority	Registrar	Central Government	Central Government / SFIO
Nature	Verification of compliance	Preliminary examination	Detailed and thorough examination
Scope	Books and papers	Affairs of the company	Entire affairs including fraud and mismanagement
Conducted by	Registrar or authorised officer	Inspector appointed by Central Govt	Inspector / SFIO
Severity	Least severe	Moderate	Most severe
Outcome	Report to Central Govt; may lead to inquiry	Report; may lead to investigation	Report; prosecution, winding up, or other action

22.3 Fraud and Penalties – Section 447

The Companies Act, 2013 takes a very serious view of fraud. Section 447 defines fraud and prescribes severe punishment for persons involved in fraud. This is one of the most stringent provisions of the Act and reflects the legislature's determination to curb corporate fraud.

Definition of Fraud – Section 447

Section Reference: Section 447: 'Fraud' in relation to affairs of a company or any body corporate, includes any act, omission, concealment of any fact or abuse of position committed by any person or any other person with the connivance in any manner, with intent to deceive, to gain undue advantage from, or to injure the interests of, the company or its shareholders or its creditors or any other person, whether or not there is any wrongful gain or wrongful loss. The definition is very wide. It includes every act of dishonesty, concealment, and abuse of position which is committed with the intent to deceive or to gain an undue advantage. The key elements of fraud under Section 447 are:

(a) Act, omission, concealment, or abuse of position: The fraud may be committed by doing something (act), by not doing something (omission), by hiding material facts (concealment), or by misusing one's position in the company (abuse of position).

(b) Intent to deceive: There must be an intention to deceive. Mere negligence or carelessness, without any dishonest intention, does not amount to fraud.

(c) Gain undue advantage or injure: The fraud must be committed to gain an undue advantage or to injure the interests of the company, its shareholders, creditors, or any other person.

(d) Whether or not there is wrongful gain or loss: The fraud is complete even if the fraudster does not actually gain anything or even if no actual loss is caused. The mere attempt with fraudulent intent is sufficient.

Punishment for Fraud

The punishment for fraud under Section 447 is as follows:

(a) General punishment: Imprisonment for a term which shall not be less than 6 months but which may extend to 10 years. AND a fine which shall not be less than the amount involved in the fraud but which may extend to three times the amount involved in the fraud.

(b) Fraud involving public interest: Where the fraud involves public interest, the term of imprisonment shall not be less than 3 years.

(c) Smaller frauds: The Companies (Amendment) Act, 2020 has introduced a proviso that where the fraud involves an amount less than

Rs. 10 lakhs, or 1% of the turnover of the company, whichever is lower, and does not involve public interest, the punishment shall be imprisonment for a term which may extend to 5 years or with fine which may extend to Rs. 50 lakhs, or with both. Section 447 applies not only to directors and officers of the company but to any person involved in the fraud, including auditors, company secretaries, chartered accountants, and even third parties who aided or abetted the fraud.

Case / Context: Satyam Computer Services Fraud (2009)

Mr. B. Ramalinga Raju, the founder and chairman of Satyam Computer Services, confessed to inflating the company's cash and bank balances by approximately Rs. 7,000 crore over a period of several years. This was one of the biggest corporate frauds in Indian history. Mr. Raju, along with several other directors and officers, was prosecuted under various provisions of the Companies Act and the Indian Penal Code. He was convicted by a special court in 2015 and sentenced to 7 years' imprisonment. This case was a turning point in Indian corporate governance and was one of the key factors which led to the strengthening of anti-fraud provisions in the Companies Act, 2013.

Case / Context: Sahara India Real Estate Scam

The Supreme Court of India in the Sahara case (2012) directed Sahara India Real Estate Corporation Ltd. and Sahara Housing Investment Corporation Ltd. to refund approximately Rs. 24,000 crore to investors, finding that the companies had issued optionally fully convertible debentures (OFCDs) without complying with the disclosure and regulatory requirements. This case highlighted the need for strict enforcement of securities law and corporate governance provisions.

Note: The stringent punishment under Section 447 is intended to act as a deterrent against corporate fraud. Before the 2013 Act, the punishment for fraud was relatively mild and did not serve as an effective deterrent. The 2013 Act has significantly increased the penalties and has also made fraud a cognisable and non-bailable offence in many cases. This has fundamentally changed the risk-reward calculus for potential fraudsters.

22.4 Compounding of Offences – Section 441

The Companies Act, 2013 recognises that not all defaults committed by companies are serious offences requiring criminal prosecution. Many defaults are minor or technical in nature and can be resolved by paying a penalty or fine without going through the lengthy process of criminal trial. The Act, therefore, provides for the 'compounding' of certain offences.

Meaning of Compounding

Compounding means the settlement of an offence by paying a prescribed sum of money, without going through the process of criminal prosecution and trial. When an offence is compounded, the criminal proceedings against the offender are dropped and the offender is deemed to have been acquitted of the offence. In simple words, compounding allows the offender to buy his way out of a criminal prosecution by paying a fine.

Provisions of Section 441

(1) Which offences can be compounded? Section 441(1) provides that any offence punishable under this Act (whether committed by a company or any officer thereof) which is punishable only with fine, or which is punishable with fine or imprisonment or both, may be compounded. However, offences which are punishable with imprisonment only (without the option of fine) cannot be compounded.

(2) Which offences cannot be compounded? Section 441(1) provides that the following offences cannot be compounded: (a) offences punishable with imprisonment only; (b) offences under Section 447 (fraud) – fraud cannot be compounded under any circumstances; (c) offences where the investigation has been initiated by the Serious Fraud Investigation Office (SFIO) and the investigation is pending.

(3) Who can compound? Section 441(1) provides that: (a) offences which are punishable with fine only may be compounded by the Regional Director or any officer authorised by the Central Government; (b) offences which are punishable with fine or imprisonment or both may be compounded by the NCLT. In the case of NCLT compounding, the Tribunal shall give a reasonable opportunity to the Registrar and the Central Government to make their representations.

(4) Limit on compounding amount: The maximum amount of compounding fee shall not exceed the maximum amount of fine prescribed for the offence [Section 441(1)].

(5) Second and subsequent offences: Section 441(2) provides that where an offence has been compounded, no proceeding or further proceeding (as the case may be) shall be taken against the offender in respect of the offence so compounded. However, if the offender commits the same offence within three years of the compounding, the subsequent offence cannot be compounded.

(6) Effect of compounding: Where any offence is compounded before the institution of any prosecution, no prosecution shall be instituted in respect of such offence against the offender in relation to whom the offence is so compounded [Section 441(3)]. Where the compounding takes place after the institution of prosecution, the composition shall be brought to the notice of the court, and the court shall discharge the accused.

Feature	Compoundable Offences	Non-Compoundable Offences
Punishment	Punishable with fine only, or fine or imprisonment or both	Punishable with imprisonment only
Fraud (Section	Cannot be compounded	Cannot be compounded

447)		
SFIO investigation	Cannot be compounded while investigation pending	Cannot be compounded
Authority	Regional Director (fine only) or NCLT (fine or imprisonment)	Must go through criminal prosecution
Repeat within 3 years	Second offence cannot be compounded	Not applicable
Effect	Deemed acquittal; prosecution dropped	Must face trial

Note: The provision for compounding of offences is a practical and pragmatic approach which benefits both the companies and the Government. Companies get an opportunity to avoid criminal prosecution and the stigma associated with it. The Government saves the time and cost of lengthy criminal trials. The Registrar and the NCLT have been compounding thousands of offences every year, ranging from delayed filing of annual returns to non-compliance with various provisions of the Act.

22.5 Central Government Powers and Exemptions

The Companies Act, 2013 gives the Central Government wide powers to make rules, issue notifications, grant exemptions, and exercise various administrative and regulatory functions. These powers enable the Government to implement the Act effectively and to adapt the law to changing economic and business conditions.

Power to Make Rules – Section 469

Section 469 gives the Central Government the power to make rules for carrying out the provisions of the Act. These rules are subordinate legislation and have the force of law. The major rules made under the Companies Act, 2013 include: Companies (Incorporation) Rules, Companies (Share Capital and Debentures) Rules, Companies (Accounts) Rules, Companies (Audit and Auditors) Rules, Companies (Appointment and Qualification of Directors) Rules, Companies (Meetings of Board and its Powers) Rules, Companies (Management and Administration) Rules, Companies (Appointment and Remuneration of Managerial Personnel) Rules, Companies (Compromises, Arrangements and Amalgamations) Rules, and several others.

The total number of rules made under the Act exceeds 40 sets of rules. Many of the substantive provisions of the Act are, in practice, contained in the rules rather than in the Act itself. Therefore, a student of company law must study the relevant rules along with the Act.

Power to Grant Exemptions – Section 462

Section Reference: Section 462(1): If the Central Government is satisfied that it is necessary in the public interest to do so, it may, by notification, and subject to such conditions and limitations, if any, as may be specified in the notification, exempt any class or classes of companies from any of the provisions of this Act. The Central Government has extensively used this power to grant exemptions to various classes of companies, especially private companies, Government companies, Section 8 companies, Nidhi companies, and companies in certain sectors (like banking, insurance, etc.). For example, the Central Government has exempted private companies from many provisions relating to managerial remuneration (Section 197), meetings (Section 96), independent directors (Section 149), and other provisions which are primarily meant for public companies and listed companies.

Power to Appoint Inspectors – Sections 210 & 212

As discussed in Section 22.2, the Central Government has the power to appoint inspectors to investigate the affairs of a company. It also has the power to direct the SFIO to investigate serious cases of fraud.

National Financial Reporting Authority (NFRA) – Section 132

Section 132 provides for the constitution of the National Financial Reporting Authority (NFRA). The NFRA is responsible for: (a) making recommendations on the formulation and laying down of accounting and auditing policies and standards; (b) monitoring and enforcing compliance with accounting and auditing standards; (c) overseeing the quality of the profession associated with ensuring compliance with accounting and auditing standards; and (d) having the power to take disciplinary action against members of the Institute of Chartered Accountants of India (ICAI) for professional misconduct.

The NFRA has been constituted with effect from 1st October, 2018. It has the power to investigate cases of professional misconduct by Chartered Accountants and audit firms and to impose penalties, including debarment from practice. The NFRA's jurisdiction extends to listed companies and prescribed classes of companies. For other companies, the ICAI continues to exercise disciplinary authority.

Special Courts – Section 435

Section 435 provides for the establishment of Special Courts for the trial of offences punishable under the Companies Act with imprisonment of two years or more. The Special Court consists of a single judge who shall be appointed by the Central Government with the concurrence of the Chief Justice of the High Court. Offences investigated by the SFIO are triable exclusively by the Special Courts. For other offences, the cases may be tried by a Magistrate of the first class or a Metropolitan Magistrate, depending on the punishment prescribed.

22.6 Insolvency and Bankruptcy Code, 2016 (Overview)

Although the Insolvency and Bankruptcy Code, 2016 (IBC) is a separate legislation and not a part of the Companies Act, 2013, it is closely connected with company law and has fundamentally changed the way corporate insolvency is handled in India. No study of modern company law is complete without an understanding of the basic framework of the IBC. This section provides a brief overview of the IBC.

Background and Objective

Before the IBC, the insolvency and bankruptcy laws in India were scattered across multiple legislations – the Presidency Towns Insolvency Act, 1909, the Provincial Insolvency Act, 1920, the Companies Act, 1956/2013, the Recovery of Debts Due to Banks and Financial Institutions Act, 1993 (RDDBFI Act), the Securitisation and Reconstruction of Financial Assets and Enforcement of Security Interest Act, 2002 (SARFAESI Act), and the Sick Industrial Companies (Special Provisions) Act, 1985 (SICA). These laws were overlapping, complex, and time-consuming. It took years, sometimes decades, to resolve insolvency cases. The NPA (Non-Performing Assets) problem in the banking sector was worsening.

The Insolvency and Bankruptcy Code, 2016 was enacted on 28th May, 2016 to consolidate and amend the laws relating to the reorganisation and insolvency resolution of corporate persons, partnership firms, and individuals in a time-bound manner. The IBC aims to maximise the value of assets of the debtor, promote entrepreneurship, ensure availability of credit, and balance the interests of all stakeholders.

Key Features of the IBC

(1) Time-bound resolution: The Corporate Insolvency Resolution Process (CIRP) must be completed within 180 days, extendable by 90 days (total 270 days). A one-time extension of 60 days was also permitted by the Supreme Court in the Essar Steel case. The maximum period including all extensions cannot exceed 330 days. If the resolution is not completed within this period, the company goes into liquidation.

(2) Creditor-in-control: The IBC shifts the power from the debtor (the defaulting company) to the creditors. A Committee of Creditors (CoC) comprising the financial creditors of the company takes all major decisions during the CIRP, including the approval of the resolution plan. The resolution plan must be approved by at least 66% of the voting share of the financial creditors.

(3) Insolvency Resolution Professional: An Insolvency Resolution Professional (IRP, later replaced by Resolution Professional or RP) is appointed to manage the affairs of the company during the CIRP. The RP takes over the management from the existing directors and conducts the CIRP under the supervision of the CoC.

(4) Moratorium – Section 14: On the commencement of the CIRP, a moratorium is declared which prohibits the institution or continuation of suits, execution of judgments, transfer or disposal of assets, recovery of security interest, and any foreclosure action by any person against the corporate debtor. This gives the company a breathing space to attempt resolution.

(5) Adjudicating Authority: The NCLT is the adjudicating authority for corporate insolvency. The NCLAT hears appeals against the NCLT's orders. Further appeals lie to the Supreme Court on questions of law.

(6) Minimum default threshold: The CIRP can be initiated when the corporate debtor has defaulted on a debt of Rs. 1 crore or more. The threshold was originally Rs. 1 lakh but was raised to Rs. 1 crore by notification dated 24th March, 2020.

(7) Waterfall mechanism for distribution – Section 53: In case of liquidation, the proceeds are distributed in the following order of priority: (a) insolvency resolution process costs and liquidation costs; (b) workmen's dues for 24 months and secured creditors; (c) employees' dues for 12 months; (d) financial debts owed to unsecured creditors; (e) Government dues (Central, State, local); (f) remaining debts; (g) preference shareholders; (h) equity shareholders.

(8) Insolvency and Bankruptcy Board of India (IBBI): The IBBI is the regulatory body established under the IBC to regulate insolvency professionals, insolvency professional agencies, and information utilities. It also makes regulations, conducts inspections, and takes disciplinary action.

Who Can Initiate CIRP?

The CIRP can be initiated by: (a) a financial creditor (e.g., a bank or financial institution) under Section 7; (b) an operational creditor (e.g., a supplier of goods or services, an employee, or a Government authority for unpaid statutory dues) under Section 9; (c) the corporate debtor itself under Section 10.

Indian Context: Some of the landmark insolvency cases resolved under the IBC include: Essar Steel (acquired by ArcelorMittal for approximately Rs. 42,000 crore), Bhushan Steel (acquired by Tata Steel for approximately Rs. 35,200 crore), Alok Industries (acquired by Reliance Industries and JM Financial ARC), Electrosteel Steels (acquired by Vedanta Group), Ruchi Soya (acquired by Patanjali Ayurved). These cases have demonstrated the effectiveness of the IBC in resolving large-scale corporate insolvency in a time-bound manner and in recovering value for the creditors.

Table 22.1: Companies Act vs. IBC – Insolvency Framework

Feature	Companies Act, 2013	Insolvency and Bankruptcy Code, 2016
Focus	Formation, management, governance of companies	Insolvency resolution and liquidation
Insolvency provisions	Winding up by Tribunal (Sections 271–365)	CIRP (Sections 6–77) + Liquidation (Sections 33–54)
Control during insolvency	Liquidator manages; Tribunal supervises	Resolution Professional manages; Committee of Creditors controls
Time limit	No fixed time limit for winding up	180 + 90 days (max 330 days) for CIRP

Priority objective	Liquidation (paying debts and dissolving)	Resolution (keeping company alive); liquidation as last resort
Creditor's role	Limited role; Tribunal decides	Central role; CoC approves resolution plan (66% vote)
Moratorium	Stay of suits (Section 279)	Comprehensive moratorium (Section 14)
Adjudicating authority	NCLT	NCLT
Regulator	MCA / Central Government	IBBI (Insolvency and Bankruptcy Board of India)
Applicable from	2013 (winding up provisions)	2016 (CIRP provisions)

Note: The IBC has been a game-changer in the Indian corporate and banking landscape. Before the IBC, the recovery rate for banks on bad loans was dismal – often less than 25%. The IBC has significantly improved the recovery rate and has changed the behaviour of defaulting promoters. The 'fear factor' of losing control of the company has made promoters more responsible in managing their debts. The IBC has also reduced the time taken for insolvency resolution from years (sometimes decades) to months. However, the IBC is still evolving, and several provisions are being tested and refined through judicial decisions and amendments.